HYMNS

FOR

THE CHURCH OF CHRIST.

EDITED BY

REV. FREDERIC H. HEDGE, D. D.,

AND

REV. FREDERIC D. HUNTINGTON.

THIRD THOUSAND.

BOSTON:
CROSBY, NICHOLS, AND COMPANY,
111 WASHINGTON STREET.
1853.

CAMBRIDGE:
METCALF AND COMPANY, STEREOTYPERS AND PRINTERS.

INDEX OF SUBJECTS.

I. SANCTUARY.

II. GOD.

III. THE WORD.

IV. CHRIST.

V. THE SPIRIT.

VI. THE CHURCH.

VII. THE HEART.

VIII. LIFE.

IX. DEATH.

X. IMMORTALITY.

XI. THE YEAR.

XII. SUPPLEMENT.

INDEX TO FIRST LINES.

I.

SANCTUARY.

OPENING OF SERVICE.

---

1. L. M.

1 How, Lord, shall vows of ours be sweet?
O, how should souls immortal meet?
How lose themselves in heaven awhile?
How win thine own eternal smile?

2 Come beautiful, as souls should be!
Come beautiful for God to see!
Come holy-fair, come heavenly-bright,
And give the All-seeing Eye delight!

3 Ye loving, of large souls and free,
Whose hours run on forgivingly,
You chief the God of Love will hear,—
Your own the incessant Pardoner!

4 Yet better songs, ye holy, raise!
More nobly live; more gladly praise!
Till beauteous round the heavenly throne
Ye worship best the Holy One.

2. C. M.

1 Now morning lifts her dewy veil,
With new-born blessings crowned;
O, haste we, then, her light to hail,
In courts of holy ground!

2 But Christ, triumphant o'er the grave,
Shines more divinely bright;
O, sing we, then, his power to save,
And walk we in his light!

3 Still, as the morning rays return,
To fancy it is given
In distant vision to discern
The radiant domes of heaven.

4 But now that our Eternal Sun
Hath shed his beams abroad,
In him we see the Holy One,
And mount at once to God.

3. C. M.

1 Now that the sun is beaming bright,
Implore we, bending low,
That He, the Uncreated Light,
May guide us as we go.

2 No sinful word, nor deed of wrong,
Nor thoughts that idly rove,
But simple truth be on our tongue,
And in our hearts be love.

3 And while the hours in order flow,
O Christ, securely fence
Our gates beleaguered by the foe, —
The gate of every sense.

4 And grant that to thine honor, Lord,
Our daily toil may tend;
That we begin it at thy word,
And in thy favor end.

4. C. M.

1 Lord, in the morning thou shalt hear
My voice ascending high;
To thee will I direct my prayer,
To thee lift up mine eye.

2 Thou art a God, before whose sight
The wicked shall not stand:
Sinners shall ne'er be thy delight,
Nor dwell at thy right hand.

3 But to thy house will I resort,
To taste thy mercies there;
I will frequent thine holy court,
And worship in thy fear.

4 The men who love and fear thy name
Shall see their hopes fulfilled;
The mighty God will compass them
With favor, as a shield.

5. 7, 4, & 6s. M.

1 Armies of God! in union
With us, through one communion,
Pour forth sweet prayers:
Our souls in love embrace,
Around the Saviour's face,
And ask his special grace
To soothe our cares.

2 Offer those golden vials
Of odors, for our trials,
Before the throne:
Till God the Father smile
On us, though we were vile,
Now counted without guile,
Through Christ alone!

3 Then raise the song of gladness,
To dissipate our sadness:
Along this vale of tears
We wend our weary way
Up towards the realms of day,
And watch, and wait, and pray,
Constant in fears!

4 Head of the hosts in glory!
We joyfully adore thee,
Thy Church on earth below,
Blending with those on high,
Where through the azure sky
Thy saints in ecstasy
For ever glow!

6. L. M.

1 Dear Lord, no other prayer I form
But for devotion pure and warm.
May warm devotion fill my soul;
May love for thee each thought control.

2 May piety increase; and prayer
Mine every thought, word, action, share;
The gift of love my sole request,
Thou, God of love! wilt grant the rest.

3 Weak praise were mine. Do thou inspire
My soul with love and living fire.
O, may this cold and lowly breast
Be warmed by thee, its God, its guest!

7. L. M.

1 Zion's true, glorious God! on thee
Praise waits in all humility.
All flesh shall unto thee repair,
To thee, O God that hearest prayer!

2 But sinful words and works still spread,
And overrun my heart and head;
Transgressions make me foul each day;
O, purge them, purge them all away!

3 Happy is he whom thou wilt choose
To serve thee in thy blessed house!
Who in thy holy temple dwells,
And, filled with joy, thy goodness tells!

8. 7s. M.

1 Sovereign and transforming Grace!
We invoke thy quickening power;
Reign the spirit of this place,
Bless the purpose of this hour.

2 Holy and creative Light!
We invoke thy kindling ray;
Dawn upon our spirits' night,
Turn our darkness into day.

3 To the anxious soul impart
Hope all other hopes above,
Stir the dull and hardened heart
With a longing and a love.

4 Give the struggling peace for strife,
Give the doubting light for gloom,
Speed the living into life,
Warn the dying of their doom.

5 Work in all, in all renew,
Day by day, the life divine;
All our wills to thee subdue,
All our hearts to thee incline.

9. 9 & 8s. M.

1 My God, I now appear before thee,
And wait thy every sign to see;
How can I know or how adore thee,
Except thy spirit breathe in me?

2 If thou, of grace the sole dispenser,
Me bless not, how can I rejoice?
Unless thy incense fill my censer,
How raise in prayer to thee my voice?

3 How can my harp give forth its sweetness
Unless thy finger sweep the string?
How can I know thy truth's completeness
Without thy sun's enlightening?

4 Thy Sabbath grant, life's work-day ended,
The spirit's and the body's rest,
The spirit by its Father tended,
The body on its Mother's breast.

10. 7s. M.

1 Lord, before thy presence come,
Bow we down with holy fear;
Call our erring footsteps home,
Let us feel that thou art near.

2 Wandering thoughts and languid powers
Come not where devotion kneels!
Let the soul expand her stores,
Glowing with the joy she feels.

3 At the portals of thine house
We resign our earth-born cares:
Nobler thoughts our souls engross,
Songs of praise and fervent prayers.

11. 7s. M.

1 All ye nations, praise the Lord;
All ye lands, your voices raise;
Heaven and earth, with loud accord,
Praise the Lord, for ever praise.

2 For his truth and mercy stand,
Past, and present, and to be,
Like the years of his right hand,
Like his own eternity.

3 Praise him, ye who know his love;
Praise him from the depths beneath;
Praise him in the heights above;
Praise your Maker, all that breathe!

12. 7s. M.

1 Glory be to God on high!
God, whose glory fills the sky;
Peace on earth to man forgiven,
Man, the well-beloved of heaven.

2 Favored mortals, raise the song!
Endless thanks to God belong;
Hearts o'erflowing with his praise,
Join the hymns your voices raise.

3 Mark the wonders of his hand!
Power, no empire can withstand;
Wisdom, angels' glorious theme;
Goodness, one eternal stream.

4 Awful Being! from thy throne
Send thy promised blessings down:
Let thy light, thy truth, thy peace,
Bid our raging passions cease.

13. C. M.

1 SING we the song of those who stand
Around the eternal throne,
Of every kindred, clime, and land,
A multitude unknown.

2 Life's poor distinctions vanish here;
To-day the young, the old,
Our Saviour and his flock appear
One Shepherd and one fold.

3 Toil, trial, suffering, still await
On earth the pilgrim's throng,
Yet learn we in our low estate
The Church Triumphant's song.

4 Worthy the Lamb for sinners slain,
Cry the redeemed above,
Blessing and honor to obtain,
And everlasting love!

5 Worthy the Lamb, on earth we sing,
Who died our souls to save!
Henceforth, O Death! where is thy sting!
Thy victory, O Grave!

14. 7s. M.

Safely through another week
God has brought us on our way;
Let us now a blessing seek,
Waiting in thy courts to-day,
Day of all the week the best,
Emblem of eternal rest.

15. L. M.

1 O Thou, to whom, in ancient time,
The lyre of Hebrew bards was strung,
Whom kings adored in song sublime,
And prophets praised with glowing tongue!

2 Not now on Zion's height alone
Thy favored worshipper may dwell,
Nor where, at sultry noon, thy Son
Sat, weary, by the patriarch's well.

3 From every place below the skies,
The grateful song, the fervent prayer,
The incense of the heart, may rise
To heaven, and find acceptance there.

4 O Thou, to whom, in ancient time,
The lyre of prophet-bards was strung,
To thee, at last, in every clime,
Shall temples rise, and praise be sung.

16. 8, 7, & 4s. M.

1 In thy name, O Lord, assembling,
We, thy people, now draw near;
Teach us to rejoice with trembling;
Speak, and let thy servants hear, —
Hear with meekness, —
Hear thy word with godly fear.

2 While our days on earth are lengthened,
May we give them, Lord, to thee;
Cheered by hope, and daily strengthened,
We would run, nor weary be,
Till thy glory,
Without clouds, in heaven we see.

3 There, in worship purer, sweeter,
All thy people shall adore,
Tasting of enjoyment greater
Than they could conceive before, —
Full enjoyment, —
Holy bliss, for evermore.

17. 7s. M.

1 Come the rich, and come the poor,
To the Christian temple door;
Let their mingled prayers ascend
To the Universal Friend.

2 Here the rich and poor may claim
Common ancestry and name;

Claim a common heritage,
In the Gospel's promise page.

3 Of the same materials wrought;
By the same Instructor taught;
Walking in life's common way;
Tending to the same decay;—

4 Rich and poor at last shall meet
At the heavenly mercy-seat,
Where the name of rich and poor
Never shall be uttered more.

18. L. M.

1 O God, whose presence glows in all
Within, around us, and above!
Thy word we bless, thy name we call,
Whose word is Truth, whose name is Love.

2 That truth be with the heart believed
Of all who seek this sacred place;
With power proclaimed, in peace received,—
Our spirits' light, thy Spirit's grace.

3 That love its holy influence pour,
To keep us meek, and make us free,
And throw its binding blessing more
Round each with all, and all with thee.

4 Send down its angel to our side,—
Send in its calm upon the breast;
For we would know no other guide,
And we can need no other rest.

19. L. M.

1 O, BOW thine ear, Eternal One!
On thee our heart adoring calls;
To thee, the followers of thy Son
Bend low within these sacred walls.

2 Here let thy holy days be kept,
And be this place to worship given,
Like that bright spot where Jacob slept,—
The house of God, the gate of heaven.

3 Here be thy praise devoutly sung;
Here let thy truth beam forth to save,
As when, of old, thy Spirit hung,
On wings of light, o'er Jordan's wave.

4 And when the lips, that with thy name
Are vocal now, to dust shall turn,
In others may devotion's flame
Be kindled here, and purely burn.

20. C. M.

1 THE offerings to thy throne which rise,
Of mingled praise and prayer,
Are but a worthless sacrifice,
Unless the heart be there.

2 Upon thine all-discerning ear
Let no vain words intrude;

No tribute but the vow sincere,—
The tribute of the good.

3 My offerings will indeed be blest,
If sanctified by thee;
If thy pure spirit touch my breast
With its own purity.

4 O, may that spirit warm my heart
To piety and love,
And to life's lowly vale impart
Some rays from heaven above!

21. C. M.

1 While thee I seek, protecting Power!
Be my vain wishes stilled;
And may this consecrated hour
With better hopes be filled.

2 Thy love the powers of thought bestowed;
To thee my thoughts would soar;
Thy mercy o'er my life has flowed,
That mercy I adore!

3 In each event of life, how clear
Thy ruling hand I see!
Each blessing to my soul more dear,
Because conferred by thee.

4 In every joy that crowns my days,
In every pain I bear,
My heart shall find delight in praise,
Or seek relief in prayer.

5 When gladness wings my favored hour,
Thy love my thoughts shall fill;
Resigned, when storms of sorrow lower,
My soul shall meet thy will.

6 My lifted eye, without a tear,
The gathering storm shall see;
My steadfast heart shall know no fear;
That heart shall rest on thee.

22. C. M.

1 Father of me and all mankind,
And all the hosts above,
Let every understanding mind
Unite to praise thy love.

2 Thy kingdom come, with power and grace,
To every heart of man;
Thy peace, and joy, and righteousness,
In all our bosoms reign.

3 The righteousness that never ends,
But makes an end of sin;
The joy that human thought transcends,
Now to our souls bring in.

4 The kingdom of established peace,
Which can no more remove;
The perfect powers of godliness,
The omnipotence of love.

23. 7s. M.

1 Light of life, seraphic fire!
Love divine, thyself impart:
Every fainting soul inspire;
Enter every drooping heart:
Every mournful sinner cheer,
Scatter all our guilty gloom;
Father! in thy grace appear,
To thy human temples come.

2 Come, in this accepted hour,
Bring thy heavenly kingdom in;
Fill us with thy glorious power,
Rooting out the seeds of sin:
Nothing more can we require,
We will covet nothing less:
Be thou all our heart's desire,
All our joy, and all our peace.

24. L. M.

1 Return, my soul, unto thy rest,
From vain pursuits and maddening cares;
From lonely woes that wring thy breast,
The world's allurements, toils, and snares.

2 Return unto thy rest, my soul,
From all the wanderings of thy thought;
From sickness unto death made whole;
Safe through a thousand perils brought.

3 Then to thy rest, my soul, return,
From passions every hour at strife;
Sin's works, and ways, and wages spurn;
Lay hold upon eternal life.

4 God is thy rest; with heart inclined
To keep his word, that word believe;
Christ is thy rest; with lowly mind,
His light and easy yoke receive.

25. L. M.

1 Father! adored in worlds above,
Thy glorious name be hallowed still;
Thy kingdom come with power and love,
And earth, like heaven, obey thy will.

2 Lord! make our daily wants thy care;
Forgive the sins which we forsake;
And, as we in thy kindness share,
Let fellow-men of ours partake.

3 Evils beset us every hour;
Thy kind protection we implore;
Thine is the kingdom, thine the power,
Be thine the glory evermore!

26. L. M.

1 Lo, God is here! Let us adore,
And humbly bow before his face;
Let all within us feel his power,
Let all within us seek his grace.

2 Lo, God is here! Him, day and night,
United choirs of angels sing:
To him, enthroned above all height,
Heaven's host their noblest homage bring.

3 Being of beings! may our praise
Thy courts with grateful fragrance fill:
Still may we stand before thy face,
Still hear and do thy sovereign will.

27. S. M.

1 Come to the house of prayer,
O ye afflicted, come:
The God of peace shall meet you there,—
He makes that house his home.

2 Come to the house of praise,
Ye who are happy now;
In sweet accord your voices raise,
In kindred homage bow.

3 Ye aged, hither come,
For ye have felt his love:
Soon shall your trembling tongues be dumb,
Your lips forget to move.

4 Ye young, before his throne,
Come, bow; your voices raise;
Let not your hearts his praise disown,
Who gives the power to praise.

5 Thou, whose benignant eye
In mercy looks on all, —
Who seest the tear of misery,
And hear'st the mourner's call, —

6 Up to thy dwelling-place
Bear our frail spirits on,
Till they outstrip time's tardy pace,
And heaven on earth be won.

28. 8 & 7s. M.

1 Love divine, all love excelling,
Joy of heaven, to earth come down!
Fix in us thy humble dwelling,
All thy faithful mercies crown.
Father! thou art all compassion,
Pure, unbounded love thou art;
Visit us with thy salvation,
Enter every longing heart.

2 Breathe, O, breathe thy loving spirit
Into every troubled breast;
Let us all in thee inherit,
Let us find thy promised rest.
Come, almighty to deliver,
Let us all thy life receive;
Graciously come down, and never,
Never more thy temples leave.

29. H. M.

1 Lord of the worlds above,
How pleasant and how fair
The dwellings of thy love,
Thine earthly temples, are!
To thine abode my heart aspires,
With warm desires to see my God.

2 O happy souls that pray
Where God appoints to hear!
O happy men that pay
Their constant service there!
They praise thee still; and happy they
Who love the way to Zion's hill.

3 They go from strength to strength,
Throughout these mortal years,
Till each arrives at length,
Till each in heaven appears:
O glorious seat, when God, our King,
Shall thither bring our willing feet!

30. L. M.

1 Forth from the dark and stormy sky,
Lord, to thine altar's shade we fly;
Forth from the world, its hope and fear,
Father, we seek thy shelter here:
Weary and weak, thy grace we pray;
Turn not, O Lord, thy guests away.

2 Long have we roamed in want and pain;
Long have we sought thy rest in vain;
Wildered in doubt, in darkness lost,
Long have our souls been tempest-tost:
Low at thy feet our sins we lay;
Turn not, O Lord, thy guests away.

31. 8 & 7s. M.

1 FAR from mortal cares retreating,
Sordid hopes and fond desires,
Here, our willing footsteps meeting,
Every heart to heaven aspires.
From the Fount of glory beaming,
Light celestial cheers our eyes;
Mercy from above proclaiming,
Peace and pardon from the skies.

2 Every stain of guilt abhorring,
Firm and bold in virtue's cause,
Still thy providence adoring,
Faithful subjects to thy laws,
Lord! with favor still attend us,
Bless us with thy wondrous love;
Thou, our sun and shield, defend us;
All our hope is from above.

32. C. M.

1 O FATHER! though the anxious fear
May cloud to-morrow's way,
No fear nor doubt shall enter here,—
All shall be thine to-day.

2 We will not bring divided hearts
To worship at thy shrine;
But each unworthy thought departs,
And leaves this temple thine.

33. S. M.

1 Lord, in this sacred hour
Within thy courts we bend,
And bless thy love, and own thy power,
Our Father and our Friend.

2 But thou art not alone
In courts by mortals trod;
Nor only is the day thine own
When man draws near to God.

3 Thy temple is the arch
Of yon unmeasured sky;
Thy Sabbath, the stupendous march
Of grand eternity.

4 Lord, may that holier day
Dawn on thy servants' sight;
And purer worship may we pay
In heaven's unclouded light.

34. C. M.

1 With sacred joy we lift our eyes
To those bright realms above, —
That glorious temple in the skies
Where dwells eternal love.

2 Before the awful throne we bow
  Of heaven's Almighty King:
Here we present the solemn vow,
  And hymns of praise we sing.

3 Thee we adore, and, Lord, to thee
  Our filial duty pay;
Thy service, unconstrained and free,
  Conducts to endless day.

4 While in thy house of prayer we kneel,
  With trust and holy fear,
Thy mercy and thy truth reveal,
  And lend a gracious ear.

35. 7s. M.

1 Lord, what offering shall we bring,
  At thine altars when we bow?
Hearts, the pure unsullied spring,
  Whence the kind affections flow;
Soft compassion's feeling soul,
  By the melting eye expressed;
Sympathy, at whose control
  Sorrow leaves the wounded breast;

2 Willing hands to lead the blind,
  Bind the wounded, feed the poor;
Love, embracing all our kind;
  Charity, with liberal store:—
Teach us, O thou Heavenly King,
  Thus to show our grateful mind,
Thus the accepted offering bring,
  Love to thee and all mankind.

36. C. M.

1 O, NOT alone with outward sign
Of fear, or voice from heaven,
The message of a truth divine,
The call of God, is given;
Awakening in the human heart
Love for the true and right,
Zeal for the Christian's better part,
Strength for the Christian's fight.

2 Though heralded by naught of fear,
Or outward sign or show;
Though only to the inward ear
It whisper soft and low;
Though dropping as the manna fell,
Unseen, yet from above,
Holy and gentle, heed it well:
The call to truth and love.

37. L. M.

1 "LET there be light!" — When from on high,
O God, that first commandment came,
Forth leaped the sun; and earth and sky
Lay in his light and felt his flame.

2 "Let there be light!" — The light of grace
And truth, a darkling world to bless,
Came with thy word, when on our race
Broke forth the Sun of Righteousness.

3 Light of our souls! how strong it grows:
That sun, how wide his beams he flings,
As up the glorious sky he goes
With light and healing in his wings!

4 Give us that light! O God, 't is given!
Hope sees it open heaven's wide halls
To those who for the truth have striven;
And Faith walks firmly where it falls.

38. 10s. M.

1 O Thou, whose power o'er moving worlds presides,
Whose voice created, and whose wisdom guides!
On darkling man in pure effulgence shine,
And cheer the clouded mind with light divine.

2 'T is thine alone to calm the pious breast
With silent confidence and holy rest;
From thee, great God! we spring; to thee we tend;
Path, motive, guide, original, and end.

39. L. M.

1 When, as returns this solemn day,
Man comes to meet his Maker, God,
What rites, what honors, shall he pay?
How spread his Sovereign's praise abroad?

2 From marble domes, and gilded spires,
Shall curling clouds of incense rise?
And gems, and gold, and garlands deck
The costly pomp of sacrifice?

3 Vain, sinful man! creation's Lord
Thy golden offerings well may spare;
But give thy heart, and thou shalt find
Here dwells a God who heareth prayer.

40. C. M.

1 O God! whose dread and dazzling brow
Love never yet forsook,
On those who seek thy presence now,
In deep compassion look.

2 For many a frail and erring heart
Is in thy holy sight,
And feet too willing to depart
From the plain way of right.

3 Yet pleased the humble prayer to hear,
And kind to all that live,
Thou, when thou seest the contrite tear,
Art ready to forgive.

4 Lord! aid us with thy heavenly grace
Our truest bliss to find;
Nor sternly judge our erring race,
So feeble, and so blind.

41. 11 & 10s. M.

1 Father, to us, thy children, humbly kneeling,
Conscious of weakness, ignorance, sin, and shame,
Give such a force of holy thought and feeling
That we may live to glorify thy name;—

2 That we may conquer base desire and passion,
That we may rise from selfish thought and will,
O'ercome the world's allurement, threat, and fashion,
Walk humbly, gently, leaning on thee still.

3 Let all thy goodness by our minds be seen,
Let all thy mercy on our souls be sealed;
Lord, if thou wilt, thy power can make us clean,
O, speak the word! Thy servants shall be healed.

42. L. M.

1 Great God! the followers of thy Son,
We bow before thy mercy-seat,
To worship thee, the Holy One,
And pour our wishes at thy feet.

2 O, grant thy blessing here to-day!
O, give thy people joy and peace!
The tokens of thy love display,
And favor that shall never cease.

41. 11 & 10s. M.

1 Father, to us, thy children, humbly kneeling,
Conscious of weakness, ignorance, sin, and shame,
Give such a force of holy thought and feeling
That we may live to glorify thy name; —

2 That we may conquer base desire and passion,
That we may rise from selfish thought and will,
O'ercome the world's allurement, threat, and fashion,
Walk humbly, gently, leaning on thee still.

Let all thy goodness by our minds be seen,
Let all thy mercy on our souls be sealed;
Lord, if thou wilt, thy power can make us clean,
O, speak the word! Thy servants shall be healed.

42. L. M.

1 Great God! the followers of thy Son,
We bow before thy mercy-seat,
To worship thee, the Holy One,
And pour our wishes at thy feet.

2 O, grant thy blessing here to-day!
O, give thy people joy and peace!
The tokens of thy love display,
And favor that shall never cease.

44. L. M.

1 Before Jehovah's awful throne,
Ye nations, bow with sacred joy;
Know that the Lord is God alone;
He can create, and he destroy.

2 We are his people, we his care,
Our souls and all our mortal frame;
What lasting honors shall we rear,
Almighty Maker, to thy name?

3 We 'll crowd thy gates with thankful songs;
High as the heavens our voices raise;
And earth, with her ten thousand tongues,
Shall fill thy courts with sounding praise.

4 Wide as the world is thy command,
Vast as eternity thy love;
Firm as a rock thy truth must stand,
When rolling years shall cease to move.

45. C. M.

1 Here holy thoughts a light have shed
From many a radiant face,
And prayers of tender hope have spread
A perfume through the place.

2 And anxious hearts have pondered here
The mystery of life,
And prayed the Eternal Spirit clear
Their doubts and aid their strife.

3 From humble tenements around
Came up the pensive train,
And in the Church a blessing found,
Which filled their homes again.

4 For faith, and peace, and mighty love,
That from the Godhead flow,
Showed them the life of heaven above
Springs from the life below.

46. 11 & 5s.

1 From the recesses of a lowly spirit,
Our humble prayer ascends; O Father! hear it,
Upsoaring on the wings of awe and meekness;
Forgive its weakness!

2 We see thy hand; it leads us, it supports us:
We hear thy voice; it counsels and it courts us:
And then we turn away; and still thy kindness
Forgives our blindness.

3 O, how long-suffering, Lord! but thou delightest
To win with love the wandering; thou invitest,
By smiles of mercy, not by frowns or terrors,
Man from his errors.

4 Father and Saviour! plant within each bosom
The seeds of holiness, and bid them blossom
In fragrance and in beauty bright and vernal,
And spring eternal.

5 Then place them in thine everlasting gardens,
Where angels walk, and seraphs are the wardens;
Where every flower escaped through death's dark portal,
Becomes immortal.

47. C. M.

1 For thy dear mercy's sake, O Lord,
Receive the prayers we pour,
And purify our hearts to taste
Thy goodness more and more.

2 Our flesh, our hearts, our spirits, Lord,
In thy clear fire refine;
Break down the self-indulgent will;
Gird us with strength divine.

3 So may all we, who here are met
This hour thy name to bless,
One day, in our eternal home,
Thine endless joys possess.

48. L. M.

1 Dear Lord! prepare our souls and train
Our hearts in thoughts of love to pray;
Teach us to know our sins, and gain
New triumphs o'er ourselves each day.

2 How oft our thoughts, in idle chase,
On vanity and sin run wild,

Our best resolves, in varying phase,
  Beguiling come, or go beguiled!

3 Caught by a glittering bait, we fall
  Sin's easy, weak, and thoughtless prey;
While, all unheeded, virtue's call
  Beckons in vain another way.

4 Dear Lord, thou hast full often said,
  There is a path, — one only way;
O, come, then, quickly to our aid,
  And teach us how and what to pray!

49. C. M.

1 God is a spirit just and wise,
  He sees our inmost mind;
In vain to heaven we raise our cries,
  And leave our souls behind.

2 Nothing but truth before his throne
  With honor can appear;
The painted hypocrites are known
  Through the disguise they wear.

3 Their lifted eyes salute the skies,
  Their bending knees the ground;
But God abhors the sacrifice
  Where not the heart is found.

4 Lord, search my thoughts, and try my ways,
  And make my soul sincere;
Then shall I stand before thy face,
  And find acceptance there.

50. 7s. M.

1 When before thy throne we kneel,
Filled with awe and holy fear,
Teach us, O our God! to feel
All thy sacred presence near.

2 Check each proud and wandering thought,
When on thy great name we call;
Man is naught, is less than naught;
Thou, our God, art all in all.

3 Weak, imperfect creatures, we
In this vale of darkness dwell;
Yet presume to look to thee,
'Midst thy light ineffable.

4 O, receive the praise that dares
Seek thy heaven-exalted throne;
Bless our offerings, hear our prayers,
Infinite and Holy One!

CLOSE OF SERVICE.

---

51. 8 & 7s. M.

1 May the grace of Christ, our Saviour,
And the Father's boundless love,
With the Holy Spirit's favor,
Rest upon us from above.

2 Thus may we abide in union
With each other and the Lord,
And possess, in sweet communion,
Joys which earth cannot afford.

52. L. M.

1 My God! how endless is thy love!
Thy gifts are every evening new;
And morning mercies from above
Gently distil, like early dew.

2 I yield my powers to thy command;
To thee I consecrate my days;
Perpetual blessings from thy hand
Demand perpetual songs of praise.

53. L. M.

1 From all that dwell below the skies
Let the Creator's praise arise;
Let the Redeemer's name be sung,
Through every land, by every tongue.

2 Eternal are thy mercies, Lord;
Eternal truth attends thy word;
Thy praise shall sound from shore to shore,
Till suns shall rise and set no more.

54. 8, 7, & 4s. M.

1 Lord! dismiss us with thy blessing,
Hope and comfort from above;
Let us each, thy peace possessing,
Triumph in redeeming love:
Still support us
While in duty's path we move.

2 Thanks we give, and adoration,
For the Gospel's joyful sound;
May the fruits of thy salvation
In our hearts and lives abound;
May thy presence
With us evermore be found.

55. 7s. M.

1 FATHER! glory be to thee,
Source of all the good we see!
Glory for the blessed light
Rising on the ancient night!

2 Glory for the hopes that come,
Streaming through the dreary tomb!
Glory for the counsel given,
Guiding us in peace to heaven!

56. C. M.

1 O WONDROUS depth of grace divine,
My soul would fain adore:
Dear Father, let me call thee mine,
And I will ask no more.

2 By thee in all things richly blest,
Low at thy feet I fall;
Thou art my Hope, my Life, my Rest,
My Father, and my all!

57. 7s. M.

1 FATHER, bless thy word to all;
Quick and powerful let it prove:
O, may sinners hear thy call!
Let thy people grow in love.

2 Thine own gracious message bless;
Follow it with power divine;
Give the Gospel great success;
Thine the work, the glory thine.

3 Father, bid the world rejoice;
Send, O, send thy truth abroad;
Let the nations hear thy voice,—
Hear it, and return to God.

58. 8 & 7s. M.

1 Lord of nature, Source of light,
In pity view thy world below;
Guide our erring footsteps right,
Through these scenes of guilt and woe.

2 Grant thy spirit; by thy kindness
Let our errors be forgiven;
Heal our sins, dispel our blindness,
Then conduct us safe to heaven.

59. 8, 7, & 4s. M.

1 Come, thou soul-transforming Spirit!
Bless the sower and the seed;
Let each heart thy grace inherit,
Raise the weak, the hungry feed;
From the Gospel
Now supply thy people's need.

2 O, may all enjoy the blessing
Which thy word 's designed to give!
Let us all, thy love possessing,
Joyfully the truth receive,
And for ever
To thy praise and glory live.

60. C. M.

1 O God, by whom the seed is given,
By whom the harvest blest;
Whose word, like manna showered from heaven,
Is planted in our breast;—

2 Preserve it from the passing feet,
And plunderers of the air;
The sultry sun's intenser heat,
And weeds of worldly care!

3 Though buried deep, or thinly strown,
Do thou thy grace supply:
The hope in earthly furrows sown
Shall ripen in the sky.

61. 8 & 7s. M.

1 Lo! the day of rest declineth,
Gather fast the shades of night;
May the Sun that ever shineth
Fill our souls with heavenly light.

2 While, thine ear of love addressing,
Thus our parting hymn we sing,
Father, give thine evening blessing;
Fold us safe beneath thy wing.

62. C. M.

1 Soon will our fleeting hours be past;
And, as the setting sun
Sinks downward in the radiant west,
Our parting beams be gone.

2 May He, from whom all blessings flow,
Our sacred rites attend,
Uniting all in wisdom's ways,
Till life's short journey end;

3 And as the rapid sands run down,
Our virtue still improve,
Till each receive the glorious crown
Of never-fading love.

63. S. M.

1 Thy name, Almighty Lord,
Shall sound through distant lands;
Great is thy grace, and sure thy word;
Thy truth for ever stands.

2 Far be thine honor spread,
And long thy praise endure,
Till morning light and evening shade
Shall be exchanged no more.

64. 7s. M.

1 Glorious in thy saints appear;
Plant thy heavenly kingdom here;
Light and life to all impart;
Shine on each believing heart;—

2 And, in every grace complete,
Make us, Lord, for glory meet;
Till we stand before thy sight,
Partners with the saints in light.

65. 7s. M.

1 Mighty One, before whose face
Wisdom had her glorious seat,
When the orbs that people space
Sprang to birth beneath thy feet!

2 Source of truth, whose rays alone
Light the mighty world of mind!
God of love, who from thy throne
Kindly watchest all mankind!

3 Shed on those who in thy name
Teach the way of truth and right,
Shed that love's undying flame,
Shed that wisdom's guiding light.

66. S. M.

1 Blest are the pure in heart,
For they shall see our God;
The secret of the Lord is theirs,
Their soul is Christ's abode.

2 Still to the lowly soul
He doth himself impart,
And for his temple and his throne
Chooseth the pure in heart.

67. L. M.

1 Thy name be hallowed evermore;
O God! thy kingdom come with power;
Thy will be done, and, day by day,
Give us our daily bread, we pray.

2 Lord! evermore to us be given
The living bread that came from heaven:
Water of life on us bestow;
Thou art the Source, the Giver thou.

68. L. M.

1 Arm of the Lord, awake! awake!
Put on thy strength, the nations shake!
Now let the world, adoring see
Triumphs of mercy wrought by thee.

2 Almighty God, thy grace proclaim
Through every clime of every name;
Let adverse powers before thee fall,
And crown the Saviour Lord of all.

69. 8 & 7s. M.

1 Glorious things of thee are spoken,
Zion, city of our God!
He whose word cannot be broken
Formed thee for his own abode.
On the Rock of Ages founded,
What can shake thy sure repose?
With salvation's walls surrounded,
Thou mayst smile at all thy foes.

2 See! the streams of living waters,
Springing from eternal love,
Well supply thy sons and daughters,
And all fear of want remove.
Who can faint while such a river
Ever flows their thirst to assuage,—
Grace, which, like the Lord, the giver,
Never fails from age to age?

3 Round each habitation hovering,
See the cloud and fire appear,
For a glory and a covering,
Showing that the Lord is near!
Fading is the worldling's pleasure,
All his boasted pomp and show;
Solid joys and lasting treasure
None but Zion's children know.

70. C. M.

1 The heaven of heavens cannot contain
The universal Lord;
Yet he in humble hearts will deign
To dwell, and be adored.

2 Where'er ascends the sacrifice
Of fervent praise and prayer,
Or on the earth, or in the skies,
The God of heaven is there.

3 His presence is diffused abroad,
Through realms, through worlds unknown;
Who seek the mercies of our God
Are ever near his throne.

71. 7s. M.

Lord, it is not life to live,
If thy presence thou deny;
Lord, if thou thy presence give,
'T is no longer death to die.
Source and Giver of repose,
Singly from thy smile it flows;
Peace and happiness are thine;
Mine they are, if thou art mine.

72. C. M.

1 Lord of the harvest, God of grace,
Send down thy heavenly rain;

In vain we plant without thine aid,
And water too in vain.

2 May no vain thoughts, those birds of prey,
Defraud us of our gain;
Nor anxious cares, those baleful thorns,
Choke up the precious grain.

3 Ne'er may our hearts be like the rock,
Where but the blade can spring,
Which, scorched with heat, becomes by noon
A dead, a useless thing.

4 But may our hearts, like fertile soil,
Receive the heavenly word;
So shall our fair and ripened fruits
Their hundred fold afford.

73. P. M.

1 Blest is the hour when cares depart,
And earthly scenes are far, —
When tears of woe forget to start,
And gently dawns upon the heart
Devotion's holy star.

2 Blest is the place where angels bend
To hear our worship rise,
Where kindred thoughts their musings blend,
And all the soul's affections tend
Beyond the veiling skies.

3 Blest are the hallowed vows that bind
Man to his work by love, —

Bind him to cheer the humble mind,
Console the weeping, lead the blind,
And guide to joys above.

74. 7 & 6s. M.

God shall bless thy going out,
Shall bless thy coming in;
Kindly compass thee about,
Till thou art saved from sin:
Lean upon thy Father's breast;
'T is he thy spirit keeps:
Rest in him, securely rest;
Thy Guardian never sleeps.

75. C. M.

1 There is a world, — and, O, how blest!
Fairer than prophets told;
And never did an angel guest
One half its peace unfold.

2 Look not abroad, with roving mind,
To seek that fair abode;
It comes where'er the lowly find
The perfect peace of God.

76. C. M.

O thou great Spirit! who along
The waters first did move,
And straight from warring chaos sprung
Light, harmony, and love;

Upon our waiting spirits brood,
  Bid all their discord cease,
And breathe upon the troubled soul
  Thy last, best gift of peace!

77. 7s. M.

1 Now may he who from the dead
  Brought the Shepherd of the sheep,
Jesus Christ, our King and Head,
  All our souls in safety keep.

2 May he teach us to fulfil
  What is pleasing in his sight;
Perfect us in all his will,
  And preserve us day and night.

78. C. M.

1 O Lord of life, and truth, and grace,
  Ere nature was begun!
Make welcome to our erring race
  Thy Spirit and thy Son.

2 We hail the Church, built high o'er all
  The heathens' rage and scoff;
Thy Providence its fencèd wall,—
  "The Lamb the light thereof."

3 Thy Christ hath reached his heavenly seat,
  Through sorrows and through scars;
The golden lamps are at his feet,
  And in his hand the stars.

4 O, may he walk among us here,
With his rebuke and love, —
A brightness o'er this lower sphere,
A ray from worlds above!

79. C. M.

1 Almighty God, thy word is cast
Like seed into the ground;
Now let the dew of heaven descend,
And righteous fruits abound.

2 Let not the foe of Christ and man
This holy seed remove;
But give it root in every heart,
To bring forth fruits of love.

3 Nor let thy word, so kindly sent
To raise us to thy throne,
Return to thee, and sadly tell
That we reject thy Son.

4 Oft as the precious seed is sown,
Thy quickening grace bestow,
That all whose souls the truth receive
Its saving power may know.

DEDICATION.

---

80. L. M.

1 This stone to thee in faith we lay,—
We build the temple, Lord, to thee,
Thine eye be open night and day,
To keep this house from error free.

2 Here, when thy people seek thy face,
And dying sinners pray to live,
Hear thou, in heaven, thy dwelling-place,
And when thou hearest, Lord, forgive.

3 Here, when thy messengers proclaim
The blessed Gospel of thy Son,
Still by the power of his great name
Be mighty signs and wonders done.

4 Thy glory never hence depart!
Yet choose not, Lord, this house alone;
Thy kingdom come to every heart;
In every bosom fix thy throne.

81. C. M.

1 O Thou, whose own vast temple stands
Built over earth and sea,
Accept the walls that human hands
Have raised to worship thee.

2 Lord, from thine inmost glory send,
Within these courts to bide,
The peace that dwelleth, without end,
Serenely by thy side.

3 May erring minds that worship here
Be taught the better way,
And they who mourn, and they who fear,
Be strengthened as they pray!

4 May faith grow firm, and love grow warm,
And pure devotion rise,
While round these hallowed walls the storm
Of earth-born passion dies!

82. C. M.

1 The patriarch's dove, on weary wing,
One leaf of olive found,
Within the narrow ark to bring,
When all the earth was drowned.

2 The dove of God, in happier hour,
O'er Jordan's sweeter wave,
In symbol showed the Spirit's power,
That all the earth would save.

3 O Lord! to this our sacred rite
Such gracious tokens grant,
As make thy temples, where they light,
Thine arks of covenant.

4 And still on life's baptizing tide,
Or sorrow's bitter sea,
Descending peace be multiplied,
And hallow hearts to thee!

83. L. M.

1 The perfect world by Adam trod
Was the first temple, built by God;
His fiat laid the corner-stone,
And heaved its pillars, one by one.

2 He hung its starry roof on high,
The broad, illimitable sky;
He spread its pavement, green and bright,
And curtained it with morning light.

3 The mountains in their places stood,
The sea, the sky, — and "all was good";
And when its first pure praises rang,
The "morning stars together sang."

4 Lord, 't is not ours to make the sea
And earth and sky a house for thee;
But in thy sight our offering stands,
An humbler temple, "made with hands."

84. L. M.

1 WHERE ancient forests widely spread,
Where bends the cataract's ocean-fall;
On the lone mountain's silent head,
There are thy temples, God of all!

2 All space is holy, for all space
Is filled by thee; — but human thought
Burns clearer in some chosen place,
Where thine own words of love are taught.

3 Here be they taught; and may we know
That faith thy servants knew of old,
Which onward bears, through weal or woe,
Till death the gates of heaven unfold.

4 Nor we alone; may those whose brow
Shows yet no trace of human cares,
Hereafter stand where we do now,
And raise to thee still holier prayers.

SABBATH.

---

85. 10s. M.

1 Types of eternal rest,—fair buds of bliss,
In heavenly flowers expanding week by week,—
The next world's gladness imaged forth in this,—
Days of whose worth the Christian's heart can speak.

2 Foretastes of heaven on earth,—pledges of joy
Surpassing fancy's flights and fiction's story,—
The preludes of a feast that cannot cloy,
And the bright out-courts of immortal glory.

3 Eternity in time,—the steps by which
We climb to future ages,—lamps that light
Man through his darker days, and thought enrich,
Yielding redemption for the week's dull flight.

4 Wakeners of prayer in man,—his resting bowers
As on he journeys in the narrow way,
Where, Eden-like, Jehovah's walking hours
Are waited for, as in the cool of day.

5 Days fixed by God for intercourse with dust,
To raise our thoughts and purify our powers,—
Periods appointed to renew our trust,—
A gleam of glory after six days' showers.

86. C. M.

1 Sleep, sleep to-day, tormenting cares,
Of earth and folly born;
Ye shall not dim the light that streams
From this celestial morn.

2 To-morrow will be time enough
To feel your harsh control;
Ye shall not violate this day,
The Sabbath of the soul.

3 Sleep, sleep for ever, guilty thoughts;
Let fires of vengeance die;
And, purged from sin, may I behold
A God of purity!

87. C. M.

1 Lord, I believe a rest remains,
To all thy people known;
A rest where pure enjoyment reigns,
And thou art loved alone;—

2 A rest, where all our soul's desire
Is fixed on things above;
Where fear, and sin, and grief expire,
Cast out by perfect love.

3 O that I now the rest might know,
Believe and enter in!
Now, Father, now the power bestow,
And let me cease from sin!

4 Remove all hardness from my heart,
All unbelief remove;
To me the rest of faith impart,
The Sabbath of thy love.

88. L. M.

1 ANOTHER six days' work is done,
Another Sabbath is begun;
Return, my soul, enjoy thy rest;
Improve the day that God has blest.

2 O that our thoughts and thanks may rise,
As grateful incense to the skies,
And draw from heaven that sweet repose,
Which none but he that feels it knows!

3 This heavenly calm within the breast
Is the dear pledge of glorious rest,
Which for the Church of God remains,
The end of cares, the end of pains.

89. S. M.

1 AGAIN the Sunday morn
Calls us to prayer and praise;
Waking our hearts to gratitude
With its enlivening rays.

2 But Christ yet brighter shone,
Quenching the morning beam;
When triumphing from death he rose,
And raised us up with him.

3 When first the Word sprang forth,
In majesty arrayed,
And bathed in streams of purest light,—
What power was there displayed!

4 But O what love!—when Christ,
For our transgressions slain,
Was by the Eternal Father raised,
For us, to life again.

90. L. M.

1 We bless thee for this sacred day,
Thou who hast every blessing given,
Which sends the dreams of earth away,
And yields a glimpse of opening heaven.

2 Rich day of holy, thoughtful rest!
May we improve thy calm repose,
And, in God's service truly blest,
Forget the world, its joys, its woes.

3 Lord! may thy truth upon the heart
Now fall and dwell as heavenly dew,
And flowers of grace in freshness start
Where once the weeds of error grew.

4 May prayer now lift her sacred wings,
Contented with that aim alone
Which bears her to the King of kings,
And rests her at his sheltering throne.

91. C. M.

1 Again the Lord of life and light
Awakes the kindling ray,
Unseals the eyelids of the morn,
And pours increasing day.

2 O, what a night was that which wrapped
The heathen world in gloom!
O, what a sun which broke, this day,
Triumphant from the tomb!

3 This day be grateful homage paid,
And loud hosannas sung;
Let gladness dwell in every heart,
And praise on every tongue.

4 Ten thousand differing lips shall join
To hail this welcome morn,
Which scatters blessings from its wings
To nations yet unborn.

92. 7s. M.

1 Morning breaks upon the tomb!
Jesus dissipates its gloom!
Day of triumph through the skies,
See the glorious Saviour rise!

2 Mortals, dry your flowing tears;
Cease those unbelieving fears;
Look on his deserted grave;
Doubt no more his power to save.

3 Ye who are of death afraid,
Triumph in the scattered shade;
Drive your anxious fears away;
See the place where Jesus lay.

4 Lo! the rising sun appears,
Shedding radiance o'er the spheres;
Lo! returning beams of light
Chase the terrors of the night.

93. C. M.

1 Blest day of God! most calm, most bright,
The first and best of days;
The laborer's rest, the saint's delight,
The day of prayer and praise;

2 My Saviour's face made thee to shine;
His rising thee did raise,
And made thee heavenly and divine
Beyond all other days.

3 The first fruits oft a blessing prove
To all the sheaves behind;
And they who do the Sabbath love,
A happy week will find.

4 This day I must to God appear;
For, Lord, the day is thine;
Help me to spend it in thy fear,
And thus to make it mine.

II.

GOD.

ADORATION.

---

94. S. M.

1 O, BLESS the Lord, my soul.
Let all within me join,
And aid my tongue to bless his name,
Whose favors are divine.

2 O, bless the Lord, my soul!
Nor let his mercies lie
Forgotten in unthankfulness,
And without praises die.

3 'T is he forgives thy sins,
'T is he relieves thy pain,
'T is he that heals thy sicknesses,
And makes thee strong again.

4 He crowns thy life with love,
He rescues from the grave,
And he from everlasting death
Hath sovereign power to save.

95. C. M.

1 Father of mercies! God of love!
My Father and my God!
I 'll sing the honors of thy name,
And spread thy praise abroad.

2 In every period of my life
Thy thoughts of love appear;
Thy mercies gild each transient scene,
And crown each passing year.

3 In all thy mercies, may my soul
A Father's bounty see;
Nor let the gifts thy grace bestows
Estrange my heart from thee.

4 Teach me, in times of deep distress,
To own thy hand, O God!
And in submissive silence bear
The lessons of thy rod.

5 Through every period of my life,
Each bright, each clouded scene,
Give me a meek and humble mind,
Still equal and serene.

6 Then may I close my eyes in death,
Redeemed from anxious fear;
For death itself, my God, is life,
If thou be with me there.

96. C. M.

1 My God! how wonderful thou art,
Thy majesty how bright!
How glorious thy mercy-seat,
In depths of burning light!

2 Yet I may love thee too, O Lord!
Almighty as thou art,
For thou hast stooped to ask of me
The love of my poor heart.

3 No earthly father loves like thee,
No mother half so mild
Bears and forbears, as thou hast done,
With me, thy sinful child.

4 My God! how wonderful thou art,
Thou everlasting Friend!
On thee I stay my trusting heart
Till faith in vision end.

97. L. M.

1 Praise to the Lord of boundless might,
With uncreated glories bright!
His presence gilds the worlds above,
The unchanging Source of light and love.

2 Shine, mighty God! with vigor shine
On this benighted heart of mine;
And let thy glories stand revealed,
As in the Saviour's face beheld.

3 My soul, revived by heaven-born day,
Thy radiant image shall display,
While all my faculties unite
To praise the Lord, who gives me light.

98. L. M.

1 Father of all! in every age,
In every clime, adored,
By saint, by savage, or by sage,
The universal Lord!

2 Thou great First Cause! least understood,
Who all my sense confined
To know but this, — that thou art good,
And that myself am blind; —

3 What conscience dictates to be done,
Or warns me not to do,
This teach me more than hell to shun,
That more than heaven pursue.

4 If I am right, thy grace impart
Still in the right to stay;
If I am wrong, O, teach my heart
To find that better way.

5 To thee, whose temple is all space,
Whose altar earth, sea, skies,
One chorus let all being raise,
All nature's incense rise.

99. L. M.

1 O Thou, whom neither time nor space
Can circle in, unseen, unknown,
Nor faith in boldest flight can trace
Save through thy Spirit and thy Son,—

2 Be ours, O *King of mercy! still*
To feel thy presence from above,
And in thy word, and in thy will,
To hear thy voice, and know thy love.

3 Great First and Last! thy blessing give!
And grant us faith, thy gift alone,
To love and praise thee while we live,
And do whate'er thou wouldst have done.

4 And when the toils of life are done,
And nature waits thy dread decree,
To find our rest beneath thy throne,
And look, in humble hope, to thee.

100. 10 & 6s. M.

1 I love my God, but with no love of mine,
For I have none to give;
I love thee, Lord; but all the love is thine,
For by thy life I live.
I am as nothing, and rejoice to be
Emptied, and lost, and swallowed up in thee,

alone, art all thy children need,
. ...re is none beside;
From thee the streams of blessedness proceed,
In thee the blest abide, —
Fountain of life, and all-abounding grace,
Our source, our centre, and our dwelling-place.

101. C. M.

1 Keep silence, all created things,
And wait your Maker's nod;
My soul exulteth while she sings
The glories of our God.

2 Life, death, and hell, and worlds unknown,
Hang on his firm decree,
He sits on no precarious throne,
Nor borrows leave to be.

3 His mighty word bade ancient Night
Her empire vast resign,
And lo! unnumbered worlds of light
In fields of azure shine.

4 His wisdom with resistless sway
Guides the eternal frame;
With wonder, let all beings pay
Their homage to his name.

102. L. M.

1 Eternal God, almighty cause
Of earth, and seas, and worlds unknown;

All things are subject to thy laws;
All things depend on thee alone.

2 Thy glorious being singly stands,
Of all within itself possessed:
Controlled by none are thy commands;
Thou in thyself alone art blessed.

3 Worship to thee alone belongs;
Worship to thee alone we give;
Thine be our hearts, and thine our songs,
And to thy glory may we live.

4 Lord, spread thy name through heathen lands;
Their idol deities dethrone;
Subdue the world to thy commands,
And reign, as thou art, God alone.

103. C. M.

1 THE Lord descended from above,
And bowed the heavens most high;
And underneath his feet he cast
The darkness of the sky.

2 On cherubim and seraphim
Full royally he rode,
And on the wings of mighty winds
Came flying all abroad.

3 He sat serene upon the floods,
Their fury to restrain;
And he, as sovereign Lord and King,
For evermore shall reign.

104. C. M.

1 Thy throne eternal ages stood,
Ere earth or heaven was made;
Thou art the ever-living God,
Were all the nations dead.

2 Eternity, with all its years,
Stands present to thy view;
To thee, there 's nothing old appears,
Great God! there 's nothing new.

3 Our lives through varying scenes are drawn,
And vexed with trifling cares,
While thine eternal thought moves on
Thine undisturbed affairs.

4 Great God! how infinite art thou!
How frail and weak are we!
Let the whole race of creatures bow,
And homage pay to thee.

105. L. M.

1 Unchangeable, all-perfect Lord!
Essential life's unbounded sea!
What lives and moves, lives by thy word;
It lives, and moves, and is, from thee!
Whate'er in earth, or sea, or sky,
Or shuns, or meets, the wandering thought,
Escapes, or strikes, the searching eye,
By thee was to existence brought.

2 Thine, Lord, is holiness, alone:
  Justice and truth before thee stand:
Yet, nearer to thy sacred throne,
  Love ever dwells at thy right hand.
And to thy love and ceaseless care,
  Father! this light, this breath, we owe;
And all we have, and all we are,
  From thee, great Source of Life! doth flow.

106. 8 & 7s. M.

1 "Lord, thy glory fills the heaven;
  Earth is with its fulness stored;
Unto thee be glory given,
  Holy, holy, holy Lord!"
Heaven is still with anthems ringing;
  Earth takes up the angels' cry,
"Holy, holy, holy," singing,
  "Lord of hosts, thou Lord most high!"

2 Ever thus in God's high praises,
  Brethren, let our tongues unite,
Whilst our thoughts his greatness raises,
  And our love his gifts excite.
With his seraph train before him,
  With his holy Church below,
Thus unite we to adore him,
  Bid we thus our anthem flow:—

3 "Lord, thy glory fills the heaven;
  Earth is with its fulness stored;
Unto thee be glory given,
  Holy, holy, holy Lord!

Thus thy glorious name confessing,
 We adopt the angels' cry,
Holy, holy, holy, — blessing
 Thee, the Lord our God most high.

107. L. M.

1 Thou, Lord, who rear'st the mountain's height,
And mak'st the cliffs with sunshine bright,
O, grant that we may own thy hand
No less in every grain of sand!

2 With forests huge, of dateless time,
Thy will has hung each peak sublime;
But withered leaves beneath the tree
Have tongues that tell as loud of thee.

3 Teach us that not a leaf can grow,
Till life from thee within it flow;
That not a grain of dust can be,
O Fount of being! save by thee; —

4 That every human word and deed,
Each flash of feeling, will, or creed,
Hath solemn meaning from above,
Begun and ended all in love.

108. 7s. M.

1 Heralds of creation! cry, —
Praise the Lord, the Lord most high!
Heaven and earth! obey the call;
Praise the Lord, the Lord of all.

2 Praise him, all ye hosts above;
Spirits perfected in love!
Sun and moon! your voices raise;
Sing, ye stars! your Maker's praise.

3 Earth! from all thy depths below
Ocean's hallelujahs flow;
Lightning, vapor, wind, and storm,
Hail and snow! his will perform.

4 High above all height his throne;
Excellent his name alone;
Him let all his works confess!
Him let all his children bless!

109. H. M.

1 All, from the sun's uprise
Unto his setting rays,
Resound in jubilees
The great Creator's praise.
Him serve alone;
In triumph bring
Your gifts, and sing
Before his throne!

2 Man drew from man his birth;
But God his noble frame
(Built of the ruddy earth)
Filled with celestial flame.
His sons we are,
By him are led,
Preserved and fed
With tender care.

3 Then to his portals press
 In your divine resorts;
With thanks his power profess,
 And praise him in his courts.
  How good! how pure!
   His mercies last;
   His promise past
  Is ever sure.

110. 11 & 6s. M.

1 Almighty One! I bend in dust before thee;
  Even so veiled cherubs bend;
In calm and still devotion I adore thee,
  All-wise, all-present Friend!
Thou to the earth its emerald robes hast given,
  Or curtained it in snow;
And the bright sun, and the soft moon in heaven,
  Before thy presence bow.

2 Thou Power sublime! whose throne is firmly seated
  On stars and glowing suns;
O, could I praise thee, — could my soul, elated,
  Waft thee seraphic tones, —
Had I the lyres of angels, — could I bring thee
  An offering worthy thee, —
In what bright notes of glory would I sing thee,
  Blest notes of ecstasy!

3 Eternity! Eternity! how solemn,
  How terrible the sound!
Here, leaning on thy promises, — a column
  Of strength, — may I be found,

O, let my heart be ever thine, while beating,
As when 't will cease to beat!
Be thou my portion, till that awful meeting
When I my God shall greet!

111. L. M.

1 Great God! in vain man's narrow view
Attempts to look thy nature through;
Our laboring powers with reverence own
Thy glories never can be known.

2 Not the high seraph's mighty thought,
Who countless years his God has sought,
Such wondrous height or depth can find,
Or fully trace thy boundless mind.

3 And yet thy kindness deigns to show
Enough for mortal minds to know;
While wisdom, goodness, power divine,
Through all thy works and conduct shine.

4 O, may our souls with rapture trace
Thy works of nature and of grace;
Explore thy sacred truth, and still
Press on to know and do thy will!

112. 7s. M.

1 Holy, holy, holy Lord!
Be thy glorious name adored;
Lord! thy mercies never fail;
Hail, celestial goodness, hail!

2 Though unworthy, Lord, thine ear,
Deign our humble songs to hear;
Purer praise we hope to bring,
When around thy throne we sing.

3 There no tongue shall silent be;
All shall join in harmony;
That, through heaven's capacious round,
Praise to thee may ever sound.

4 Lord! thy mercies never fail;
Hail, celestial goodness, hail!
Holy, holy, holy Lord!
Be thy glorious name adored.

113. 7s. M.

1 Let us, with a gladsome mind,
Praise the Lord, for he is kind;
For his mercies shall endure,
Ever faithful, ever sure.

2 Let us sound his name abroad,
For of gods he is the God;
Who, with all-commanding might,
Filled the new-made world with light;

3 Caused the golden-tressèd sun
All day long his course to run;
And the moon to shine by night,
'Mongst her spangled sisters bright.

4 All his creatures he doth feed;
His full hand supplies their need;
Let us, therefore, warble forth
His high majesty and worth.

114. C. M.

1 O God! we praise thee, and confess
That thou the only Lord
And everlasting Father art,
By all the earth adored.

2 To thee all angels cry aloud;
To thee the powers on high,
Both cherubim and seraphim,
Continually do cry.

3 O holy, holy, holy Lord,
Whom heavenly hosts obey!
The world is with the glory filled
Of thy majestic sway.

4 The apostles' glorious company,
And prophets, crowned with light,
With all the martyrs' noble host,
Thy constant praise recite.

5 The holy Church throughout the world,
O Lord! confesses thee,
That thou eternal Father art,
Of boundless majesty.

115. C. M.

1 SHINE forth, Eternal Source of light!
And make thy glories known;
Fill our enlarged, adoring sight
With lustre all thine own.

2 Vain are the charms and faint the rays
The brightest creatures boast;
And all their grandeur and their praise
Is in thy presence lost.

3 To know the Author of our frame
Is our sublimest skill;
True science is to read thy name,
True life to obey thy will.

4 For this I long, for this I pray,
And following on pursue,
Till visions of eternal day
Fix and complete the view.

116. L. M.

1 LET one loud song of praise arise
To God, whose goodness ceaseless flows;
Who dwells enthroned above the skies,
And life and breath on all bestows.

2 Let all of good this bosom fires
To him, sole good, give praises due;
Let all the truth himself inspires
Unite to sing him only true.

3 In ardent adoration joined,
Obedient to thy holy will,
Let all our faculties combined
Thy just commands, O God! fulfil.

4 O, may the solemn breathing sound,
Like incense, rise before thy throne,
Where thou, whose glory knows no bound,
Great Cause of all things, dwell'st alone.

117. L. M.

1 Lift up your hearts! Yes, I will lift
My heart and soul, dear Lord, to thee,
Who every good and perfect gift
Vouchsaf'st so lavishly and free.

2 All that is best from thee comes down
On us, with rich and ample store,
Thy bounteous hands our wishes crown
With good, increasing more and more.

3 Then, while I live, with ardent eye
Let me look up to thee, and learn,
From blessings here, to look on high,
And purer blessings there discern!

4 All thou hast given is thine, then take
Me, thine own gift, for all thine own,
And teach me every day to make
New vows of love to thee alone!

118. L. M.

1 High in the heavens, eternal God!
Thy goodness in full glory shines;
Thy truth shall break through every cloud
That veils and darkens thy designs.

2 For ever firm thy justice stands,
As mountains their foundations keep;
Wise are the wonders of thy hands;
Thy judgments are a mighty deep.

3 Life, like a fountain, rich and free,
Springs from the presence of my Lord;
And in thy light our souls shall see
The glories promised in thy word.

119. C. M.

1 Eternal Source of life and light!
Supremely good and wise!
To thee we bring our grateful vows,
To thee lift up our eyes.

2 Our dark and erring minds illume
With truth's celestial rays;
Inspire our hearts with sacred love,
And tune our lips to praise.

GOD'S PRESENCE, POWER, AND WISDOM.

---

120. 6s. M.

1 THE God who reigns alone
O'er earth, and sea, and sky,
Let man with praises own,
And sound his honors high.

2 Him all in heaven above,
Him all on earth below,
The exhaustless Source of love,
The great Creator, know.

3 He formed the living flame,
He gave the reasoning mind,
Then only he may claim
The worship of mankind.

4 So taught his only Son,
Blest messenger of grace!
The Eternal is but one,
No second holds his place.

121. C. M.

1 JEHOVAH God! thy gracious power
On every hand we see;
O, may the blessings of each hour
Lead all our thoughts to thee!

2 If on the wings of morn we speed
To earth's remotest bound,
Thy hand will there our footsteps lead,
Thy love our path surround.

3 Thy power is in the ocean deeps,
And reaches to the skies;
Thine eye of mercy never sleeps,
Thy goodness never dies.

4 In all the varying scenes of time,
On thee our hopes depend;
Through every age, in every clime,
Our Father, and our Friend!

122. C. P. M.

1 I SING of God, the mighty source
Of all things, the stupendous force
On which all things depend;
From whose right arm, beneath whose eyes,
All period, power, and enterprise
Commence, and reign, and end.

2 The world, the clustering spheres, he made,
The glorious light, the soothing shade;
Dale, plain, and grove and hill;

The multitudinous abyss,
Where nature joys in secret bliss,
And wisdom hides her skill.

3 Tell them, I AM, Jehovah said
To Moses, while earth heard in dread,
And, smitten to the heart,
At once above, beneath, around,
All nature, without voice or sound,
Replied, O Lord, THOU ART!

123. L. M.

1 GOD wounds the heart, and he makes whole;
He calms the tempest of the soul:
When he shuts up in long despair,
Who can remove the heavy bar?

2 He frowns, and darkness veils the moon,
The fainting sun grows dim at noon;
The pillars of heaven's starry roof
Tremble and start at his reproof.

3 These are a portion of his ways:
But who shall dare describe his face?
Who can endure his light, or stand
To hear the thunders of his hand?

124. L. M.

1 GREAT Former of this various frame
Our souls adore thine awful name;

And bow, and tremble, while we praise
The Ancient of eternal days.

2 Our days a transient period run,
And change with every circling sun;
And, in the firmest state we boast,
A moth can crush us into dust.

3 But let the creatures fall around;
Let death consign us to the ground;
Let the last general flame arise,
And melt the arches of the skies;

4 Calm as the summer's ocean, we
Can all the wreck of nature see,
While grace secures us an abode,
Unshaken as the throne of God.

125. L. M.

1 Lord, thou hast searched and seen me through,
Thine eye commands, with piercing view,
My rising and my resting hours,
My heart and flesh, with all their powers.

2 My thoughts, before they are my own,
Are to my God distinctly known;
He knows the words I mean to speak,
Ere from my opening lips they break.

3 Within thy circling power I stand;
On every side I find thy hand:
Awake, asleep, at home, abroad,
I am surrounded still with God.

4 O, may these thoughts possess my breast,
Where'er I rove, where'er I rest;
Nor let my weaker passions dare
Consent to sin, for God is there.

126. L. M.

1 SEARCHER of hearts, to thee are known
The inmost secrets of my breast;
At home, abroad, in crowds, alone,
Thou mark'st my rising and my rest, —
My thoughts far off, through every maze,
Source, stream, and issue, — all my ways.

2 How from thy presence should I go,
Or whither from thy spirit flee,
Since all above, around, below,
Exist in thine immensity?
If up to heaven I take my way,
I meet thee in eternal day; —

3 If in the grave I make my bed,
With worms and dust, lo! thou art there;
If, on the wings of morning sped,
Beyond the ocean I repair,
I feel thine all-controlling will,
And thy right hand upholds me still.

4 Search me, O God! and know my heart;
Try me, my secret soul survey;
And warn thy servant to depart
From every false and evil way:
So shall thy truth my guidance be
To life and immortality.

127. C. M.

1 Great Ruler of all nature's frame,
We own thy power divine;
We hear thy breath in every storm,
For all the winds are thine.

2 Wide as they sweep their sounding way,
They work thy sovereign will;
And, awed by thy majestic voice,
Confusion shall be still.

3 Thy mercy tempers every blast
To those who seek thy face,
And mingles with the tempest's roar
The whispers of thy grace.

4 Those gentle whispers let me hear,
Till all the tumult cease,
And gales of paradise shall lull
My weary soul to peace.

128. L. M.

1 Thy ways, O Lord, with wise design,
Are framed upon thy throne above,
And every dark or bending line
Meets in the centre of thy love.

2 My favored soul shall meekly learn
To lay her reason at thy throne;
Too weak thy secrets to discern,
I'll trust thee for my guide alone.

129. C. M.

1 God, in the high and holy place,
Looks down upon the spheres;
Yet in his providence and grace
To every eye appears.

2 He bows the heavens; the mountains stand,
A highway for our God:
He walks amidst the desert-land;
'T is Eden where he trod.

3 The forests in his strength rejoice;
Hark! on the evening breeze,
As once of old, the Lord God's voice
Is heard among the trees.

4 If God hath made this world so fair,
Where sin and death abound,
How beautiful beyond compare
Will Paradise be found!

130. C. M.

1 To thee, my God, my days are known,
My soul enjoys the thought;
My actions all before thy face,
Nor are my faults forgot.

2 Each secret breath devotion breathes
Is vocal to thine ear;
And all my walks of daily life
Before thine eye appear.

3 Each golden hour of beaming light
Is gilded by thy rays;
And dark affliction's midnight gloom
A present God surveys.

4 Full in thy view through life I pass,
And in thy view I die;
And, when each mortal bond is broke,
Shall find my God is nigh.

131. C. M.

1 Eternal Wisdom! thee we praise;
Thee the creation sings;
With thy great name, rocks, hills, and seas,
And heaven's high palace, rings.

2 Thy hand, how wide it spread the sky!
How glorious to behold!
Tinged with a blue of heavenly dye,
And starred with sparkling gold!

3 The noisy winds stand ready there
Thy orders to obey;
With sounding wings they sweep the air,
To make thy chariot way.

4 There, like a trumpet loud and strong,
Thy thunder shakes our coast,
While the red lightnings wave along, —
The banners of thine host.

5 The rolling mountains of the deep
Observe thy strong command;

Thy breath can raise the billows steep,
  Or sink them to the sand.

6 Infinite strength and equal skill
  Shine through the worlds abroad,
Our souls with vast amazement fill,
  And speak the builder, God.

132. L. M.

1 Ere mountains reared their forms sublime,
  Or heaven and earth in order stood,
Before the birth of ancient time,
  From everlasting thou art God.

2 A thousand ages, in their flight,
  With thee are as a fleeting day;
Past, present, future, to thy sight
  At once their various scenes display.

3 But our brief life 's a shadowy dream,
  A passing thought, that soon is o'er,
That fades with morning's earliest beam,
  And fills the musing mind no more.

4 To us, O Lord, the wisdom give,
  Each passing moment so to spend,
That we at length with thee may live,
  Where life and bliss shall never end.

133. C. M.

1 In all my vast concerns with thee,
  In vain my soul would try

To shun thy presence, Lord, or flee
  The notice of thine eye.

2 Thine all-surrounding sight surveys
  My rising and my rest;
My public walks, my private ways,
  And secrets of my breast.

3 My thoughts lie open to the Lord,
  Before they 're formed within;
And ere my lips pronounce the word
  He knows the sense I mean.

4 O wondrous knowledge, deep and high!
  Where can a creature hide?
Within thy circling arms I lie,
  Beset on every side.

5 So let thy grace surround me still,
  And like a bulwark prove,
To guard my soul from every ill,
  Secured by sovereign love.

134. L. M.

1 All-powerful, self-existent God,
  Who all creation dost sustain!
Thou wast, and art, and art to come,
  And everlasting is thy reign.

2 Fixed and eternal as thy days,
  Each glorious attribute divine,
Through ages infinite, shall still
  With undiminished lustre shine.

3 Fountain of being! Source of good!
Immutable thou dost remain!
Nor can the shadow of a change
Obscure the glories of thy reign.

4 Earth may with all her powers dissolve,
If such the great Creator's will;
But thou for ever art the same,
I AM is thy memorial still.

135. C. M.

1 BEYOND, beyond the boundless sea,
Above that dome of sky,
Farther than thought itself can flee,
Thy dwelling is on high;
Yet dear the awful thought to me,
That thou, my God, art nigh.

2 We hear thy voice, when thunders roll
Through the wide fields of air;
The waves obey thy dread control;
Yet still thou art not there.
Where shall I find him, O my soul,
Who yet is everywhere?

3 O, not in circling depth or height,
But in the conscious breast,
Present to faith, though veiled from sight,
There does his spirit rest.
O, come, thou Presence Infinite,
And make thy creature blest!

GOD'S LOVE.

---

136. C. M.

1 O GIFT of gifts! O grace of faith!
My God! how can it be
That thou, who hast discerning love,
Shouldst give that gift to me?

2 How many hearts thou mightst have had
More innocent than mine!
How many souls more worthy far
Of that sweet touch of thine!

3 Ah, Grace! into unlikeliest hearts
It is thy boast to come,
The glory of thy light to find
In darkest spots a home.

4 The crowd of cares, the weightiest cross,
Seem trifles less than light,—
Earth looks so little and so low
When faith shines full and bright.

5 O, happy, happy that I am!
If thou canst be, O Faith!
The treasure that thou art in life,
What wilt thou be in death?

137. 8 & 7s. M.

1 God is love; his mercy brightens
All the path in which we rove;
Bliss he wakes, and woe he lightens:
God is wisdom, God is love.

2 Chance and change are busy ever;
Man decays, and ages move;
But his mercy waneth never:
God is wisdom, God is love.

3 E'en the hour that darkest seemeth
Will his changeless goodness prove;
From the gloom his brightness streameth.
God is wisdom, God is love.

4 He with earthly cares entwineth
Hope and comfort from above;
Everywhere his glory shineth:
God is wisdom, God is love.

138. C. M.

1 Lord! thou art good: all nature shows
Its mighty Author kind;
Thy bounty through creation flows,
Full, free, and unconfined.

2 The whole, and every part, proclaims
Thine infinite good-will;
It shines in stars, and flows in streams,
And blooms on every hill.

3 We view it o'er the spreading main,
And heavens which spread more wide;
It drops in gentle showers of rain,
And rolls in every tide.

4 My admiration let it raise!
My best affections move!
Employ my tongue in songs of praise,
And fill my heart with love!

139. 7s. M.

1 Father! thy paternal care
Has my guardian been, my guide!
Every hallowed wish and prayer
Has thy hand of love supplied;
Thine is every thought of bliss
Left by hours and days gone by;
Every hope thy offspring is,
Beaming from futurity.

2 Every sun of splendid ray,
Every moon that shines serene,
Every morn that welcomes day,
Every evening's twilight scene,
Every hour which wisdom brings,
Every incense at thy shrine,
These, — and all life's holiest things,
And its fairest, — all are thine.

3 And for all, my hymns shall rise
Daily to thy gracious throne:
Thither let my asking eyes
Turn unwearied,—righteous One!
Through life's strange vicissitude,
There reposing all my care;
Trusting still, through ill and good,
Fixed, and cheered, and counselled there.

140. 8 & 7s. M.

1 FATHER, source of every blessing,
Tune my heart to grateful lays;
Streams of mercy, never ceasing,
Call for ceaseless songs of praise.

2 Teach me some melodious measure
Sung by raptured saints above;
Fill my soul with sacred pleasure,
While I sing redeeming love.

3 Thou didst seek me when a stranger,
Wandering from the fold above;
Thou, to save my soul from danger,
Didst redeem me with thy love.

4 By thy hand restored, defended,
Safe through life thus far I 've come;
Safe, O Lord, when life is ended,
Bring me to my heavenly home.

141. 8, 7, & 4s. M.

1 Every human tie may perish;
Friend to friend unfaithful prove;
Mothers cease their own to cherish;
Heaven and earth at last remove;
But no changes
Can avert the Father's love.

2 In the furnace God may prove thee,
Thence to bring thee forth more bright;
But can never cease to love thee;
Thou art precious in his sight:
God is with thee,—
God, thine everlasting light.

142. C. P. M.

1 My God, thy boundless love I praise;
How bright, on high, its glories blaze,
How sweetly bloom below!
It streams from thine eternal throne;
Through heaven its joys for ever run,
And o'er the earth they flow.

2 'T is love that paints the purple morn,
And bids the clouds, in air upborne,
Their genial drops distil:
In every vernal beam it glows,
And breathes in every gale that blows,
And glides in every rill.

3 Then let the love that makes me blest
With cheerful praise inspire my breast,
And ardent gratitude;
And all my thoughts and passions tend
To thee, my Father and my Friend,
My soul's eternal good.

143. 8s. M.

1 Yield to me now, for I am weak,
But confident in self-despair;
Speak to my heart, in blessings speak;
Be conquered by my instant prayer:
Speak, or thou never hence shalt move,
And tell me if thy name be Love.

2 'T is Love! 't is Love! thou diedst for me;
I hear thy whisper in my heart;
The morning breaks, the shadows flee;
Pure, universal Love thou art:
To me, to all, thy mercies move,
Thy nature and thy name is Love.

3 My prayer hath power with God; the grace
Unspeakable I now receive;
Through faith I see thee face to face;
I see thee face to face, and live!
In vain I have not wept and strove;
Thy nature and thy name is Love.

144. L. M.

1 How high Thou art! our songs can own
No music Thou couldst stoop to hear;
But still the Son's expiring groan
Is vocal in the Father's ear.

2 How pure Thou art! our hands are dyed
With curses, red with murder's hue;
But He hath stretched His hands to hide
The sins that pierced them from thy view.

3 How strong Thou art! we tremble lest
The thunders of thine arm be moved;
But He is lying on thy breast,
And thou must clasp thy Best-beloved!

4 How kind Thou art! Thou didst not choose
To joy in Him for ever so;
But that embrace thou wouldst not lose
For vengeance, didst for love forego!

5 High God, and pure, and strong, and kind!
The low, the foul, the feeble, spare!
Thy brightness in His face we find,—
Behold our darkness only there!

145. L. M.

1 WHAT would we give to our beloved?
The hero's heart to be unmoved,—
The poet's star-tuned harp to sweep,—

The senate's shout to patriot vows, —
The monarch's crown to light the brows?
"He giveth his belovèd sleep."

2 "Sleep soft, beloved!" we sometimes say,
But have no power to charm away
Sad dreams that through the eyelids creep:
But never doleful dream again
Shall break their happy slumber, when
"He giveth his belovèd sleep."

3 O earth, so full of dreary noise!
O men, with wailing in your voice!
O delvèd gold, the wailer's heap!
O strife, O curse, that o'er it fall!
God makes a silence through you all,
And giveth his belovèd sleep!

4 Yea! men may wonder while they scan, —
A living, thinking, feeling man
In such a rest his heart to keep!
But angels say, — and through the word,
I ween, their blessed smile is heard, —
"He giveth his belovèd sleep."

146. L. M.

1 The Lord my pasture shall prepare
And feed me with a shepherd's care;
His presence shall my wants supply
And guard me with a watchful eye:
My noonday walks he shall attend,
And all my midnight hours defend.

2 When in the sultry glebe I faint,
Or on the thirsty mountain pant,
To fertile vales and dewy meads
My weary, wandering steps he leads;
Where peaceful rivers, soft and slow,
Amid the verdant landscape flow.

3 Though in the paths of death I tread,
With gloom and terror overspread,
My steadfast heart shall know no ill,
For thou, O Lord, art with me still;
Thy friendly crook shall give me aid
And guide me in the fearful shade.

147. S. M.

1 The Lord my shepherd is,
I shall be well supplied:
Since he is mine, and I am his,
What can I want beside?

2 He leads me to the place
Where heavenly pasture grows,
Where living waters gently pass,
And full salvation flows.

3 If e'er I go astray,
He doth my soul reclaim,
And guides me in his own right way,
For his most holy name.

4 While he affords his aid
I cannot yield to fear;
Tho' I should walk thro' death's dark shade,
My Shepherd 's with me there.

148. C. M.

1 When all thy mercies, O my God,
My rising soul surveys,
Transported with the view, I 'm lost
In wonder, love, and praise.

2 Unnumbered comforts on my soul
Thy tender care bestowed,
Before my infant heart conceived
From whom those comforts flowed.

3 When worn with sickness, oft hast thou
With health renewed my face;
And, when in sin and sorrow sunk,
Revived my soul with grace.

4 Ten thousand thousand precious gifts
My daily thanks employ;
Nor is the least a cheerful heart,
That tastes those gifts with joy.

GOD'S FORGIVENESS.

---

149. L. M.

1 Show pity, Lord! O Lord, forgive;
Let a repenting sinner live:
Are not thy mercies large and free?
May not the contrite trust in thee?

2 A broken heart, my God! my King!
Is all the offering I can bring;
The God of grace will ne'er despise
A broken heart for sacrifice.

150. L. M.

1 Forgive us for thy mercy's sake,
Our multitude of sins forgive!
And for thy own possession take,
And bid us to thy glory live:
Live in thy sight, and gladly prove
Our faith by our obedient love.

2 The covenant of forgiveness seal,
And all thy mighty wonders show!
Our hidden enemies expel,
And conquering them to conquer go,
Till all of pride and sin be slain,
And not one evil thought remain.

3 O, put it in our inward parts,
The living law of perfect love!
Write the new precept on our hearts;
We shall not then from thee remove,
But in thy glorious image shine,
Thy people, and for ever thine.

151. C. M.

1 SEARCHER of hearts, before thy face
I all my soul display;
And, conscious of its innate arts,
Entreat thy strict survey.

2 If, lurking in its inmost folds,
I any sin conceal,
O, let a ray of light divine
The secret guile reveal.

3 If tinctured with that odious gall
Unknowing I remain,
Let grace, like a pure silver stream,
Wash out the hateful stain.

4 To humble penitence and prayer
Be gentle pity given;
Speak ample pardon to my heart,
And grant an inward heaven.

152. 7s. M.

1 Blest Instructor, from thy ways
Who can tell how oft he strays?
Purge me from the guilt that lies
Wrapt within my heart's disguise.

2 Let my tongue, from error free,
Speak the words approved by thee;
To thine all-observing eyes
Let our thoughts accepted rise.

3 While I thus thy name adore,
And thy healing grace implore,
Blest Redeemer! bow thine ear;
God, my strength! propitious hear.

153. 7s. M.

1 Father, when in dust to thee
Low we bow the adoring knee;
When, repentant, to the skies
Scarce we lift our streaming eyes;
O, by all the pain and woe
Suffered by thy Son below,
Bending from thy throne on high,
Hear our solemn litany.

2 By his birth and early years,
By his human griefs and fears,
By his fasting and distress
In the lonely wilderness,

By his victory in the hour
Of the subtle tempter's power;
Father, look with pitying eye;
Hear our solemn litany.

3 By his hour of dark despair,
By his agony of prayer,
By his purple robe of scorn,
By his wounds and crown of thorn,
By his cross, his pangs and cries,
By his perfect sacrifice;
Father, look with pitying eye;
Hear our solemn litany.

154. L. M.

1 Earth has a joy unknown in heaven,
The new-born peace of sin forgiven!
Tears of such pure and deep delight,
Ye angels! never dimmed your sight.

2 Ye saw, of old, on chaos rise
The beauteous pillars of the skies:
Ye know where morn, exulting, springs,
And evening folds her drooping wings.

3 Bright heralds of the Eternal Will,
Abroad his errands ye fulfil;
Or, throned in floods of beamy day,
Symphonious in his presence play.

4 But I amid your choirs shall shine,
And all your knowledge will be mine:
Ye on your harps must lean to hear
A secret chord that mine will bear.

155. L. M.

1 'T IS not Thy chastening hand I fear,
For that is love and mercy still;
I know to Thee thy child is dear,
Howe'er I wander from thy will;
I fear not that Thou shouldst depart,
Only that I should close my heart;
Thy love hath ever flowed to me,
But I am cold and false to thee.

2 O, give me then an earnest heart,
Another's woes more prompt to feel,
And let my wounds more keenly smart,
If but another's I may heal;
Be it through want, or woe, or pain,
But draw me to thyself again,
And let me feel my sins forgiven;
I dwell with Thee, and thus in heaven.

156. C. M.

1 COULD we but hear all nature's voice,
From glowworm up to sun,
'T would speak in one concordant sound,
Thy will, O God, be done!

2 But hark! a sadder, mightier prayer,
From all men's hearts that live:
Thy will be done in earth and heaven,
And thou my sins forgive!

GOD'S HELP AND PROTECTION.

---

157. L. M.

1 Whither, O, whither should I fly,
But to my loving Father's breast;
Secure within thine arms to lie,
And safe beneath thy wings to rest!

2 In all my ways thy hand I own,
Thy ruling providence I see:
Assist me still my course to run,
And still direct my paths to thee.

3 I have no skill the snare to shun,
But thou, O God, my wisdom art;
I ever into ruin run;
But thou art greater than my heart.

4 Foolish, and impotent, and blind,
Lead me a way I have not known;
Bring me where I my heaven may find,
The heaven of loving thee alone,

158. S. M.

1 God, who is just and kind,
Will those who err instruct,
And in the paths of righteousness
Their wandering steps conduct.

2 The humble soul he guides;
Teaches the meek his way;
Kindness and truth he shows to all
Who his just laws obey.

3 Give me the tender heart
That mingles fear with love;
And lead me through whatever path
Thy wisdom shall approve.

4 O, ever keep my soul
From error, shame, and guilt!
Nor suffer the fair hope to fail,
Which on thy truth is built.

159. L. M.

1 Be with me, Lord, where'er I go;
Teach me what thou wouldst have me do;
Suggest whate'er I think or say;
Direct me in thy narrow way.

2 Prevent me lest I harbor pride,
Lest I in mine own strength confide;
Show me my weakness, let me see
I have my power, my all from thee.

3 Enrich me always with thy love;
My kind protection ever prove;
Thy signet put upon my breast,
And let thy Spirit on me rest.

4 O, may I never do my will,
But thine and only thine fulfil;
Let all my time and all my ways
Be spent and ended to thy praise.

160. C. M.

1 THRICE happy souls, who, born from heaven,
While yet they sojourn here,
Do all their days with God begin,
And spend them in his fear.

2 'Midst hourly cares, may love present
Its incense to thy throne;
And, while the world our hands employs,
Our hearts be thine alone.

3 As different scenes of life arise,
Our grateful hearts would be
With thee, amidst the social band,
In solitude with thee.

4 In solid, pure delights like these,
Let all our days be past;
Nor shall we then impatient wish,
Nor shall we fear the last.

161. 8, 7, & 4s. M.

1 Guide me, O thou great Jehovah,
Pilgrim through this barren land:
I am weak, but thou art mighty;
Hold me with thy powerful hand:
Bread of heaven,
Feed me till I want no more.

2 Open now the crystal fountain,
Whence the healing streams do flow;
Let the fiery, cloudy pillar
Lead me all my journey through:
Strong Deliverer,
Be thou still my strength and shield.

3 When I tread the verge of Jordan,
Bid my anxious fears subside;
Bear me through the swelling current;
Land me safe on Canaan's side;
Songs of praises
I will ever give to thee.

162. L. M.

1 My Helper, God! I bless thy name!
The same thy power, thy grace the same:
The tokens of thy friendly care
Open, and crown, and close the year.

2 Amidst ten thousand deaths I stand,
Supported by thy guardian hand;

And see, when I survey my ways,
Ten thousand monuments of praise.

3 Thus far thine arm hath led me on;
Thus far I make thy mercy known;
And, while I tread this desert land,
New blessings shall new songs demand.

163. L. M.

1 Thus far on life's perplexing path,
Thus far thou, Lord, our steps hast led,
Snatched from the world's pursuing wrath,
Unharmed though floods o'erhung our head:
Like ransomed Israel on the shore,
Here then we pause, look back, adore.

2 Strangers and pilgrims here below,
Like all our fathers, in their day,
We to the land of promise go,
Lord, by thine own appointed way:
Still guide, illumine, cheer our flight,
In cloud by day, in fire by night.

3 When we have numbered all our years,
And stand at length on Jordan's brink,
Though the flesh fail with mortal fears,
O, let not then the spirit sink;
But strong in faith, and hope, and love,
Plunge through the stream, to rise above!

164. L. M.

1 O God, the Lord of place and time,
Who orderest all things prudently;
Brightening with beams the opening prime,
And glowing in the mid-day sky;

2 Quench thou the fires of hate and strife,
The wasting fever of the heart,
From perils guard our feeble life,
And to our souls thy peace impart.

165. L. M.

1 Thou, who canst guide the wandering star
Through trackless realms of ether's space,
Who calm'st the elemental war,
Whose hand from pole to pole I trace,—

2 In wisdom Thou hast placed me here,
Thou, when thou wilt, canst take me hence;
Ah! while I tread this earthly sphere,
Extend to me thy wide defence.

3 To thee, my God, to thee I call!
Whatever weal or woe betide,
By thy command I rise or fall,
In thy protection I confide.

4 If, when this dust 's to dust restored,
My soul shall float on airy wing,
How shall thy glorious name adored
Inspire her feeble voice to sing!

166. 8, 6, & 10s. M.

1 God is our refuge and defence,
Our shield his dread omnipotence.
Earth may beneath us shrink,
The ancient mountains hoar
Down in the deep tide sink, —
Let the wild deluge roar!
Jehovah is our refuge and defence!

2 There is a river calm and pure,
Whose streams refresh and well secure
The dwelling-place of God.
Blest city, fair and bright,
His favored saints' abode,
Where the Lord reigns in light, —
No foe can shake his strong foundations sure.

3 God is our refuge and our shield,
What then can make us fear or yield?
Wars at his bidding cease,
He breaks the bow and spear,
He reigns in truth and peace;
Let all adore and fear
Our God and Saviour, Israel's help and shield!

167. C. M.

1 My God! my Majesty divine!
My very presence bright!
Thou life, thou love, thou joy of mine!
My soul's own Infinite!

2 Art thou not mine? for my poor sake,
Dost thou not wondrously?
Dost not thou of thy glory take
To give it unto me?

3 Are not my sins the witnesses
That thou art not at home?
Doth not my penitence express
That thou again wilt come?

4 And when I sorely strove with sin,
Wast thou not strong for me?
O, did we not together win
That precious victory?

5 Waits not my soul, for thee to show
The work it must fulfil?
Art thou not hidden in my woe?
And there how gracious still!

6 When fulness of delight is mine,
Stands not thy glory by,
And helps each happy hour to shine
With wondrous radiancy?

7 Thou God of mine! eternal be
The fulness of thy grace!
O, still be pleased to shine in me!
Keep, keep thy dwelling-place!

168. C. M.

1 In lowliest confidence we wait
For thine appointed day;

"Thy kingdom come! thy will be done!"
This only let us pray.

2 Forgive us, Father, O, forgive
Our still increasing debt
Of sin, as we forgiveness grant
To those who us forget.

3 When stormy passion o'er the brink
Our tossing souls would urge,
O, lead us not within the gulf
Of that o'erwhelming surge!

4 But from the power of sin and death,
The soul's worst enemy,
Deliver us, — thou who alone
Canst set the prisoner free.

169. L. M.

1 When Israel, of the Lord beloved,
Out from the land of bondage came,
Her fathers' God before her moved,
An awful guide, in smoke and flame.

2 By day, along the astonished lands
The cloudy pillar glided slow;
By night, Arabia's crimsoned sands
Returned the fiery column's glow.

3 Thus present still, though now unseen,
When brightly shines the prosperous day,
Be thoughts of thee a cloudy screen,
To temper the deceitful ray!

4 And, O, when gathers on our path,
In shade and storm, the frequent night,
Be thou, long-suffering, slow to wrath,
A burning and a shining light.

170. L. M.

1 Leader of Israel's host, and guide
Of all who seek the land above,
Beneath thy shadow we abide,
The cloud of thy protecting love;
Our strength thy grace, our rule thy word,
Our end the glory of the Lord.

2 By thine unerring spirit led,
We shall not in the desert stray;
We shall not full direction need,
Nor miss our providential way;
As far from danger as from fear,
While love, almighty love, is near.

171. C. M.

1 Father of light! conduct my feet
Through life's dark, dangerous road;
Let each advancing step still bring
Me nearer to my God.

2 Let heaven-eyed prudence be my guide;
And when I go astray,
Recall my feet from folly's paths,
To wisdom's better way.

3 That heavenly wisdom from above
Abundantly impart;
And let it guard, and guide, and warm,
And penetrate my heart,

4 Till it shall lead me to thyself,
Fountain of bliss and love!
And all my darkness be dispersed
In endless light above.

172. L. M.

1 Through all the various shifting scene
Of life's mistaken ill or good,
Thy hand, O God! conducts unseen
The beautiful vicissitude.

2 Thou givest, with paternal care,
Howe'er unjustly we complain,
To all, their necessary share
Of joy and sorrow, health and pain.

3 All things on earth, and all in heaven,
On thine eternal will depend;
And all for greater good were given,
Would man pursue the appointed end.

4 Be this my care! — to all beside
Indifferent let my wishes be;
Passion be calm, and dumb be pride,
And fixed my soul, great God! on thee.

173. C. M.

1 O, help us, Lord! each hour of need
Thy heavenly succor give;
Help us in thought, and word, and deed,
Each hour on earth we live.

2 O, help us, when our spirits bleed,
With contrite anguish sore,
And when our hearts are cold and dead,
O, help us, Lord, the more.

3 O, help us through the prayer of faith
More firmly to believe;
For still the more the servant hath,
The more he shall receive.

4 O, help us, Father! from on high;
We know no help but thee;
O, help us so to live and die,
As thine in heaven to be.

174. L. M.

1 O Thou, to whose all-searching sight
The darkness shineth as the light,
Search, prove my heart, it pants for thee;
O, burst its bonds, and set it free!

2 If in this maze of life I stray,
Be thou my guide, be thou my way;
No foes, no violence I fear,
No harm, while thou, my God, art near

3 If rising floods my soul o'erflow,
Or sinks my heart in waves of woe,
O God, thy timely aid impart,
And raise my head, and cheer my heart.

4 If rough and thorny be my way,
My strength proportion to my day;
Till toil, and grief, and pain shall cease,
And all is calm, and joy, and peace.

175. S. M.

1 I WANT a true regard,
A single, steady aim,
Unmoved by threatening or reward,
To thee and thy great name.

2 Swift to my rescue come;
Thine own this moment seize;
Gather my wandering spirit home,
And keep in perfect peace.

3 Long as our trials last,
Long as the cross we bear,
O, let our souls on thee be cast
In never-ceasing prayer!

176. 7 & 6s. M.

1 To the haven of thy breast,
O God of love, I fly!
Be my refuge and my rest,
Whene'er the storm is high.

2 In the day of my distress,
Thou hast my succor been;
In my hour of helplessness,
Restraining me from sin.

3 First and last, in me perform
The work thou hast begun:
Be my shelter from the storm,
My shadow from the sun.

4 O, how swiftly dost thou move,
In every trial hour!
Still protect me with thy love,
And shield me with thy power.

177. S. M.

1 O, LEAD me to the Rock
That 's high above my head,
And make the covert of thy wings
My shelter and my shade.

2 Within thy presence, Lord,
For ever I 'll abide;
Thou art the tower of my defence,
The refuge where I hide.

178. C. M.

1 AUTHOR of good! we rest on thee;
Thine ever watchful eye
Alone our real wants can see,
Thy hand alone supply.

2 O, let thy fear within us dwell,
Thy love our footsteps guide!
That love shall vainer loves expel;
That fear all fears beside.

3 And since, by passion's force subdued,
Too oft, with stubborn will,
We blindly shun the latent good,
And grasp the specious ill;

4 Not what we wish, but what we want,
Let mercy still supply;
The good, unasked, O Father! grant,
The ill, though asked, deny.

179. 7s. M.

1 They who on the Lord rely
Safely dwell, though danger 's nigh;
Lo, his sheltering wings are spread
O'er each faithful servant's head.

2 When they wake, or when they sleep,
Angel guards their vigils keep;
Death and danger may be near,
Faith and love have naught to fear.

180. S. M.

1 'Tis God the spirit leads
In paths before unknown:
The work to be performed is ours;
The strength is all his own.

2 Assisted by his grace,
We still pursue our way;
And hope at last to reach the prize,
Secure in endless day.

3 'T is he that works to will,
'T is he that works to do;
He is the power by which we act,
His be the glory too.

181. L. M.

1 Amidst a world of hopes and fears,
A wild of cares, and toils, and tears,
Where foes alarm, and dangers threat,
And pleasures kill, and glories cheat;

2 Shed down, O Lord! a heavenly ray
To guide me in the doubtful way;
And o'er me hold thy shield of power,
To guard me in the dangerous hour.

3 Teach me the flattering paths to shun,
In which the thoughtless many run,
Who for a shade the substance miss,
And grasp their ruin in their bliss.

4 May never pleasure, wealth, or pride
Allure my wandering soul aside;
But through this maze of mortal ill,
Safe lead me to thy heavenly hill.

182. C. M.

1 O Thou, from whom all goodness flows,
I lift my soul to thee;
In all my sorrows, conflicts, woes,
Good Lord, remember me.

2 When on my aching, burdened heart,
My sins lie heavily,
Thy pardon grant, new peace impart;
Good Lord, remember me.

3 When trials sore obstruct my way,
And ills I cannot flee,
O, let my strength be as my day:
Good Lord, remember me.

4 When in the solemn hour of death
I wait thy just decree,
Be this the prayer of my last breath,
Good Lord, remember me.

183. L. M.

1 The billows swell, the winds are high,
Clouds overcast my wintry sky;
Out of the depths to thee I call;
My fears are great, my strength is small.

2 O Lord, the pilot's part perform,
And guard and guide me through the storm;
Defend me from each threatening ill;
Control the waves; say, "Peace! be still!"

3 Amidst the roaring of the sea,
My soul still hangs her hope on thee;
Thy constant love, thy faithful care,
Is all that saves me from despair.

4 Though tempest-tost and half a wreck,
My Saviour through the floods I seek;
Let neither winds nor stormy main
Force back my shattered bark again.

184. L. M.

1 Thou, who, upon the eternal throne,
Dost weigh the fates of all below,
And ever wear'st the radiant crown
Of worlds unnumbered round thy brow:
Thy wisdom formed the plan sublime
Of what man's future course shall be;
The path didst show which I must climb
To reach my final destiny.

2 Till then, let power divine protect,
And heavenly peace my spirit cheer,
My footsteps here below direct,
Till I before thy face appear.
The present seed I now shall sow
To ripen for eternity;
O, let it to perfection grow,
Then take thy pilgrim home to thee.

GOD IN NATURE.

---

185. 7s. M.

1 Nature with eternal youth
Ever bursts upon thy sight,
All her works are types of truth!
Mirrors of celestial light!

2 But the soul, when veiled in sin,
And eclipsed with fear and doubt,
From the darkened world within
Throws its shade on that without;—

3 While to those who, pure in heart,
For the truth their powers employ,
She will constant good impart,
And diffuse perpetual joy.

4 If the mind would nature see,
Let her cherish virtue more;
Goodness bears the golden key
That unlocks her palace door!

186. L. M.

1 God of the rolling orbs above,
Thy name is written clearly bright
In the warm day's unvarying blaze,
Or evening's golden shower of light:
For every fire that fronts the sun,
And every spark that walks alone
Around the utmost verge of heaven,
Were kindled at thy burning throne.

2 God of the world, the hour must come,
And nature's self to dust return;
Her crumbling altars must decay;
Her incense-fires shall cease to burn:
But still her grand and lovely scenes
Have made man's warmest praises flow,
For hearts grow holier as they trace
The beauty of the world below.

187. L. M.

1 O Thou, that once on Horeb stood
Revealed within the burning tree,
To-day, as well, in each green wood,
Be seen by hearts that yearn for thee.
Each shining leaf is bright with God,
Each bough a prophet's "budding rod,"
Each by thy flaming sun illumed,
Yet each, like Horeb's, unconsumed.

2 O Thou, whose hand poured Jordan's stream,
Whose angel-dove hung o'er its wave,
To hallow with a heavenly gleam
The Son whose love a world would save;—
Bring from the waters at our side
Some whisper, gentle as their tide,
Saying, like Christ on Galilee,—
That holier lake,— Peace, Peace to thee!

3 We pray, O Lord, who touched the mount,
We pray through Him who stilled the sea,—
May every outward sight a fount
Of inward life and courage be.
The radiant bush, the white-winged dove,
The fire of faith, the peace of love,
Uplift our souls, and urge them on
To take the cross, to wear the crown.

188. 8, 6, & 4s. M.

1 Sweet day! so cool, so calm, so bright,
Bridal of earth and sky;
The dew shall weep thy fall to-night,
For thou must die!

2 Sweet rose! in air whose odors wave,
And color charms the eye;
Thy root is ever in its grave,
And thou must die!

3 Sweet spring! of days and roses made,
Whose charms for beauty vie;
Thy days depart, thy roses fade,
For thou must die!

4 Only a sweet and holy soul
Hath tints that never fly;
While flowers decay, and seasons roll,
It cannot die.

189. 7s. M.

1 Heaven and earth, and sea and air,
God's eternal praise declare;
Up, my soul! awake and raise
Grateful hymns and songs of praise.

2 See the sun, with glorious ray,
Pierce the clouds at opening day;
Moon and stars, in splendor bright,
Praise their God through silent night.

3 See how earth, with beauty decked,
Tells a heavenly Architect;
Woods and fields, with lowing kine,
Show their Maker all divine.

4 See the birds, how, pair by pair,
Swift they cleave the yielding air;
Thunder, lightning, storm, and wind,
God doth at his will unbind.

5 See the billows tumbling o'er,
Chafing with incessant roar;
Hear them, as they sink and swell,
Loud their Maker's praises tell.

6 Through the world, great God, I trace
Wonders of thy power and grace:
Write more deeply on my heart
What I am, and what thou art.

190. 9 & 8s. M.

1 The sun is still for ever sounding
With brother spheres his rival song,
As on his destined journey bounding,
With thunder step he speeds along.

2 And fleetly, thought surpassing, fleetly
The earth's green pomp is spinning round;
Where Paradise alternates sweetly
With night terrific and profound.

3 There foams the sea, its broad wave beating
Against the tall cliff's rocky base,
And rock and sea away are fleeting
In everlasting spheral chase.

4 And storms with rival fury heaving
From land to sea, from sea to land,
Still, as they rave, a chain are weaving
Of deepest efficacy grand.

5 There burning desolation blazes,
Precursor of the thunder's way,
But, Lord, thy servants own with praises
The milder movement of thy day.

6 The sight gives angels strength, though greater
Than angels' utmost thought sublime;
And all thy wondrous works, Creator,
Are glorious as in Eden's prime!

191. C. M.

1 Unheard the dews around me fall,
And heavenly influence shed;
And, silent on this earthly ball,
Celestial footsteps tread.

2 Night reigns, in silence, o'er the pole,
And spreads her gems unheard;
Her lessons penetrate the soul,
Yet borrow not a word.

3 Noiseless the sun emits his fire,
And pours his golden streams;
And silently the shades retire
Before his rising beams.

4 O, grant my soul an ear to hear
Thy deep and silent voice;
To bend in lowly, filial fear,
And in thy love rejoice.

192. C. M.

1 Praise ye the Lord, immortal choirs,
That fill the worlds above;
Praise him who formed you of his fires,
And feeds you with his love.

2 Shine to his praise, ye crystal skies,
The floor of his abode;
Or veil in shade your thousand eyes,
Before your brighter God.

3 Shout to the Lord, ye surging seas,
In your eternal roar;
Let wave to wave resound his praise,
And shore reply to shore.

4 Wave your tall heads, ye lofty pines,
To Him that bids you grow;
Sweet clusters, bend the fruitful vines
On every thankful bough.

5 Thus while the meaner creatures sing,
Ye mortals, take the sound;
Echo the glories of your King
Through all the earth around.

193. C. M.

1 The green earth sends its incense up,
From every mountain shrine,
From every flower and dewy cup,
That greeteth the sunshine.

2 The clouds weep o'er the fallen world,
E'en as repentant love,
Ere, to the blessed breeze unfurled,
They fade in light above.

3 The sky is as a temple's arch;
The blue and wavy air
Is glorious with the spirit-march
Of messengers of prayer.

4 The gentle moon, the kindling sun,
The many stars, are given,
As shrines to burn earth's incense on,
The altar-fires of heaven.

194. L. M.

1 Father of lights! we sing thy name,
Who kindlest up the lamp of day;
Wide as he spreads his golden flame,
His beams thy power and love display.

2 Fountain of good! from thee proceed
The copious drops of genial rain,
Which o'er the hill, and through the mead,
Revive the grass, and swell the grain.

3 O, let not our forgetful hearts
O'erlook the tokens of thy care;
But what thy liberal hand imparts,
Still own in praise, still ask in prayer.

4 So shall our suns more grateful shine,
And showers in sweeter drops shall fall,
When all our hearts and lives are thine,
And thou, O God! enjoyed in all.

195. 8s. M.

1 Blessed be thy name for ever,
Thou of life the Guard and Giver!
Thou canst guard thy creatures sleeping,
Heal the heart long broke with weeping:

God of stillness and of motion,
Of the desert and the ocean,
Of the mountain, rock, and river,
Blessed be thy name for ever!

2 Thou who slumberest not, nor sleepest,
Blest are they thou kindly keepest.
God of evening's parting ray,
Of midnight gloom, and dawning day,
That rises from the azure sea
Like breathings of eternity;
God of life! that fade shall never,
Blessed be thy name for ever!

196. L. M.

1 The turf shall be my fragrant shrine;
My temple, Lord, that arch of thine,
My censer's breath the mountain airs,
And silent thoughts my only prayers.
My choir shall be the moonlit waves,
When murmuring homeward to their caves,
Or when the stillness of the sea
E'en more than music breathes of thee.

2 I'll seek, by day, some glade unknown,
All light and silence like thy throne,
And the pale stars shall be, at night,
The only eyes that watch my rite.
Thy heaven, on which 't is bliss to look,
Shall be my pure and shining book,
Where I can read, in words of flame,
The glories of thy wondrous name.

3 There 's nothing bright, above, below,
From flowers that bloom, to stars that glow,
But in its light my soul can see
Some feature of thy Deity.
There 's nothing dark, below, above,
But in its gloom I trace thy love,
And meekly wait that moment when
Thy touch shall turn all bright again.

197. C. M.

1 The Lord our God is clothed with might;
The winds obey his will;
He speaks, and in the heavenly height
The rolling sun stands still.

2 Rebel, ye waves, and o'er the land
With threatening aspect roar;
The Lord uplifts his awful hand,
And chains you to the shore.

3 Ye winds of night, your force combine:
Without his high behest,
Ye shall not, in the mountain pine,
Disturb the sparrow's nest.

4 His voice sublime is heard afar;
In distant peals it dies;
He binds the whirlwinds to his car,
And sweeps the howling skies.

5 Ye nations, bend; in reverence bend;
Ye monarchs, wait his nod,
And bid the choral song ascend
To celebrate our God.

198. L. M.

1 Thou art, O God, the life and light
Of all this wondrous world we see;
Its glow by day, its smile by night,
Are but reflections caught from thee;
Where'er we turn, thy glories shine,
And all things fair and bright are thine.

2 When day, with farewell beam, delays
Among the opening clouds of even,
And we can almost think we gaze,
Through opening vistas into heaven,—
Those hues that mark the sun's decline,
So soft, so radiant, Lord, are thine.

3 When night, with wings of starry gloom,
O'ershadows all the earth and skies,
Like some dark, beauteous bird, whose plume
Is sparkling with unnumbered eyes,—
That sacred gloom, those fires divine,
So grand, so countless, Lord, are thine.

4 When youthful spring around us breathes,
Thy spirit warms her fragrant sigh;
And every flower that summer wreathes
Is born beneath thy kindling eye:
Where'er we turn, thy glories shine,
And all things fair and bright are thine.

199. C. M.

1 THERE is a book, who runs may read,
Which heavenly truth imparts;
And all the lore its scholars need,
Pure eyes and Christian hearts.

2 The works of God, above, below,
Within us and around,
Are pages in that book, to show
How God himself is found.

3 The glorious sky, embracing all,
Is like the Father's love;
Wherewith encompassed, great and small
In peace and order move.

4 Two worlds are ours: 't is only sin
Forbids us to descry
The mystic heaven and earth within,
Plain as the earth and sky.

5 Thou who hast given me eyes to see
And love this sight so fair,
Give me a heart to find out thee,
And read thee everywhere.

200. C. P. M.

1 BEGIN, my soul, the exalted lay;
Let each enraptured thought obey,
And praise the Almighty's name.

Lo, heaven and earth, and seas and skies,
In one melodious concert rise
To swell the inspiring theme.

2 Thou heaven of heavens, his vast abode,
Ye clouds, proclaim your Maker, God;
Ye thunders, speak his power.
Lo, on the lightning's rapid wings
In triumph rides the King of kings:
The astonished worlds adore.

3 Ye deeps, with roaring billows rise
To join the thunders of the skies, —
Praise Him who bids you roll.
His praise in softer notes declare,
Each whispering breeze of yielding air,
And breathe it to the soul.

4 Let man, by nobler passions swayed,
The feeling heart, the reasoning head,
In heavenly praise employ:
Spread the Creator's name around,
Till heaven's wide arch repeat the sound, —
The general burst of joy.

201. 7s. M.

1 Praise to God, immortal praise,
For the love that crowns our days!
Bounteous Source of every joy,
Let thy praise our tongues employ.

2 All that Spring, with bounteous hand,
Scatters o'er the smiling land, —

All that liberal Autumn pours
From her rich, o'erflowing stores,—

3 These to thee, our God, we owe,
Source whence all our comforts flow!
And for these, in happy days,
We will pay our grateful praise.

4 Grateful, never-ending praise,
Lord, to thee my soul shall raise;
And, when every blessing 's flown,
Love thee for thyself alone.

202. L. M.

1 My God! all nature owns thy sway;
Thou giv'st the night and thou the day:
When all thy loved creation wakes,
When morning, rich in lustre, breaks,
And bathes in dew the opening flower,
To thee we owe her fragrant hour;
And when she pours her choral song,
Her melodies to thee belong.

2 Or when, in paler tints arrayed,
The evening slowly spreads her shade,
That soothing shade, that grateful gloom,
Can, more than day's enlivening bloom,
Still every fond and vain desire,
And calmer, purer thoughts inspire;
From earth the longing spirit free,
And lead the softened heart to thee.

3 As o'er thy work the seasons roll,
And soothe, with change of bliss, the soul,
O, never may their smiling train
Pass o'er the human sense in vain!
But, oft as on their charms we gaze,
Attune the wondering soul to praise;
And be the joys that most we prize
The joys that from thy favor rise!

203. 8 & 7s. M.

1 PRAISE the Lord! ye heavens, adore him;
Praise him, angels in the height;
Sun and moon, rejoice before him;
Praise him, all ye stars of light!

2 Praise the Lord, for he hath spoken;
Worlds his mighty voice obeyed;
Laws which never can be broken
For their guidance he hath made.

3 Praise the Lord, for he is glorious;
Never shall his promise fail;
God hath made his saints victorious,
Sin and death shall not prevail.

4 Praise the God of our salvation,
Hosts on high his power proclaim;
Heaven and earth, and all creation,
Praise and magnify his name!

204. L. M.

1 The spacious firmament on high,
With all the blue, ethereal sky,
And spangled heavens, a shining frame,
Their great Original proclaim.
The unwearied sun, from day to day,
Doth his Creator's power display;
And publishes to every land
The work of an almighty hand.

2 Soon as the evening shades prevail,
The moon takes up the wondrous tale,
And nightly to the listening earth
Repeats the story of her birth:
Whilst all the stars which round her burn,
And all the planets in their turn,
Confirm the tidings as they roll,
And spread the truth from pole to pole.

3 What though, in solemn silence, all
Move round this dark, terrestrial ball;
What though no real voice nor sound
Amidst their radiant orbs be found;
In reason's ear they all rejoice,
And utter forth a glorious voice;
For ever singing, as they shine,
"The hand that made us is divine."

205. C. M.

1 I sing the mighty power of God,
That made the mountains rise;

That spread the flowing seas abroad,
And built the lofty skies.

2 I sing the wisdom that ordained
The sun to rule the day;
The moon shines full at his command,
And all the stars obey.

3 I sing the goodness of the Lord,
That filled the earth with food;
He formed the creatures with his word,
And then pronounced them good.

4 Lord, how thy wonders are displayed,
Where'er I turn mine eye;
If I survey the ground I tread,
Or gaze upon the sky!

5 There 's not a plant or flower below,
But makes thy glories known;
And clouds arise, and tempests blow,
By order from thy throne.

6 Creatures, as numerous as they be,
Are subject to thy care;
There 's not a place where we can flee,
But God is present there.

III.

THE WORD.

THE WORD.

---

206. C. M.

1 Word of the ever-living God!
Will of his glorious Son!
Without thee how could earth be trod,
Or heaven itself be won?

2 Yet, to unfold thy hidden worth,
Thy mysteries to reveal,
That Spirit which first gave thee forth
Thy volume must unseal!

3 And we, if we aright would learn
The wisdom it imparts,
Must to its heavenly teaching turn
With simple, childlike hearts!

207. S. M.

1 How perfect is thy word,
And all thy judgments just!
For ever sure thy promise, Lord,
And men securely trust.

2 My gracious God, how plain
Are thy directions given!
O, may I never read in vain,
But find the path to heaven.

3 I hear thy word with love,
And I would fain obey;
Send thy good Spirit from above,
To guide me, lest I stray.

4 While with my heart and tongue
I spread thy praise abroad;
Accept the worship and the song,
My Father and my God.

208. L. M.

1 The heavens declare thy glory, Lord!
In every star thy wisdom shines;
But when our eyes behold thy word,
We read thy name in fairer lines.

2 Sun, moon, and stars convey thy praise
Round the whole earth, and never stand;
So, when thy truth began its race,
It touched and glanced on every land.

3 Nor shall thy spreading Gospel rest,
Till through the world thy truth has run;
Till Christ has all the nations blest,
That see the light, or feel the sun.

4 Thy richest mercy here we view,
In souls renewed, and sins forgiven;
Lord! cleanse our sins, our souls renew,
And make thy word our guide to heaven.

209. L. M.

1 Teach me, O, teach me, Lord! thy way;
So to my life's remotest day,
By thy unerring precepts led,
My willing feet its paths shall tread.

2 Informed by thee, with sacred awe
My heart shall meditate thy law;
And, with celestial wisdom filled,
To thee its full obedience yield.

3 Give me to know thy words aright,
Thy words, my soul's supreme delight;
That, purged from thirst of gold, my mind
In them its better wealth may find.

4 O, turn from vanity mine eye;
To me thy quickening strength supply;
And with thy promised mercy cheer
A heart devoted to thy fear.

210. L. M.

1 Upon the Gospel's sacred page
The gathered beams of ages shine;
And, as it hastens, every age
But makes its brightness more divine.

2 On mightier wing, in loftier flight,
From year to year does knowledge soar,
And, as it soars, the Gospel light
Adds to its influence more and more.

3 Truth, strengthened by the strength of thought,
Pours inexhaustible supplies,
Whence sagest teachers may be taught,
And wisdom's self become more wise.

4 More glorious still as centuries roll,
New regions blest, new powers unfurled,
Expanding with the expanding soul,
Its waters shall o'erflow the world;—

5 Flow to restore, but not destroy;
As when the cloudless lamp of day
Pours out its floods of light and joy,
And sweeps each lingering mist away.

211. C. M.

1 A GLORY gilds the sacred page,
Majestic like the sun:
It gives a light to every age;
It gives, but borrows none.

2 The hand that gave it still supplies
The gracious light and heat:
His truths upon the nations rise;
They rise, but never set.

3 Let everlasting thanks be thine,
For such a bright display,

As makes a world of darkness shine
With beams of heavenly day.

4 My soul rejoices to pursue
The steps of Him I love,
Till glory break upon my view
In brighter worlds above.

212. L. M.

1 Lamp of our feet! whose hallowed beam
Deep in our hearts its dwelling hath,
How welcome is the cheering gleam
Thou sheddest o'er our lowly path!
Light of our way! whose rays are flung
In mercy o'er our pilgrim road,
How blessed, its dark shades among,
The star that guides us to our God.

2 In the sweet morning's hour of prime,
Thy blessed words our lips engage,
And round our hearths at evening time
Our children spell the holy page;
The waymark through long distant years,
To guide their wandering footsteps on,
Till thy last loveliest beam appears,
Inscribed upon the church-yard stone.

3 Lamp of our feet! which day by day
Are passing to the quiet tomb,
If on it fall thy peaceful ray,
Our last low dwelling hath no gloom.

How beautiful their calm repose
  To whom thy blessed hope is given,
Whose pilgrimage on earth is closed
  By the unfolding gates of heaven!

213. C. M.

1 Let all the heathen writers join
    To form one perfect book,
  Great God, if once compared with thine,
    How mean their writings look!

2 Not the most perfect rules they gave
    Could show one sin forgiven,
  Nor lead a step beyond the grave;
    But thine conduct to heaven.

3 Our faith, and love, and every grace,
    Fall far below thy word;
  But perfect truth and righteousness
    Dwell only with the Lord.

214. S. M.

1 It is the one true light,
    When other lamps grow dim,
  'T will never burn less purely bright,
    Nor lead astray from Him.
    It is Love's blessed band,
    That reaches from the throne
  To him — whoe'er he be — whose hand
    Will seize it for his own!

2 It is the golden key
Unto celestial wealth,
Joy to the sons of poverty,
And to the sick man, health!
The gently proffered aid
Of one who knows and best
Supplies the beings he has made
With what will make them blest.

3 It is the sweetest sound
That infant years can hear,
Travelling across that holy ground,
With God and angels near.
There rests the weary head,
There age and sorrow go;
And how it smooths the dying bed,
O, let the Christian show!

215. L. M.

1 God, in the Gospel of his Son,
Makes his eternal counsels known;
'T is here his richest mercy shines,
And truth is drawn in fairest lines.

2 Wisdom its dictates here imparts,
To form our minds, to cheer our hearts,
Its influence makes the sinner live;
It bids the drooping saint revive.

3 Our raging passions it controls,
And comfort yields to contrite souls;
It brings a better world to view,
And guides us all our journey through.

4 May this blest volume ever lie
Close to my heart, and near my eye,
Till life's last hour my soul engage,
And be my chosen heritage.

216. H. M.

1 MARK the soft-falling snow,
And the descending rain!
To heaven, from whence it fell,
It turns not back again;
But waters earth through every pore,
And calls forth all her secret store.

2 Arrayed in beauteous green
The hills and valleys shine,
And man and beast are fed
By providence divine:
The harvest bows its golden ears,
The copious seed of future years.

3 "So," saith the God of grace,
"My Gospel shall descend,
Almighty to effect
The purpose I intend;
Millions of souls shall feel its power,
And bear it down to millions more."

217. S. M.

1 BEHOLD, the morning sun
Begins his glorious way!
His beams through all the nations run,
And life and light convey.

2 But where the Gospel comes,
It spreads diviner light;
It calls dead sinners from their tombs,
And gives the blind their sight.

3 My gracious God, how plain
Are thy directions given!
O, may we never read in vain,
But find the path to heaven.

4 I hear thy word with love,
And I would fain obey;
Send thy good Spirit from above,
To guide me, lest I stray.

218. S. M.

1 Imposture shrinks from light,
And dreads the curious eye;
But sacred truths the test invite,
They bid us search and try.

2 With understanding blest,
Created to be free,
Our faith on man we dare not rest,
Subject to none but thee.

3 Lord, give the light we need;
With soundest knowledge fill;
From noxious error guard our creed,
From prejudice our will.

4 The truth thou shalt impart,
May we with firmness own;
Abhorring each evasive art,
And fearing thee alone.

219. C. M.

1 Father of mercies! in thy word
What endless glory shines!
For ever be thy name adored
For these celestial lines.

2 Here may the wretched sons of want
Exhaustless riches find;
Riches above what earth can grant,
And lasting as the mind.

3 Here the Redeemer's gentle voice
Spreads heavenly peace around:
And life and everlasting joys
Attend the blissful sound.

4 Divine Instructor! gracious Lord!
Be thou for ever near;
Teach me to love thy sacred word,
And read salvation there.

220. C. M.

1 Lamp of our feet! whereby we trace
Our path, when wont to stray;
Stream from the fount of heavenly grace!
Brook by the traveller's way!

2 Bread of our souls! whereon we feed;
True manna from on high!
Our guide, and chart! wherein we read
Of realms beyond the sky.

3 Pillar of fire, through watches dark!
Or radiant cloud by day!
When waves would whelm our tossing bark,
Our anchor and our stay!

4 Childhood's preceptor! manhood's trust!
Old age's firm ally!
Our hope, when we go down to dust,
Of immortality!

221. 7s. M.

1 WORD by God the Father sent,
Lord of all, Omnipotent!
Word for sinners' need supplied,
As their comfort and their guide!

2 Word of life, both pure and strong!
Word for which the heathen long!
Spread abroad, till out of night
All the world awake to light.

3 Up! for lo, earth's surface o'er,
Waving fields with ripening store!
Countless sheaves are spread around,
Few, O, few the reapers found!

4 Lord of harvest, great and kind!
Rouse to action heart and mind;
Let the gathering nations all
See thy light and hear thy call.

222. L. M.

1 The starry firmament on high,
And all the glories of the sky,
Yet shine not to thy praise, O Lord,
So brightly as thy written word:
The hopes that holy word supplies,
Its truths divine and precepts wise,—
In each a heavenly beam I see,
And every beam conducts to thee.

2 Almighty Lord! the sun shall fail,
The moon forget her nightly tale,
And deepest silence hush on high
The radiant chorus of the sky;—
But fixed for everlasting years,
Unmoved amid the wreck of spheres,
Thy word shall shine in cloudless day,
When heaven and earth have passed away

IV.

CHRIST.

ADVENT AND NATIVITY.

---

223. P. M.

1 O LOVELY Voices of the sky,
Which hymned the Saviour's birth!
Are ye not singing still on high,
Ye that sang, "Peace on earth"?
To us yet speak the strains,
Wherewith, in time gone by,
Ye blest the Syrian swains,
O Voices of the sky!

2 O clear and shining Light, whose beams
That hour heaven's glory shed
Around the palms, and o'er the streams,
And on the shepherds' head!
Be near, through life and death,
As in that holiest night
Of hope, and joy, and faith;
O clear and shining Light!

3 O Star which led to Him whose love
Brought down man's ransom free!

Where art thou? — 'midst the host above,
May we still gaze on thee?
In heaven thou art not set,
Thy rays earth may not dim;
Send them to guide us yet,
O Star which led to Him!

224. L. M.

1 When, marshalled on the nightly plain,
The glittering host bestud the sky,
One star alone, of all the train,
Can fix the sinner's wandering eye.

2 Hark! hark! to God the chorus breaks,
From every host, from every gem;
But one alone the Saviour speaks, —
It is the Star of Bethlehem!

3 Once on the raging seas I rode;
The storm was loud, the night was dark;
The ocean yawned, and rudely blowed
The wind that tossed my foundering bark.

4 Deep horror then my courage froze;
Death-struck, I ceased the tide to stem;
When suddenly a star arose, —
It was the Star of Bethlehem.

5 It was my guide, my light, my all;
It bade my dark forebodings cease;
And, through the storm and danger's thrall,
It led me to the port of peace.

6 Now, safely moored, my perils o'er,
I 'll sing, first in night's diadem,
For ever, and for evermore, —
The Star — the Star of Bethlehem!

225. S. M.

1 Behold the sun, how bright
From yonder east he springs,
As if the soul of life and light
Were breathing from his wings.

2 So bright the Gospel broke
Upon the souls of men;
So fresh the dreaming world awoke
In truth's full radiance then.

3 Before yon sun arose,
Stars clustered through the sky;
But, O, how dim, how pale, were those,
To his one burning eye!

4 So truth lent many a ray,
To bless the pagan's night;
But, Lord, how faint, how cold, were they,
To thy one glorious light!

226. 6 & 4s. M.

1 Thou, whose almighty word
Chaos and darkness heard,
And took their flight!

Hear us, we humbly pray,
And where the Gospel day
Sheds not its glorious ray,
Let there be light!

2 Thou, who didst come to bring,
On thy redeeming wing,
Healing and sight!
Health to the sick in mind,
Light to the inly blind,
O, now to all mankind
Let there be light!

3 Descend thou from above,
Spirit of truth and love,
Speed on thy flight!
Move o'er the waters' face,
Spirit of hope and grace,
And in earth's darkest place
Let there be light!

227. C. M.

1 Now gird your patient loins again,
Your wasting torches trim!
The chief of all the sons of men,
Shall we not welcome him?
Fill all his courts with sacred songs,
And from the temple wall
Wave garlands o'er the joyful throngs
That crowd his festival!

2 And still more freshly in the mind
Store up the hopes sublime

Which then were born for all mankind,
  So blessed was the time;
And, underneath these hallowed eaves,
  A Saviour will be born
In every heart that him receives,
  On his triumphal morn.

228. 8 & 6s. M.

1 DEPART awhile, each thought of care,
  Be earthly things forgotten all,
And speak, my soul, thy grateful prayer,
  Obedient to the sacred call.
For hark! the pealing chorus swells;
  Devotion chants the hymn of praise,
And now of joy and hope it tells,
  Till, fainting on the ear, it says,—
    Glory to thee, O Lord!

2 Thine, wondrous babe of Galilee!
  Fond theme of David's harp and song,
Thine are the notes of minstrelsy,
  To thee its ransomed chords belong.
And hark! again the chorus swells,
  The song is wafted on the breeze,
And to the listening earth it tells,
  In accents soft and sweet as these,—
    Glory to thee, O Lord!

3 My heart doth feel that still he 's near,
  To meet the soul in hours like this;
Else, why, O, why, that falling tear,
  When all is peace and love and bliss?

But hark! that Bethlehem chorus swells
Anew its thrilling vesper strain,
And still of joy and hope it tells,
And bids creation sing again,—
Glory to thee, O Lord!

229. L. M.

1 O DAY to which the seas and sky,
And earth and heaven, glad welcome sing
O day which healed our misery,
And brought on earth salvation's King!

2 Immortal hope of all mankind,
In whom the Father's face we see,
To him this day, throughout the world,
His people pour their prayers through thee

3 And we, O Lord, whose eyes are touched
By thine own beam of light divine,
Offer our songs of thankful praise
On this blest natal day of thine.

230. 8 & 7s. M.

1 HARK! what mean those holy voices,
Sweetly sounding through the skies?
Lo! the angelic host rejoices;
Heavenly hallelujahs rise.

2 Listen to the wondrous story,
Which they chant in hymns of joy:
" Glory in the highest, glory!
Glory be to God most high!

3 "Peace on earth, good-will from heaven,
Reaching far as man is found;
Souls redeemed and sins forgiven; —
Loud our golden harps shall sound.

4 "Christ is born, the great Anointed;
Heaven and earth his praises sing!
O, receive whom God appointed,
For your Prophet, Priest, and King!"

231. C. M.

1 While shepherds watched their flocks by night,
All seated on the ground,
The angel of the Lord came down,
And glory shone around.

2 "Fear not," said he, — for mighty dread
Had seized their troubled mind, —
"Glad tidings of great joy I bring
To you and all mankind."

3 Thus spake the seraph, and forthwith
Appeared a shining throng
Of angels, praising God, and thus
Addressed their joyful song: —

4 "All glory be to God on high,
And to the earth be peace!
Good-will henceforth, from heaven to men,
Begin and never cease!"

232. 8, 7, & 4s. M.

1 Angels, from the realms of glory,
Wing your flight o'er all the earth!
Ye, who sang creation's story,
Now proclaim Messiah's birth:
Come and worship, —
Worship Christ, the new-born King.

2 Shepherds, in the field abiding,
Watching o'er your flocks by night,
God with man is now residing;
Yonder shines the heavenly light:
Come and worship, —
Worship Christ, the new-born King.

3 Saints, before the altar bending,
Watching long in hope and fear,
Suddenly, the Lord descending,
In his temple shall appear:
Come and worship, —
Worship Christ, the new-born King.

4 Sinners, bowed in true repentance,
Doomed for guilt to endless pains,
Justice now revokes the sentence;
Mercy calls you; break your chains:
Come and worship, —
Worship Christ, the new-born King.

233. P. M.

1 Wake! the welcome day appeareth,
Every heart with joy it cheereth!
Wake! the Lord's great year behold!
That which holy men of old,
Those who throng the sacred pages,
Waited for through countless ages:
Hallelujah! Hallelujah!

2 Patriarchs erst and priests aspiring,
Kings and prophets long desiring,
Saw not this before they died.
Lo the Light to them denied!
See its beams to earth directed!
Welcome, O thou long-expected!
Hallelujah! Hallelujah!

3 In our stead himself he offers,
On the accursèd tree he suffers,
That his death's sweet savor may
Take our curse for aye away,
Cross and curse for us enduring,
Hope and heaven to us securing:
Hallelujah! Hallelujah!

4 Rent the temple curtain's centre;
Come, ye nations, freely enter
Through the veil the holy place!
Freely stand before his face,
Here your grateful tributes bringing:
Come thou Bride, for ever singing,
Hallelujah! Hallelujah!

234. C. M.

1 'T WAS in the East, the mystic East,
Where Time his race began,
And new-born nature spread the feast
For new-created man, —

2 The tree of life was planted first,
So holy Scriptures tell,
Before the earth with sin was cursed,
And man from Eden fell.

3 That tree untasted passed away,
And sin and sorrow grew;
And tarried long the wished-for day
To waiting Israel due; —

4 Till from the land where Jordan old
Still washes Judah's shore,
Where God's own hand the page unroll[illegible]
Of Judah's sacred lore,

5 Sprung, to requite that early loss,
From David's royal root,
Another Tree, whose stem the cross,
And Christendom its fruit.

6 Blest be the Tree of life divine!
The hand that gave it blest!
Lord, through the earth extend its line,
And give the nations rest!

7 In us implant its sacred seed,
And with thy grace bedew,
And let it, ripening into deed,
For aye itself renew.

235. L. M.

1 When Jordan hushed his waters still,
And silence slept on Zion's hill;
When Bethlehem's shepherds through the night
Watched o'er their flocks by starry light;—

2 Hark! from the midnight hills around,
A voice of more than mortal sound
In distant hallelujahs stole,
Wild murmuring o'er the raptured soul.

3 "O Zion! lift thy waiting eye,
The long-expected hour is nigh;
The joys of nature rise again,
The Prince of Salem comes to reign.

4 "He comes, to cheer the trembling heart,
Bids Satan and his host depart;
Again the day-star gilds the gloom,
Again the bowers of Eden bloom."

236. 11 & 10s. M.

1 Brightest and best of the sons of the morning,
Dawn on our darkness and lend us thine aid;
Star of the East, the horizon adorning,
Guide where the infant Redeemer is laid.

2 Cold on his cradle the dew-drops are shining;
Low lies his head with the beasts of the stall;
Angels bend o'er him, in slumber reclining,—
Monarch, Redeemer, Restorer of all.

3 Say, shall we yield him, in costly devotion,
Odors of Edom, and offerings divine?
Gems of the mountain, and pearls of the ocean,
Myrrh from the forest, or gold from the mine?

4 Vainly we offer each ample oblation,
Vainly with gold would his favor secure;
Richer by far is the heart's adoration,
Dearer to God are the prayers of the poor.

237. C. M.

1 JOHN was the prophet of the Lord,
To go before his face;
The herald which the Prince of Peace
Sent to prepare his ways.

2 "Behold the Lamb of God," he cries,
"That takes our guilt away;
I saw the Spirit o'er his head,
On his baptizing day.

3 "Be every vale exalted high,
Sink every mountain low;
The proud must stoop, and humble souls
Shall his salvation know.

4 "Behold the Morning Star arise,
Ye that in darkness sit;
He marks the path that leads to peace,
And guides our doubtful feet."

238. C. M.

1 Calm on the listening ear of night
  Come heaven's melodious strains,
Where wild Judea stretches far
  Her silver-mantled plains.

2 Celestial choirs from courts above
  Shed sacred glories there;
And angels, with their sparkling lyres,
  Make music on the air.

3 The answering hills of Palestine
  Send back the glad reply;
And greet, from all their holy heights,
  The day-spring from on high.

4 O'er the blue depths of Galilee
  There comes a holier calm,
And Sharon waves, in solemn praise,
  Her silent groves of palm.

5 "Glory to God!" the sounding skies
  Loud with their anthems ring,
"Peace to the earth, good-will to men,
  From heaven's Eternal King!"

6 Light on thy hills, Jerusalem!
  The Saviour now is born!
And bright on Bethlehem's joyous plains
  Breaks the first Christmas morn.

239. C. M.

1 We come not with a costly store,
O Lord, like them of old,
The masters of the starry lore,
From Ophir's shore of gold;
No weepings of the incense-tree
Are with the gifts we bring,
No odorous myrrh of Araby
Blends with our offering.

2 But still our love would bring its best;
A spirit keenly tried
By fierce affliction's fiery test,
And seven times purified:
The fragrant graces of the mind,
The virtues that delight
To give their perfume out, will find
Acceptance in thy sight.

240. 8 & 7s. M.

1 Come, thou long-expected Saviour,
Born to set thy people free,
From our fears and sins deliver,
Let us find our rest in thee:
Israel's strength and consolation,
Hope of all the earth thou art,
Dear desire of every nation,
Joy of every longing heart.

2 Born thy people to deliver;
Born a child, — and yet a King;
Born to reign in us for ever,
Now thy precious kingdom bring:
By thine own indwelling spirit,
Rule in all our hearts alone;
Let us all in thee inherit,
Raise us to thy glorious throne.

241. S. M.

1 Behold the Prince of Peace!
The chosen of the Lord,
God's well beloved Son, fulfils
The sure prophetic word.

2 No royal pomp adorns
This King of Righteousness;
But meekness, patience, truth, and love
Compose his princely dress.

3 The spirit of the Lord,
In rich abundance shed,
On this great prophet gently lights,
And rests upon his head.

4 Jesus, thou light of men!
Thy doctrine life imparts:
O, may we feel its quickening power,
To warm and glad our hearts!

242. 7s. M.

1 Sons of men, behold from far,
Hail the long-expected star!
Star of truth that gilds the night,
And guides bewildered men aright.

2 Mild it shines on all beneath,
Piercing through the shades of death;
Scattering error's wide-spread night;
Kindling darkness into light.

3 Nations all, remote and near,
Haste to see your Lord appear;
Haste, for him your hearts prepare,
Meet him manifested there!

4 There behold the day-spring rise,
Pouring light on mortal eyes;
See it chase the shades away,
Shining to the perfect day.

243. C. M.

1 Hark, the glad sound! the Saviour comes,
The Saviour promised long;
Let every heart a throne prepare,
And every voice a song.

2 He comes the prisoners to release,
In wretched bondage held:
The gates of brass before him burst,
The iron fetters yield.

3 He comes the broken heart to bind,
The bleeding soul to cure;
And, with the treasures of his grace,
Enrich the humble poor.

4 Our glad hosannas, Prince of Peace!
Thy welcome shall proclaim;
And heaven's eternal arches ring
With thy belovèd name.

244. S. M.

1 We meditate the day
Of triumph and of rest,
When shown of God, and shaped in clay,
The Word was manifest.

2 The angels saw and sung;
Earth listened far and wide;
Believed and preached, — a faith, — a tongue,
The Word was glorified.

3 Lord, give it gracious sweep,
And here its errand bless,
Whose mercy sent it o'er the deep,
To glad a wilderness.

4 Ray out its starry light,
To guide our pilgrim way;
A sign of hope through this world's night,
And brighter than its day.

5 Again thy witness-voice!
Again thy spirit-dove!
That hearts may in its trust rejoice,
And soften with its love.

245. C. M.

1 The race that long in darkness pined
Have seen a glorious light;
The people dwell in day, who dwelt
In death's surrounding night.

2 To hail thy rise, thou better Sun,
The gathering nations come,
Joyous as when the reapers bear
The harvest treasures home.

3 To us a child of hope is born,
To us a Son is given;
Him shall the tribes of earth obey,
Him, all the hosts of heaven.

4 His name shall be the Prince of Peace,
Whose rule shall stretch abroad,
The Wonderful, the Counsellor,
The great and mighty Lord.

5 His power, increasing, still shall spread;
His reign no end shall know;
Justice shall guard his throne above,
And peace abound below.

246. L. M.

1 The wondering sages trace from far,
Bright in the west, a morning star;
A light illumes the western skies,
Seen never in the east to rise.

2 Born of eternity, its rays
A glory shed on human ways;
Its brightness chases night away,
And kindles darkness into day.

3 O Jesus! brightest Morning Star!
This earth illumine near and far,
That all men in these latter days
May know thee, and proclaim thy praise.

247. 7s. M.

1 WAKE the song of jubilee;
Let it echo o'er the sea!
Now is come the promised hour;
Jesus reigns with sovereign power!

2 Now the desert lands rejoice,
And the islands join their voice;
Yea, the whole creation sings,—
Jesus is the King of kings!

3 He shall reign from pole to pole,
With supreme, unbounded sway;
He shall reign, when, like a scroll,
Yonder heavens have passed away!

4 Hallelujah! for the Lord
God Omnipotent shall reign!
Hallelujah! let the word
Echo round the earth and main!

EVENTS IN CHRIST'S MINISTRY.

---

248. C. M.

1 SEE, from on high, a light divine
  On Jesus' head descend!
And hear the sacred voice from heaven,
  That bids us all attend.

2 "This is my well-beloved Son,"
  Proclaimed the voice divine;
"Hear him," his Heavenly Father said,
  "For all his words are mine."

3 His mission thus confirmed from heaven,
  The great Messiah came,
And heavenly wisdom showed to man
  In God his Father's name.

4 The path of heavenly peace he showed,
  That leads to bliss on high;
Where all his faithful followers here
  Shall live, no more to die.

249. L. M.

1 Messiah Lord! who, wont to dwell
In lowly shape and cottage cell,
Didst not refuse a guest to be
At Cana's poor festivity, —

2 O, when our soul from care is free,
Then, Saviour, would we think on thee;
And, seated at the festal board,
In fancy's eye behold the Lord.

3 Then may we seem, in fancy's ear,
Thy manna-dropping tongue to hear,
And think, — "If now his searching view
Each secret of our spirit knew!"

4 So may such joy, chastised and pure,
Beyond the bounds of earth endure
Nor pleasure in the wounded mind
Shall leave a rankling sting behind.

250. L. M.

1 Around Bethesda's healing wave,
Waiting to hear the rustling wing,
Which spoke the angel nigh, who gave
Its virtue to that holy spring,
With patience and with hope endued,
Were seen the gathered multitude.

2 Bethesda's pool has lost its power!
No angel, by his glad descent,

Dispenses that diviner dower,
  Which with its healing waters went.
But he, whose word surpassed its wave,
Is still omnipotent to save.

3 Saviour! thy love is still the same
  As when that healing word was spoke;
Still in thine all-redeeming name
  Dwells power to burst the strongest yoke!
O, be that power, that love displayed,
Help those whom thou alone canst aid!

251. L. M.

1 O'ER the dark wave of Galilee
  The gloom of twilight gathers fast,
And on the waters drearily
  Descends the fitful evening blast.

2 The weary bird hath left the air,
  And sunk into his sheltered nest;
The wandering beast has sought his lair,
  And laid him down to welcome rest.

3 Still, near the lake, with weary tread,
  Lingers a form of human kind;
And on his lone, unsheltered head
  Flows the chill night-damp of the wind.

4 Why seeks he not a home of rest?
  Why seeks he not a pillowed bed?
Beasts have their dens, the bird its nest;
  He hath not where to lay his head.

5 Such was the lot he freely chose,
To bless, to save the human race;
And through his poverty there flows
A rich, full stream of heavenly grace.

252. L. M.

1 Ride on, ride on in majesty!
Hark! all the tribes hosanna cry!
Thy humble beast pursues his road,
With palms and scattered garments strowed.

2 Ride on, ride on in majesty!
In lowly pomp ride on to die!
O Christ! thy triumphs now begin,
O'er captive death and conquered sin.

3 Ride on, ride on in majesty!
The wingèd squadrons of the sky
Look down with sad and wondering eyes,
To see the approaching sacrifice.

4 Ride on, ride on in majesty!
Thy last and fiercest strife is nigh;
The Father on his sapphire throne
Expects his own anointed Son!

253. C. M.

1 As Jesus sought his wandering sheep,
With weary toil oppressed,
He came to Martha's lowly roof,
A loved and honored guest.

2 While Martha serves with busy feet,
In reverential mood,
Meek Mary sits beside the Judge,
And feeds on heavenly food.

3 Yea, Martha soon herself shall sit,
The eternal word to hear,
And shall forget the festal board,
To feast on holier cheer.

4 Sole rest of all that come to thee,
O'er all our works preside,
That we may have in thee, at last,
The part that shall abide.

254. L. M.

1 When Jesus' friend had ceased to be,
Still Jesus' heart its friendship kept.
"Where have ye laid him?"—"Come and see!"
But ere his eyes could see, they wept.

2 Lord! not in sepulchres alone
Corruption's worm is rank and free;
The shroud of death our bosoms own,—
The shades of sorrow! Come and see!

3 Come, Lord! God's image cannot shine
Where sin's funereal darkness lowers;
Come! turn those weeping eyes of thine
Upon these sinning souls of ours!

4 And let those eyes, with shepherd care,
Their moving watch above us keep;

Till love the strength of sorrow wear,
And as thou weepedst, we may weep!

5 For surely we may weep to know
So dark and deep our spirits' stain;
That, had thy blood refused to flow,
Thy very tears had flowed in vain.

255. L. M.

1 Lord! in thy garden agony,
No light seemed on thy soul to break,
No form of seraph lingered nigh,
Nor yet the voice of comfort spake, —

2 Till, by thine own triumphant word,
The victory over ill was won;
Till the sweet, mournful cry was heard,
"Thy will, O God, not mine, be done!"

3 Lord, bring these precious moments back,
When, fainting, against sin we strain;
Or in thy counsels fail to track
Aught but the present grief and pain.

4 In weakness, help us to contend;
In darkness, yield to God our will;
And true hearts, faithful to the end,
Cheer by thine holy angels still!

256. L. M.

1 A voice upon the midnight air,
Where Kedron's moonlit waters stray,

Weeps forth in agony and prayer,
"O Father, take this cup away!"

2 Ah, thou who sorrow'st unto death!
We conquer in thy mortal fray;
And Earth for all her children saith,
"O God, take not this cup away!"

3 O Lord of sorrow! meekly die;
Thou 'lt heal or hallow all our woe;
Thy name refresh the mourner's sigh,
Thy peace revive the faint and low.

4 Great Chief of faithful souls, arise!
None else can lead the martyr band,
Who teach the brave how peril flies,
When faith, unarmed, uplifts the hand.

5 Thy parting blessing, Lord, we pray;
Make but one fold below, above;
And when we go the last, lone way,
O, give the welcome of thy love!

257. C. M.

1 Dark was the night, and cold the ground,
On which the Lord was laid;
His sweat like drops of blood ran down;
In agony he prayed, —

2 "Father, remove this bitter cup,
If such thy sacred will;
If not, content to drink it up,
Thy pleasure I fulfil."

3 Go to the garden, sinner; see
Those precious drops that flow;
The heavy load he bore for thee,
For thee he lies so low.

4 Then learn of him the cross to bear;
Thy Father's will obey;
And, when temptations press thee near,
Awake to watch and pray.

258. L. M.

1 The morning dawns upon the place
Where Jesus spent the night in prayer;
Through brightening glooms behold his face,
No form or comeliness is there.

2 Last eve, by those he called his own
Betrayed, forsaken, or denied,
He met his enemies alone,
In all their malice, rage, and pride.

3 But hark! he prays, — 't is for his foes;
He speaks, — 't is comfort to his friends;
Answers, — and paradise bestows;
"'T is finished!" — here the conflict ends.

4 "Truly this was the Son of God!"
Though in a servant's mean disguise,
And bruised beneath the Father's rod,
Not for himself, — for man he dies.

259. 8 & 6s. M.

1 'T WAS the day when God's Anointed
Died for us the death appointed,
Bleeding on the dreadful cross;
Day of darkness, day of terror,
Deadly fruit of ancient error,
Nature's fall, and Eden's loss!

2 Haste, prepare the bitter chalice!
Gentile hate and Jewish malice
Lift the royal victim high,—
Like the serpent wonder-gifted
Which the prophet once uplifted,—
For a sinful world to die!

3 Conscious of the deed unholy,
Nature's pulses beat more slowly,
And the sun his light denied;
Darkness wrapped the sacred city,
And the earth with fear and pity
Trembled when the Just One died.

4 It is finished, Man of sorrows!
From thy cross our nature borrows
Strength to bear and conquer thus.
While exalted there we view thee,
Mighty Sufferer, draw us to thee,
Sufferer victorious!

5 Not in vain for us uplifted,
Man of sorrows wonder-gifted!
May that sacred symbol be.

Eminent amid the ages,
Guide of heroes and of sages,
May it guide us still to thee!

6 Still to thee, whose love unbounded
Sorrow's deep for us hath sounded,
Perfected by conflicts sore.
Glory to thy cross for ever!
Star that points our high endeavor
Whither thou hast gone before.

260. L. M.

1 "'T is finished!" — so the Saviour cried,
And meekly bowed his head, and died:
"'T is finished!" — yes, the race is run,
The battle fought, the victory won.

2 "'T is finished!" — all that heaven foretold
By prophets in the days of old;
And truths are opened to our view,
That kings and prophets never knew.

3 "'T is finished!" — Son of God, thy power
Hath triumphed in this awful hour;
And yet our eyes with sorrow see
That life to us was death to thee.

4 "'T is finished!" — let the joyful sound
Be heard through all the nations round;
"'T is finished!" — let the triumph rise,
And swell the chorus of the skies.

261. 7s. M.

1 Angel, roll the rock away!
Death, yield up thy mighty prey!
See, he rises from the tomb,
Glowing in immortal bloom.

2 Powers of heaven, seraphic fires!
Sing and sweep your sounding lyres;
Sons of men! in humble strain,
Sing your mighty Saviour's reign.

3 Every note with wonder swell,
And the Saviour's triumph tell:
Where, O death, is now thy sting?
Where thy terrors, vanquished king?

262. 7s. M.

1 Christ the Lord is risen to-day,
Sons of men and angels say:
Raise your joys and triumphs high;
Sing, ye heavens, and, earth, reply!

2 Love's redeeming work is done,
Fought the fight, the victory won:
Jesus' agony is o'er,
Darkness veils the earth no more.

3 Soar we now where Christ hath led,
Following our exalted Head;
Made like him, like him we rise, —
Ours the cross, the grave, the skies.

263. C. M.

1 Ye humble souls, that seek the Lord,
Chase all your fears away,
And bow with pleasure down to see
The place where Jesus lay.

2 Then raise your eyes and tune your songs,
The Saviour lives again!
Not all the bolts and bars of death
The Conqueror could detain.

3 High o'er the angelic bands, he rears
His once dishonored head;
And through unnumbered years he reigns,
Who dwelt among the dead.

4 With joy like his, shall every saint
His empty tomb survey;
Then rise with his ascending Lord,
Through all his shining way.

264. 6 & 4s. M.

1 On earth was darkness spread,
One boundless night;
"Let there be light," God said,—
And there was light!

2 There hung a deeper gloom
O'er quick and dead,
But Jesus burst the tomb,
And darkness fled.

3 God by his word arrayed
Darkness with light;
God by his Son displayed
Day without night.

4 For thee, O man! arose
Creation's ray;
For thee, too, brighter glows
Salvation's day.

5 The beams first poured on earth
For mortals shone;
The light of later birth
Immortals own.

265. P. M.

1 LIFT your glad voices in triumph on high,
For Jesus hath risen, and man cannot die.
Vain were the terrors that gathered around him,
And short the dominion of death and the grave;
He burst from the fetters of darkness that bound him,
Resplendent in glory, to live and to save.
Loud was the chorus of angels on high,—
"The Saviour hath risen, and man shall not die."

2 Glory to God, in full anthems of joy;
The being he gave us, death cannot destroy.
Sad were the life we must part with to-morrow,
If tears were our birthright, and death were our end;
But Jesus hath cheered the dark valley of sorrow,
And bade us, immortal, to heaven ascend.
Lift, then, your voices in triumph on high,
For Jesus hath risen, and man shall not die.

266. 7 & 8s. M.

1 Jesus lives! no longer now
Can thy terrors, Death, appall me;
Jesus lives! and well I know,
From the dead he will recall me;
Better life will then commence,
This shall be my confidence.

2 Jesus lives! to him the throne
Over all the world is given;
I shall go where he is gone,
Live and reign with him in heaven:
God is pledged, weak doubtings, hence!
This shall be my confidence.

3 Jesus lives! I know full well,
Naught from him my heart can sever;
Life nor death, nor powers of hell,
Joy nor grief, henceforth, for ever.
God will power and grace dispense,
This shall be my confidence.

4 Jesus lives! henceforth is death
Entrance into life immortal;
Calmly I can yield my breath,
Fearless tread the frowning portal;
Thou, when faileth flesh and sense,
Lord, wilt be my confidence!

OFFICES TO THE SOUL.

---

267. 7s. M.

1 Jesus, lover of my soul,
Let me to thy bosom fly,
While the nearer waters roll,
While the tempest still is high:
Hide me, O my Saviour, hide,
Till the storms of life be past;
Safe into the haven guide;
O, receive my soul at last!

2 Thou, O Christ, art all I want;
More than all in thee I find:
Raise the fallen, cheer the faint,
Heal the sick, and lead the blind.
Thou of life the fountain art;
Freely let me take of thee;
Spring thou up within my heart;
Rise to all eternity.

268. L. M.

1 How sweetly flowed the Gospel's sound
From lips of gentleness and grace,
When listening thousands gathered round,
And joy and reverence filled the place.

2 From heaven he came, of heaven he spoke,
To heaven he led his followers' way;
Dark clouds of gloomy night he broke,
Unveiling an immortal day.

3 "Come, wanderers, to my Father's home,
Come, all ye weary ones, and rest!"
Yes, Sacred Teacher, we will come,
Obey thee, love thee, and be blest.

269. L. M.

1 My dear Redeemer, and my Lord,
I read my duty in thy word:
But in thy life the law appears,
Drawn out in living characters.

2 Such was thy truth, and such thy zeal,
Such deference to thy Father's will,
Such love, and meekness so divine,
I would transcribe and make them mine.

3 Cold mountains and the midnight air
Witnessed the fervor of thy prayer;
The desert thy temptations knew,
Thy conflict, and thy victory too.

4 Be thou my pattern; may I bear
More of thy gracious image here;
Then God, the Judge, shall own my name
Amongst the followers of the Lamb.

270. 7s. M.

1 Go to dark Gethsemane,
Ye that feel temptation's power,
Your Redeemer's conflict see,
Watch with him one bitter hour;
Turn not from his griefs away,
Learn of Jesus Christ to pray.

2 Follow to the judgment hall,
View the Lord of life arraigned;
O the wormwood and the gall!
O the griefs his soul sustained!
Shun not suffering, shame, or loss;
Learn of him to bear the cross.

3 Calvary's mournful mountain climb;
There, admiring at his feet,
Mark that miracle of time,
Love's own sacrifice complete;
"It is finished," hear him cry;
Learn of Jesus Christ to die.

4 Early hasten to the tomb
Where they laid his breathless clay;
All is solitude and gloom;
Who has taken him away?
Christ is risen, he meets our eyes:
Saviour, teach us so to rise.

271. L. M.

1 The fiery steed and flaming car
Stood waiting on the azure road,
To take the blest Elijah far,
To him who called,—Elijah's God.

2 And in his brother prophet's view,
As now his heavenward course he bore,
How deep the joy Elisha knew,
To catch the sacred robe he wore!

3 Ascended Saviour! so may we
Receive thy white and shining dress,
Stand clothed in all thy purity,
The garment of thy righteousness.

4 And thus, by thee presented, stand
Within our gracious Father's sight,
The heirs to an immortal land
Of love, and peace, and joy, and light!

272. C. M.

1 The winds were howling o'er the deep,
Each wave a watery hill:
The Saviour wakened from his sleep;
He spake, and all was still.

2 The madman in a tomb had made
His mansion of despair:
Woe to the traveller who strayed,
With heedless footsteps, there!

3 He met that glance so thrilling sweet,
He heard those accents mild;
And, melting at Messiah's feet,
Wept like a weanèd child.

4 O madder than the raving man!
O deafer than the sea!
How long the time since Christ began
To call in vain to me!

5 Yet could I hear him once again,
As I have heard of old,
Methinks he should not call in vain
His wanderer to the fold.

273. 6s. M.

1 Cheer up, desponding soul,
Thy longing pleased I see:
'T is part of that great whole,
Wherewith I longed for thee!

2 Wherewith I longed for thee,
And left my Father's throne,
From death to set thee free,
And claim thee for my own!

3 To claim thee for my own,
I suffered on the cross;
O, were my love but known,
All else would be as dross!

4 All else would be as dross!
And souls, through grace divine,
Would count their gains but loss,
To live for ever mine!

274. C. P. M.

1 O, COULD we speak the matchless worth,
O, could we sound the glories forth,
Which in our Saviour shine,
We 'd soar, and touch the heavenly strings,
And vie with Gabriel, while he sings,
In notes almost divine.

2 We 'd sing the characters he bears,
And all the forms of love he wears,
Exalted on his throne:
In loftiest songs of sweetest praise,
We would, to everlasting days,
Make all his glories known.

3 O, the delightful day will come,
When Christ our Lord will bring us home,
And we shall see his face;
Then, with our Saviour, Brother, Friend,
A blest eternity we 'll spend,
Triumphant in his grace.

275. L. M.

1 JESUS, thou source of calm repose,
All fulness dwells in thee divine;
Our strength, to quell the proudest foes;
Our light, in deepest gloom to shine;
Thou art our fortress, strength, and tower,
Our trust and portion, evermore.

2 Jesus, our Comforter thou art;
Our rest in toil, our ease in pain;
The balm to heal each broken heart,
In storms our peace, in loss our gain;
Our joy, beneath the worldling's frown;
In shame, our glory and our crown;—

3 In want, our plentiful supply;
In weakness, our almighty power;
In bonds, our perfect liberty;
Our refuge in temptation's hour;
Our comfort, amidst grief and thrall;
Our life in death; our all in all.

276. L. M.

1 Thou art the Way,—and he who sighs
Amid this starless waste of woe,
To find a pathway to the skies,
A light from heaven's eternal glow,
By thee must come, thou Gate of love,
Through which the saints undoubting trod,
Till faith discovers, like the dove,
An ark, a resting-place in God.

2 Thou art the Truth,—whose steady day
Shines on through earthly blight and bloom
The pure, the everlasting ray,
The lamp that shines even in the tomb;
The light that out of darkness springs,
And guideth those that blindly go;
The word whose precious radiance flings
Its lustre upon all below.

3 Thou art the Life, — the blessed well,
With living waters gushing o'er,
Which those that drink shall ever dwell
Where sin and thirst are known no more.
Thou art the mystic pillar given,
Our lamp by night, our light by day;
Thou art the sacred bread from heaven;
Thou art the Life, the Truth, the Way.

277. L. M.

1 Thou, Lord! by mortal eyes unseen,
And by thine offspring here unknown,
To manifest thyself to men,
Hast set thine image in thy Son.

2 O Thou! at whose almighty word
Fair light at first from darkness shone,
Teach us to know our glorious Lord,
And trace the Father in the Son.

3 While we thine image there displayed
With love and admiration view,
Form us in likeness to our Head,
That we may bear thine image too.

278. C. M.

1 How blest thy creature is, O God,
When, with a single eye,
He views the lustre of thy word,
The day-spring from on high!

2 The soul, a dreary province once
Of Satan's dark domain,
Feels a new empire formed within,
And owns a heavenly reign.

3 The glorious orb, whose golden beams
The fruitful year control,
Since first, obedient to thy word,
He started from the goal,—

4 Has cheered the nations with the joys
His orient rays impart:
But, Jesus, 't is thy light alone
Can shine upon the heart.

279. L. M.

1 Long as the darkening cloud abode,
So long did ancient Israel rest;
Nor moved they, till the guiding Lord
In brighter garments stood confessed.

2 Father of spirits, Light of light,
Lift up the cloud, and rend the veil;
Shine forth in fire amid that night
Whose blackness makes the heart to fail.

3 'T is done! to Christ the power is given;
His death has rent the veil away;
Our great Forerunner entered heaven,
And oped the gate of endless day.

4 Adoring nations hail the dawn,
All kingdoms bless the noontide beam,
And light, unfolding life's full morn,
Is vast creation's deathless theme.

280. 7s. M.

1 Come! said Jesus' sacred voice,
Come, and make my paths your choice;
I will guide you to your home;
Weary pilgrim, hither come!

2 Thou who, houseless, sole, forlorn,
Long hast borne the proud world's scorn,
Long hast roamed the barren waste,
Weary pilgrim, hither haste!

3 Ye who, tossed on beds of pain,
Seek for ease, but seek in vain;
Ye, whose swollen and sleepless eyes
Watch to see the morning rise;

4 Ye, by fiercer anguish torn,
In remorse for guilt who mourn,
Here repose your heavy care:
Who the stings of guilt can bear?

5 Sinner, come! for here is found
Balm that flows for every wound,
Peace that ever shall endure,
Rest eternal, sacred, sure.

281. S. M.

1 O, cease, my wandering soul,
On restless wing to roam;
All this wide world, to either pole,
Has not for thee a home.

2 Behold the ark of God;
Behold the open door;
O, haste to gain that dear abode,
And rove, my soul, no more!

3 There, safe thou shalt abide,
There, sweet shall be thy rest,
And every longing satisfied,
With full salvation blest.

282. L. M.

1 Jesus, and can it ever be,
A mortal man ashamed of thee?
Scorned be the thought by rich and poor;
My soul shall scorn it more and more.

2 Ashamed of Jesus! yes, I may,
When I 've no sins to wash away,
No tears to wipe, no joys to crave,
And no immortal soul to save.

3 Ashamed of Jesus! that dear friend,
On whom my hopes of heaven depend?
No; when I blush, be this my shame,
That I no more revere his name.

4 Till then, — nor is the boasting vain, —
Till then I boast a Saviour slain;
And O, may this my portion be,
That Saviour 's not ashamed of me!

283. C. M.

1 JESUS, thine all-victorious love
Shed in my heart abroad:
Then shall my feet no longer rove,
Rooted and fixed in God.

2 My steadfast heart, from falling free,
Shall then no longer move;
But God be all the world to me,
And all my heart be love.

284. 7s. M.

1 EARTH has nothing sweet or fair,
Lovely forms or beauties rare,
But before my eyes they bring
Christ, of beauty Source and Spring.

2 When the morning paints the skies,
When the golden sunbeams rise,
Then my Saviour's form I find
Brightly imaged on my mind.

3 When the day-beams pierce the night,
Oft I think on Jesus' light,
Think how bright that light will be,
Shining through eternity.

4 Come, Lord Jesus! and dispel
This dark cloud in which I dwell,
And to me the power impart
To behold thee as thou art.

285. 8 & 7s. M.

1 Jesus, I my cross have taken,
All to leave and follow thee;
I am poor, despised, forsaken,—
Thou henceforth my all shalt be.

2 Let the world despise and leave me,
It has left my Saviour too;
Human hearts and looks deceive me,
Thou art not, like them, untrue.

3 Man may trouble and distress me,
'T will but drive me to thy breast;
Life with trials hard may press me,
Heaven will bring me sweeter rest.

4 Soul, then know thy full salvation;
Rise o'er sin, and fear, and care;
Joy to find in every station
Something still to do or bear.

5 Haste thee on from grace to glory,
Armed with faith, and winged with prayer;
An eternal day before thee
Waits for God to guide thee there.

286. 7s. M.

1 When, my Saviour, shall I be
Perfectly resigned to thee?
Poor and vile in my own eyes,
Only in thy wisdom wise?

2 Only thee content to know,
Ignorant of all below?
Only guided by thy light?
Only mighty in thy might?

3 So I may thy spirit know,
Let it as it listeth blow:
Let the manner be unknown,
So I may with thee be one;—

4 Fully in my life express
All the heights of holiness;
Sweetly let my spirit prove
All the depths of humble love.

287. C. M.

1 O, SEE how Jesus trusts himself
Unto our childish love,
As though by his free ways with us
Our earnestness to prove!

2 His sacred name a common word
On earth he loves to hear;
There is no majesty in him
Which love may not come near.

3 The light of love is round his feet,
His paths are never dim;
And he comes nigh to us when we
Dare not come nigh to him.

4 Let us be simple with him, then,
Not backward, stiff, or cold,
As though our Bethlehem could be
What Sinai was of old.

288. L. M.

1 Come, O thou universal good!
Balm of the wounded conscience, come!
Haven to take the shipwrecked in,
My everlasting rest from sin!

2 Come, O my comfort and delight!
My strength, and health, and shield, and sun,
My boast, my confidence, and might,
My joy, my glory, and my crown.

289. C. M.

1 Jesus, the very thought of thee
With sweetness fills my breast;
But sweeter far thy face to see,
And in thy presence rest.

2 Nor voice can sing, nor heart can frame,
Nor can the memory find,
A sweeter sound than thy blest name,
O Saviour of mankind!

3 O hope of every contrite heart!
O joy of all the meek!
To those who fall, how kind thou art!
How good to those who seek!

4 But what to those who find? Ah! this
Nor tongue nor pen can show,
The love of Jesus, what it is,
None but his loved ones know.

5 Jesus, our only joy be thou,
  As thou our prize wilt be;
Jesus, be thou our glory now,
  And through eternity.

290. C. M.

1 O Jesus, Lord of all below,
  Thou fount of life and fire,
Surpassing all the joys we know,
  All that we can desire.

2 May every heart confess thy name,
  And ever thee adore,
And, seeking thee, itself inflame
  To seek thee more and more.

3 Thee may our tongue for ever bless,
  Thee may we love alone,
And ever in our lives express
  The image of thine own.

291. 7s. M.

1 Christ, whose glory fills the skies,
  Christ, the true, the only light,
Sun of Righteousness, arise!
  Triumph o'er the shades of night;
Day-spring from on high, be near!
Day-star, in my heart appear!

2 Dark and cheerless is the morn,
  If thy life is hid from me;

Joyless is the day's return,
Till thy mercy's beams I see;
Till they inward light impart,
Warmth and gladness to my heart.

3 Visit, then, this soul of mine;
Pierce the gloom of sin and grief;
Fill me, radiant Sun divine;
Scatter all my unbelief;
More and more thyself display,
Shining to the perfect day.

292. 7 & 6s. M.

1 My spirit longeth for Thee
To dwell within my breast;
Although I am unworthy
Of so divine a Guest!

2 Of so divine a Guest
Unworthy though I be,
Yet hath my heart no rest
Until it come to Thee!

3 Until it come to Thee,
In vain I look around;
In all that I can see,
No rest is to be found!

4 No rest is to be found,
But in thy bleeding love:
O, let my wish be crowned,
And send it from above!

293. C. M.

1 Christ leads me through no darker rooms
Than he went through before:
He that into God's kingdom comes
Must enter by this door.

2 Come, Lord, when grace hath made me meet
Thy blessed face to see;
For if thy work on earth be sweet,
What must thy glory be?

3 Then I shall end my sad complaints,
And weary, sinful days,
And join with those triumphant saints
That sing Jehovah's praise.

4 My knowledge of that life is small;
The eye of faith is dim;
But 't is enough that Christ knows all,
And I shall be with him!

294. L. M.

1 "See how he loved!" exclaimed the Jews,
As tender tears from Jesus fell;
My grateful heart the thought pursues,
And on the theme delights to dwell.

2 See how he loved,—who travelled on,
Teaching the doctrine from the skies;
Who bade disease and pain begone,
And called the sleeping dead to rise.

3 See how he loved, — who never shrank
From toil or danger, pain or death;
Who all the cup of sorrow drank,
And meekly yielded up his breath.

4 Such love can we, unmoved, survey?
O, may our breasts with ardor glow,
To tread his steps, his laws obey,
And thus our warm affections show!

295. L. M.

1 How beauteous were the marks divine,
That in thy meekness used to shine,
That lit thy lonely pathway, trod
In wondrous love, O Son of God!

2 O, who like thee so calm, so bright,
So pure, so made to live in light?
O, who like thee did ever go
So patient through a world of woe?

3 O, who like thee so humbly bore
The scorn, the scoffs, of men before?
So meek, forgiving, godlike, high,
So glorious in humility?

4 The bending angels stooped to see
The lisping infant clasp thy knee,
And smile, as in a father's eye,
Upon thy mild divinity.

5 And death, which sets the prisoner free,
Was pang and scoff and scorn to thee;
Yet love through all thy torture glowed,
And mercy with thy life-blood flowed.

296. 10s. M.

1 O THOU great Friend to all the sons of men,
Who once appearedst in humblest guise below,
Sin to rebuke, to break the captive's chain,
And call thy brethren forth from want and woe,—

2 We look to thee! thy truth is still the light
Which guides the nations, groping on their way,
Stumbling and falling in disastrous night,
Yet hoping ever for the perfect day.

3 Yes! thou art still the Life; thou art the Way
The holiest know;—Light, Life, and Way of heaven!
And they who dearest hope, and deepest pray,
Toil by the light, life, way, which thou hast given.

297. L. M.

1 To thee, O God! we homage pay,
Source of the light that rules the day!
Who, while he gilds all nature's frame,
Reflects thy rays and speaks thy name.

2 In louder strains we sing that grace
Which gives the Sun of Righteousness,
Whose nobler light salvation brings,
And scatters healing from his wings.

3 Still on our hearts may Jesus shine
With beams of light and love divine;
Quickened by him, our souls shall live,
And cheered by him shall grow and thrive.

4 O, may his glories stand confessed,
From north to south, from east to west;
Successful may his Gospel run,
Wide as the circuit of the sun.

298. C. M.

1 Not to the terrors of the Lord,
The tempest, fire, and smoke;
Not to the thunder of that word
Which God on Sinai spoke;—

2 But we are come to Zion's hill,
The city of our God,
Where milder words declare his will,
And spread his love abroad.

3 Behold the innumerable host
Of angels, clothed in light!
Behold the spirits of the just,
Whose faith is turned to sight!

4 The saints on earth, and all the dead,
But one communion make;
All join in Christ, their living Head,
And of his grace partake.

299. S. M.

1 The law by Moses came;
But peace, and truth, and love
Were brought by Christ, — a nobler name, —
Descending from above.

2 Amidst the house of God
Their different works were done;
Moses a faithful servant stood,
But Christ a faithful Son.

3 Then to his new commands
Be strict obedience paid;
O'er all his Father's house he stands
The Sovereign and the Head.

300. 7s. M.

1 Saviour of the sin-sick soul,
Give me faith to make me whole!
Finish thy great work of grace,
Cut it short in righteousness.

2 Speak, the second time, "Be clean!"
Take away my inbred sin;
Every stumbling-block remove;
Cast it out by perfect love.

3 Nothing less will I require,
Nothing more can I desire:
None but Christ to me be given;
None but Christ in earth or heaven!

4 O that I might now decrease!
O that all I am might cease!
Let me into nothing fall,
Let my Lord be all in all!

301. S. M.

1 JESUS, I fain would find
Thy zeal for God in me,
Thy yearning pity for mankind,
Thy burning charity.

2 In me thy spirit dwell!
In me thy mercy move!
So shall the fervor of my zeal
Be the pure flame of love.

302. 7s. M.

1 PILGRIM, burdened with thy sin,
Come the way to Zion's gate;
There, till mercy speaks within,
Knock and weep, and watch and wait;
Knock, — he knows the sinner's cry;
Weep, — he loves the mourner's tears;
Watch, — for saving grace is nigh;
Wait, — till heavenly grace appears.

2 Hark; it is the Saviour's voice,
"Welcome, pilgrim, to thy rest!"
Now within the gate rejoice,
Safe and owned, and bought and blest;

Safe from all the lures of vice,
  Owned by joys the contrite know,
Bought by love, and life the price,
  Blest the mighty debt to owe.

3 Holy pilgrim, what for thee
  In a world like this remains?
From thy guarded breast shall flee
  Fear and shame, and doubt and pains;
Fear the hope of heaven shall flee,
  Shame from glory's view retire,
Doubt in full belief shall die,
  Pain in endless bliss expire.

303. L. M.

1 Come, Jesus! come! return again;
  With brighter beam thy servants bless,
Who long to feel thy perfect reign,
  And share thy kingdom's happiness!

2 A feeble race, by passion driven,
  In darkness and in doubt we roam,
And lift our anxious eyes to heaven,
  Our hope, our harbor, and our home.

3 Yet, 'mid the wild and wintry gale,
  When death rides darkly on the sea,
And strength and earthly daring fail,
  Our hopes, Redeemer, rest on thee!

304. L. M.

1 THE sage his cup of hemlock quaffed,
And calmly drained the fatal draught:
Such pledge did Grecian justice give
To one who taught men how to live.

2 The Christ, in piety assured,
The anguish of his cross endured:
Such pangs did Jewish bigots try
On him who taught us how to die.

3 Mid prison-walls, the sage could trust
That men would grow more wise and just;
From Calvary's mount, the Christ could see
The dawn of immortality.

4 Who know to live, and know to die,
Their souls are safe, their triumph nigh:
Power may oppress, and priestcraft ban;
Justice and faith are God in man.

305. 8 & 7s. M. (Peculiar.)

1 HEAD of the Church triumphant,
We joyfully adore thee;
Till thou appear, thy members here
Shall sing like those in glory:
We lift our hearts and voices
With blest anticipation;
And cry aloud, and give to God
The praise of our salvation.

2 Thou dost conduct thy people
Through torrents of temptation;
Nor will we fear, while thou art near,
The fire of tribulation:
The world, with sin and Satan,
In vain our march opposes;
By thee we shall break through them all,
And sing the song of Moses.

3 By faith we see the glory
To which thou shalt restore us;
The cross despise for that high prize
Which thou hast set before us:
And if thou count us worthy,
We each, as dying Stephen,
Shall see thee stand, at God's right hand,
To take us up to heaven.

306. C. M.

1 Thou, O my Jesus, thou didst me
Upon the cross embrace;
For me didst bear the nails and spear,
And manifold disgrace,—

2 And griefs and torments numberless,
And sweat of agony,
Yea, death itself; and all for one
That was thine enemy.

3 Then, why, O blessed Jesus Christ,
Should I not love thee well?
Not for the hope of winning heaven,
Nor of escaping hell;

4 Not with the hope of gaining aught,
Not seeking a reward;
But as thyself hast lovèd me,
O ever-loving Lord.

307. 6, 10, & 4s. M.

1 SAVIOUR and dearest friend,
Who dying groaned for me,
Thoughtless of self, all weakness do I bend
At thought of thee.

2 O, didst thou weep my tears?
Then will I weep no more;
The anguish I have felt for bitter years
Pierced thee before.

3 My sorrows hast thou borne,
Sinless and Crucified!
Trembling, I thank thee, and no more will mourn,
Since thou hast died.

4 Bowing unto the storm
That beats upon my head,
I see thy pitying, perfect-fashioned form
Suffering instead.

5 Thine is the heart thus bought;
I cannot call it mine;
Perish ambition! be each hope, each thought,
Henceforth divine!

308. 7s. M.

1 Hark, my soul, it is the Lord!
'T is thy Saviour, hear his word.
Jesus speaks, and says to thee,
" Say, poor sinner, lov'st thou me?

2 " I delivered thee when bound,
And when bleeding healed thy wound;
Sought thee wandering, set thee right,
Turned thy darkness into light.

3 " Mine is an unchanging love,
Higher than the heights above,
Deeper than the depths beneath,
Free and faithful, strong as death."

4 Lord, it is my chief complaint
That my love is still so faint;
Yet I love thee and adore;
O for grace to love thee more!

309. 7s. M.

1 Feeble, helpless, how shall I
Learn to live and learn to die?
Who, O God, my guide shall be?
Who shall lead thy child to thee?

2 Blessed Father, gracious One,
Thou hast sent thy holy Son;
He will give the light I need,
He my trembling steps will lead.

3 Through this world, uncertain, dim,
Let me ever learn of him;
From his precepts wisdom draw,
Make his life my solemn law.

4 Thus in deed, and thought, and word,
Led by Jesus Christ the Lord,
In my weakness, thus shall I
Learn to live and learn to die.

310. L. M.

1 I KNOW that my Redeemer lives,—
What joy the blest assurance gives!
He lives, he lives, who once was dead;
He lives, my everlasting Head!

2 He lives, to bless me with his love;
He lives, to plead for me above;
He lives, my hungry soul to feed;
He lives, to help in time of need.

3 He lives, and grants me daily breath;
He lives, and I shall conquer death;
He lives, my mansion to prepare;
He lives, to bring me safely there.

4 He lives, all glory to his name;
He lives, my Saviour, still the same;
What joy the blest assurance gives,—
I know that my Redeemer lives!

311. 7s. M.

1 Rock of Ages, cleft for me,
Let me hide myself in thee!
Let the water and the blood,
From thy riven side which flowed,
Be of sin the double cure,
Cleanse me from its guilt and power.

2 Not the labors of my hands
Can fulfil thy law's demands:
Could my zeal no respite know,
Could my tears for ever flow,
All for sin could not atone;
Thou must save, and thou alone!

3 Nothing in my hand I bring;
Simply to thy cross I cling;
Naked, come to thee for dress;
Helpless, look to thee for grace;
Foul, I to thy fountain fly;
Wash me, Saviour, or I die!

4 Whilst I draw this fleeting breath,
When my eye-strings break in death,
When I soar through tracts unknown,
See thee on thy judgment-throne,
Rock of Ages, cleft for me,
Let me hide myself in thee.

312. 8 & 7s. M.

1 Saviour, source of every blessing,
Tune my heart to grateful lays;
Streams of mercy never ceasing
Call for ceaseless songs of praise.

2 Teach me some melodious measure,
Sung by raptured saints above;
Fill my soul with sacred pleasure,
While I sing redeeming love.

3 Thou didst seek me when a stranger,
Wandering from the fold of God;
Thou, to save my soul from danger,
Didst redeem me with thy blood.

4 By thy hand restored, defended,
Safe through life thus far I 've come;
Safe, O Lord, when life is ended,
Bring me to my heavenly home.

313. 6 & 4s. M.

1 My faith looks up to thee,
Thou Lamb of Calvary,
Saviour Divine!
Lord, hear me while I pray;
"Take all my guilt away!"
O, let me from this day
Be wholly thine!

2 May thy rich grace impart
Strength to my fainting heart,
My zeal inspire;
As thou hast died for me,
O, may my love to thee
Pure, warm, and changeless be,—
A living fire.

3 While life's dark maze I tread,
And griefs around me spread,
Be thou my guide;
Bid darkness turn to day,
Wipe sorrow's tears away,
Nor let me ever stray
From thee aside.

4 When ends life's transient dream,
When death's cold, sullen stream
Shall o'er me roll,
Blest Saviour, then, in love,
Fear and distrust remove;
O, bear me safe above,—
A ransomed soul.

THE CROSS.

314. 8 & 7s. M.

1 Sweet the moments, rich in blessing,
Which before the cross I spend;
Life, and health, and peace possessing,
From the sinner's dying Friend:
Here alone I find my heaven,
Humbly on the Lamb to gaze;
Feel how much has been forgiven,
To his own eternal praise!

2 Love and grief my heart dividing,
Here I 'll spend my latest breath;
Constant still in faith abiding,
Life deriving from his death:
May I still enjoy this feeling,
In all need to Jesus go,
Prove each day his wounds more healing,
And himself more deeply know!

315. 8, 6, & 4s. M.

1 Father, who in the olive shade,
When the dark hour came on,
Didst, with a breath of heavenly aid,
Strengthen thy Son,—

2 O, by the anguish of that night,
Send us down blest relief;
Or, to the chastened, let thy might
Hallow this grief!

3 And thou, that, when the starry sky
Saw the dread strife begun,
Didst teach adoring faith to cry,
"Thy will be done!"—

4 By thy meek spirit, thou of all
That e'er have mourned, the chief,
Blest Saviour, if the stroke must fall,
Hallow this grief!

316. L. M.

1 By sufferings only can we know
The nature of the life we live;
The temper of our souls they show,
How true, how pure, the love we give.
To leave my love in doubt would be
No less disgrace than misery!

2 I welcome, then, with heart sincere,
The cross my Saviour bids me take;

No load, no trial, is severe,
That 's borne or suffered for his sake:
And thus my sorrow shall proclaim
A love that 's worthy of the name.

317. S. M.

1 Behold the amazing sight,
The Saviour lifted high!
Behold the Father's chief delight
Expire in agony!

2 For love of us he bled,
And all in torture died;
'T was love that bowed his fainting head,
And oped his gushing side.

3 In him our hearts unite,
Nor share his grief alone,
But from his cross pursue their flight
To his triumphant throne.

318. 8 & 7s. M.

1 In the cross of Christ I glory,
Towering o'er the wrecks of time;
All the light of sacred story
Gathers round its head sublime.

2 When the woes of life o'ertake me,
Hopes deceive, and fears annoy,
Never shall the cross forsake me;
Lo! it glows with peace and jov

3 When the sun of bliss is beaming
Light and love upon my way,
From the cross the radiance streaming
Adds more lustre to the day.

4 Bane and blessing, pain and pleasure,
By the cross are sanctified;
Peace is there that knows no measure,
Joys that through all time abide.

319. L. M.

1 When I survey the wondrous cross
On which the Prince of glory died,
My richest gain I count but loss,
And pour contempt on all my pride.

2 See from his head, his hands, his feet,
Sorrow and love flow mingled down!
Did e'er such love and sorrow meet?
Or thorns compose so rich a crown?

3 Were the whole realm of nature mine,
That were a present far too small;
Love so amazing, so divine,
Demands my soul, my life, my all.

320. 7s. M.

1 'T is my happiness below,
Not to live without the cross;
But the Saviour's power to know,
Sanctifying every loss.

2 Trials must and will befall;
But with humble faith to see
Love inscribed upon them all,
This is happiness to me.

3 Trials make the promise sweet;
Trials give new life to prayer;
Bring me to my Father's feet,
Lay me low, and keep me there.

321. L. M.

1 Is it not strange, the darkest hour
That ever dawned on sinful earth
Should touch the heart with softest power,
And give our sweetest comforts birth?

2 That to the cross our eyes should turn
For cheering light, and strength to save,
Sooner than where the Easter sun
Shines glorious on the open grave?

3 Yet so it is: for duly there
The storms of life are lulled to rest;
Stilled by the Saviour's trusting prayer,
Soothed by the peace within his breast.

4 My Saviour! whom 't is life to see,
Thy promise in thy cross appears;
Its power, its peace, O, grant to me!
Its perfect love to still my fears.

322. C. M.

1 We tread the path our Master trod:
We bear the cross he bore;
And every thorn that wounds our feet
His temples pierced before.

2 Oft do our eyes with joy o'erflow,
And oft are bathed in tears;
Yet naught but heaven our hopes can raise,
And naught but sin our fears.

3 We purge our mortal dross away,
Refining as we run;
And while we die to earth and sense,
Our heaven is here begun.

323. C. P. M.

1 Self-love no grace in sorrow sees,
Consults her own peculiar ease, —
'T is all the bliss she knows;
But nobler aims true Love employ, —
In self-denial is her joy,
In suffering her repose.

2 Sorrow and Love go side by side;
Nor height nor depth can e'er divide
Their heaven-appointed bands;
Those dear associates still are one,
Nor, till the race of life is run,
Disjoin their wedded hands.

3 Thy choice and mine shall be the same,
Inspirer of that holy flame,
Which must for ever blaze!
To take the cross and follow thee,
Where love and duty lead, shall be
My portion and my praise.

324. 8 & 7s. M.

1 Cross, reproach, and tribulation,
Ye to me are welcome guests,
When I have this consolation,
That my soul in Jesus rests.

2 The reproach of Christ is glorious;
Those who here his burden bear
In the end shall prove victorious,
And eternal gladness share.

3 Bear, then, the reproach of Jesus,
Ye who live a life of faith!
Lift triumphant songs and praises,
Even in martyrdom and death.

4 Bonds and stripes, and evil story,
Are our honorable crowns;
Pain is peace, and shame is glory,
Gloomy dungeons are as thrones.

325. 7s. M.

1 Every bird that upward springs
Bears the cross upon his wings;

We without it cannot rise
Upward to our native skies.

2 Every ship that meets the waves
By the cross their fury braves;
We, on life's wide ocean tost,
If we have it not, are lost.

3 Hope it gives us when distressed,
When we faint it gives us rest;
Satan's craft and Satan's might
By the cross are put to flight.

4 That from sin earth might be free,
Jesus bore it, — so must we;
Ne'er through faintness lay it down:
First the cross, and then the crown!

326. C. M.

1 The Saviour, — what a noble flame
Was kindled in his breast,
When, hasting to Jerusalem,
He marched before the rest!

2 With all his sufferings full in view,
And woes to us unknown,
Forth to the task his spirit flew;
'T was love that urged him on.

3 Lord, while thy bleeding glories here
Engage our wondering eyes,
We learn our lighter cross to bear,
And hasten to the skies.

327. 6 & 10s. M.

1 Thou who didst stoop below,
To drain the cup of woe,
Wearing the form of frail mortality, —
Thy toil and conflict done,
Thy crown of victory won, —
Hast passed from earth,—passed to thy home on high.

2 Our eyes behold thee not,
Yet hast thou not forgot
Those who have placed their hope, their trust, in thee;
Before thy Father's face
Thou hast prepared a place,
That where thou art, there they may also be.

3 O Thou who art our life,
Be with us through the strife!
Was not thy head by earth's fierce tempests bowed?
Raise thou our eyes above,
To see a Father's love
Beam, like the bow of promise, through the cloud.

V.

THE SPIRIT.

QUICKENER, SANCTIFIER, AND COMFORTER.

---

328. C. M.

1 Lo! when the Spirit of our God
Came down his flock to find,
A voice from heaven was heard abroad,
A rushing, mighty wind.

2 It fills the Church of God; it fills
The sinful world around:
Only in stubborn hearts and wills
No place for it is found.

3 To other strains our souls are set:
A giddy whirl of sin
Fills ear and heart, and will not let
Heaven's harmonies come in.

4 Come, Lord, come, Wisdom, Love, and Power,
Open our ears to hear!
Let us not miss the accepted hour:
Save, Lord, by love or fear.

329. 7 & 6s. M.

1 Open, Lord, my inward ear,
And bid my heart rejoice;
Bid my quiet spirit hear
The comfort of thy voice;
Never in the whirlwind found,
Or where earthquakes rock the place,
Still and silent is the sound,
The whisper of thy grace.

2 From the world of sin and noise
And tumult I withdraw;
For the small and inward voice
I wait with humble awe;
Silent am I now and still,
Dare not in thy presence move;
To my waiting soul reveal
The secret of thy love.

330. L. M.

1 Hath not thy heart within thee burned
At evening's calm and holy hour,
As if its inmost depths discerned
The presence of a loftier power?

2 As they who once with Jesus trod
With kindling breast his accents heard,
But knew not that the Son of God
Was uttering every burning word,—

3 Father of Jesus! thus thy voice
Speaks to our hearts in tones divine;
Our spirits tremble and rejoice,
But know not that the voice is thine.

4 Still be thy hallowed accents near!
To doubt and passion whisper peace;
Direct us on our journey here,
And bid, in heaven, our wanderings cease.

331. 8 & 4s. M.

1 My heart lies dead; and no increase
Doth my dull husbandry improve:
O, let thy graces, without cease,
Drop from above.

2 Thy dew doth every morning fall:
And shall the dew outstrip thy Dove?—
The dew, for which earth cannot call,
"Drop from above!"

3 The world is tempting still my heart
Unto a hardness void of love;
Let heavenly grace, to cross its art,
Drop from above.

4 O, come! for thou dost know the way!
Or if to me thou wilt not move,
Remove me where I need not say,
"Drop from above!"

332. C. M.

1 We ask not, Lord, thy cloven flame,
Or tongues of various tone;
But long thy praises to proclaim
With fervor, in our own.

2 We neither have nor seek the power
Ill demons to control;
But thou in dark temptation's hour
Shalt chase them from the soul.

3 No heavenly harpings soothe our ear,
No mystic dreams we share;
Yet hope to feel thy comfort near,
And bless thee in our prayer.

4 When tongues shall cease, and power decay,
And knowledge empty prove,
Do thou thy trembling servants stay
With faith, and hope, and love.

333. 6 & 10s. M.

1 Wilt Thou not visit me?
The plant beside me feels thy gentle dew;
Each blade of grass I see,
From thy deep earth its quickening moisture drew.

2 Wilt Thou not visit me?
Thy morning calls on me with cheering tone;
And every hill and tree
Lend but one voice, the voice of thee alone

3 Come! for I need thy love,
More than the flower the dew, or grass the rain;
Come, like thy holy dove,
And let me in thy sight rejoice to live again.

4 Yes! Thou wilt visit me;
Nor plant nor tree thine eye delights so well,
As when, from sin set free,
Man's spirit comes with thine in peace to dwell.

334. S. M.

1 The Spirit, in our hearts,
Is whispering, "Sinner, come!"
The Bride, the Church of Christ, proclaims
To all his children, "Come!"

2 Let him that heareth say
To all about him, Come!
Let him that thirsts for righteousness
To Christ, the fountain, come!

3 Yes, whosoever will,
O, let him freely come,
And freely drink the stream of life;
'T is Jesus bids him come.

4 Lo! Jesus, who invites,
Declares, "I quickly come!"
Lord, even so! I wait thine hour;
Jesus, my Saviour, come!

335. S. M.

1 Come, Holy Spirit, come!
Let thy bright beams arise;
Dispel the sorrow from our minds,
The darkness from our eyes.

2 Convince us all of sin;
Lead us to thine abode,
And to our wondering view reveal
Thy mercies, O our God!

3 Revive our drooping faith,
Our doubts and fears remove,
And kindle in our breasts the flame
Of never-dying love.

4 'T is thine to cleanse the heart,
To sanctify the soul,
To pour fresh life in every part,
And new-create the whole.

5 Dwell, Spirit, in our hearts!
Our minds from bondage free;
Then shall we know, and praise, and love,
And rise at length to thee.

336. C. M.

1 When God, of old, came down from heaven,
In power and wrath he came;
Before his feet the clouds were riven,
Half darkness and half flame.

2 But when he came the second time,
He came in power and love;
Softer than gales at morning prime
Hovered his holy Dove.

3 The fires that rushed on Sinai down
In sudden torrents dread,
Now gently light a glorious crown
On every sainted head.

4 Like arrows went those lightnings forth,
Winged with the sinner's doom;
But these, like tongues, o'er all the earth
Proclaiming life to come.

337. S. M.

1 O, COME, and dwell in me,
Spirit of power within!
And bring the glorious liberty
From sorrow, fear, and sin.

2 The seed of sin's disease,
Spirit of health, remove,—
Spirit of finished holiness,
Spirit of perfect love!

3 Hasten the joyful day
Which shall my sins consume;
When old things shall be done away,
And all things new become.

338. L. M.

1 Health of the weak, to make them strong!
Refuge of sinners, and their song!
Comfort of each afflicted breast!
Haven of hope in realms of rest!
Lord of the patriarchs gone before!
Light of the prophets' learned lore!
Deign from thy throne to look on me,
And hear my lowly litany.

2 Lead me, O Spirit, to the Son,
To taste and feel what he has done;
To lay me low before his cross,
And reckon all besides as dross;
To speak, and think, and will, and move,
And love, as thou wouldst have me love:
O, look upon this bended knee,
And hear my heart's own litany!

339. L. M.

1 Come, O Creator Spirit blest!
And in our souls take up thy rest;
Come, with thy grace and heavenly aid,
To fill the hearts which thou hast made.

2 Great Paraclete! to thee we cry:
O highest gift of God most high!
O fount of life! O fire of love!
And sweet anointing from above!

3 Kindle our senses from above,
And make our hearts o'erflow with love;
With patience firm, and virtue high,
The weakness of our flesh supply.

4 Far from us drive the foe we dread,
And grant us thy true peace instead;
So shall we not, with thee for guide,
Turn from the path of life aside.

340. 7s. M.

1 Gracious Spirit! Love divine!
Let thy light within me shine;
All my guilty fears remove;
Fill me with thy heavenly love.

2 Life and peace to me impart;
Seal salvation on my heart;
Dwell thyself within my breast,
Earnest of immortal rest.

3 Let me never from thee stray;
Keep me in the narrow way;
Fill my soul with joy divine;
Keep me, Lord, for ever thine.

341. 7s. M.

1 Holy Spirit! Lord of light!
From thy clear celestial height,
Come, thou Light of all that live!
Thy pure beaming radiance give!

2 Come, thou Father of the poor!
Come, with treasures which endure;
Thou, of all consolers best,
Visiting the troubled breast,

3 Thou in toil art comfort sweet;
Pleasant coolness in the heat;
Solace in the midst of woe;
Dost refreshing peace bestow.

4 Light immortal! Light divine!
Visit thou these hearts of thine;
If thou take thy grace away,
Nothing pure in man will stay.

5 Heal our wounds,— our strength renew;
On our dryness pour thy dew;
Wash the stains of guilt away;
Guide the steps that go astray.

6 Give us comfort when we die;
Give us life with thee on high;
In thy sevenfold gifts descend;
Give us joys which never end.

342. C. M.

1 Spirit of God! thy churches wait,
With wishful, longing eyes;
Let us no more lie desolate;
O, bid thy light arise!

2 Thy light, that on our souls hath shone,
Leads us in hope to thee;

Let us not feel its rays alone,—
Alone thy people be.

3 O, bring our dearest friends to God;
Remember those we love;
Fit them, on earth, for thine abode;
Fit them for joys above.

343. L. M.

1 Like morning, when her early breeze
Breaks up the surface of the seas,
That, in their furrows, dark with night,
Her hand may sow the seeds of light,—

2 Thy grace can send its breathings o'er
The spirit dark and lost before;
And, freshening all its depths, prepare
For truth divine to enter there.

3 Till David touched his sacred lyre,
In silence lay the unbreathing wire;
But when he swept its chords along,
Then angels stooped to hear the song.

4 So sleeps the soul, till thou, O Lord,
Shalt deign to touch its lifeless chord;
Till, waked by thee, its breath shall rise
In music worthy of the skies.

344. L. M.

1 I WANT the spirit of power within,
Of love, and of a healthful mind;
Of power to conquer every sin,
Of love to God and all mankind;
Of health that pain and death defies,
Most vigorous when the body dies.

2 O that the Comforter would come,
Nor visit as a transient guest,
But fix in me his constant home,
And keep possession of my breast;
And make my soul his loved abode,
The temple of indwelling God!

345. 8 & 7s. M.

1 LIGHT of those whose dreary dwelling
Borders on the shades of death!
Come, and, by thy love's revealing,
Dissipate the clouds beneath;
The new heaven and earth's Creator!
In our deepest darkness rise,
Scattering all the night of nature,
Pouring eyesight on our eyes.

2 Still we wait for thine appearing;
Life and joy thy beams impart,
Chasing all our fears, and cheering
Every poor benighted heart:

Come, and manifest the favor
 Promised to thy ransomed race;
Come, thou glorious God and Saviour!
 Come, and bring thy Gospel grace.

346. P. M.

1 Our blest Redeemer, ere he breathed
 His tender, last farewell,
A Guide, a Comforter, bequeathed
 With us to dwell.

2 He came in tongues of living flame,
 To teach, convince, subdue;
All-powerful as the wind he came,
 As viewless too.

3 He came sweet influence to impart,
 A gracious, willing guest,
While he can find one humble heart
 Wherein to rest.

4 And every virtue we possess,
 And every victory won,
And every thought of holiness,
 Are his alone.

5 Spirit of purity and grace!
 Our weakness pitying see;
O, make our hearts thy dwelling-place,
 And worthier thee!

347. L. M.

1 Come, blessed Spirit, Source of light,
Whose power and grace are unconfined,
Dispel the gloomy shades of night,
The thicker darkness of the mind.

2 To mine illumined eyes display
The glorious truth thy word reveals;
Cause me to run the heavenly way;
The book unfold, unloose the seals.

3 Thine inward teachings make me know,
The mysteries of redeeming love;
The emptiness of things below,
The excellence of things above.

4 While through this dubious maze I stray,
Spread, like the sun, thy beams abroad,
To show the dangers of the way,
And guide my feeble steps to God.

348. S. M.

1 Say not the law divine
Is hidden far from thee;
That heavenly law within may shine,
And there its brightness be.

2 Soar not, my soul, on high,
To bring it down to earth;
No star within the vaulted sky
Is of such priceless worth.

3 Thou need'st not launch thy bark
Upon a shoreless sea,
Breasting its waves to find the ark,
To bring this dove to thee.

4 Cease, then, my soul, to roam,
Thy wanderings all are vain:
That holy word is found at home;
Within thy heart its reign.

349. L. M.

1 At anchor laid, remote from home,
Toiling, I cry, sweet Spirit, come!
Celestial breeze, no longer stay,
But swell my sails, and speed my way.

2 Fain would I mount, fain would I glow,
And loose my cable from below;
But I can only spread my sail;
Thou, thou must breathe the auspicious gale.

350. L. M.

1 O Source of uncreated light!
By whom the worlds were raised from night,
Come, visit every pious mind;
Come, pour thy joys on human kind.

2 Plenteous in grace, descend from high,
Rich in thy matchless energy;
From sin and sorrow set us free,
And make us temples worthy thee.

3 Cleanse and refine our earthly parts,
Inflame and sanctify our hearts,
Our frailties help, our vice control,
Submit the senses to the soul.

4 Thrice holy fount! thrice holy fire!
Our hearts with heavenly love inspire;
Make us eternal truths receive,
Aid us to live as we believe.

351. L. M.

1 Blest Spirit! source of grace divine!
What soul-refreshing streams are thine!
O, bring these healing waters nigh,
Or we must droop, and fall, and die!

2 No traveller through desert lands,
'Midst scorching suns, and burning sands,
More eager longs for cooling rain,
Or pants the current to obtain.

3 Our longing souls aloud would sing,
Spring up, celestial fountain, spring;
To a redundant river flow,
And cheer this thirsty land below.

4 May this blest river, near my side,
Through all my journey gently glide;
Then, in Emanuel's land above,
Spread to a sea of joy and love.

VI.

THE CHURCH.

ORDINATION AND INSTALLATION.

---

352. L. M.

1 O Thou, who art above all height!
Our God, our Father, and our Friend!
Beneath thy throne of love and light,
Let thine adoring children bend.

2 Since thy young servant now hath given
Himself, his powers, his hopes, his youth,
To the great cause of truth and heaven,
Be thou his guide, O God of truth!

3 Here may his doctrines drop like rain,
His speech like Hermon's dew distil,
Till green fields smile, and golden grain,
Ripe for the harvest, waits thy will.

4 And when he sinks in death, — by care,
Or pain, or toil, or years oppressed, —
O God! remember then our prayer,
And take his spirit to thy rest.

353. L. M.

1 We bid thee welcome in the name
Of Jesus, our exalted Head:
Come as a servant; so he came;
And we receive thee in his stead.

2 Come as a teacher sent from God,
Charged his whole counsel to declare;
Lift o'er our ranks the prophet's rod,
While we uphold thy hands with prayer.

3 Come as a messenger of peace,
Filled with the Spirit, fired with love;
Live to behold our large increase,
And die to meet us all above.

354. L. M.

1 Ye Christian heralds! go, proclaim
Salvation in Immanuel's name:
To distant climes the tidings bear,
And plant the rose of Sharon there.

2 He 'll shield you with a wall of fire,
With holy zeal your hearts inspire,
Bid raging winds their fury cease,
And calm the savage breast to peace.

3 And when our labors all are o'er,
Then shall we meet to part no more,—
Meet, with the ransomed throng to fall,
And crown the Saviour Lord of all.

355. C. M.

1 O God! thy children gathered here,
Thy blessing now we wait;
Thy servant, girded for his work,
Stands at the temple's gate.

2 A holy purpose in his heart
Has deepened calm and still;
Now from his childhood's Nazareth
He comes, to do thy will.

3 O Father! keep his soul alive
To every hope of good;
And may his life of love proclaim
Man's truest brotherhood!

4 O Father! keep his spirit quick
To every form of wrong;
And in the ear of sin and self
May his rebuke be strong!

5 And as he doth Christ's footsteps press,
If e'er his faith grow dim,
Then, in the dreary wilderness,
Thine angels strengthen him!

356. 7s. M.

1 Lift aloud the voice of praise!
God, our Father and our Friend,
Hear the prayer and song we raise,
Weak, yet trusting, we would bend.

2 Lo! another servant brought
To the heritage of God;—
May he teach as Christ hath taught,
Tread the path his Saviour trod.

3 To the vineyard may he come,
Girded with celestial might;
Skilled to draw thy children home,
Taught to give the darkened light.

4 Unto thee a people bend,—
Bind us heart to heart in love;
Flock and pastor, we would tend
Ever toward our home above.

357. L. M.

1 O Thou in whose eternal name
Went forth the Apostles' ardent host,
Baptize us with the hallowed flame
That fell from heaven at Pentecost!

2 The fearless faith that cries, "Repent!"
Thy servant's earnest message fill;
By Thee the living word was sent,
Thy presence make it living still.

3 And while thy people bend and pray
Towards thy benignant throne of light,
Give answer in the dawning day
Of Freedom, Mercy, Truth, and Right.

4 Immortal Truth! it lives in Thee;
Our hope shall lean on Thee alone!

Thy Christ be all our liberty,
  And all our strength and will thy own!

5 Father, whose heavenly kingdom lies
  In every meek, believing breast,
Reveal before thy children's eyes
  That kingdom's coming, and its rest!

6 Give thy Son's herald, from above,
  The anointing of thy spirit's breath;
The faith that worked in Christ by love,
  The trust that triumphed in his death!

BAPTISM.

---

358. L. M.

1 This child we dedicate to thee,
O God of grace and purity!
Shield it from sin and threatening wrong,
And let thy love its life prolong.

2 O, may thy Spirit gently draw
Its willing soul to keep thy law;
May virtue, piety, and truth,
Dawn even with its dawning youth.

3 Grant that, with true and faithful heart,
We too may act the Christian's part,
Cheered by each promise thou hast given,
And laboring for the prize in heaven.

359. S. M.

1 The Saviour gently calls
Our children to his breast;

He folds them in his gracious arms;
Himself declares them blest.

2 "Let them approach," he cries,
"Nor scorn their humble claim;
The heirs of heaven are such as these, —
For such as these I came."

3 Gladly we bring them, Lord,
Devoting them to thee;
Imploring, that, as we are thine,
Thine may our offspring be.

360. C. M.

1 BAPTIZED into our Saviour's death,
Our souls to sin must die;
With Christ our Lord we live anew,
With Christ ascend on high.

2 There by his Father's side he sits,
Enthroned divinely fair,
Yet owns himself our Brother still,
And our Forerunner there.

3 Rise from these earthly trifles, rise
On wings of faith and love;
Above our choicest treasure lies, —
And be our hearts above.

4 But earth and sin will draw us down,
When we attempt to fly;
Lord, send thy strong, attractive power
To fix our souls on high.

361. S. M.

1 See Israel's Shepherd stand,
With all-engaging charms;
Hark, how he calls the tender lambs,
And folds them in his arms!

2 Permit them to approach,
"Forbid them not," he cried;
"Of such my Father's kingdom is,
And such with him abide."

3 We bring them, gracious Lord,
And yield them up to thee;
Joyful that we ourselves are thine,
Thine let our offspring be.

4 If orphans they are left,
Thy guardian love we trust;
That love can heal our bleeding hearts,
When weeping o'er their dust.

362. S. M.

1 Our children thou dost claim,
And mark them out for thine;
Ten thousand blessings to thy name
For goodness so divine!

2 Thee let the fathers own,
And thee the sons adore:
Joined to the Lord in solemn vows,
To be forgot no more.

3 Our offspring, still thy care,
Shall own their fathers' God;
To latest times thy blessing share,
And sound thy praise abroad.

363. S. M.

1 To thee, O God in heaven,
This little one we bring,
Giving to thee what thou hast given,
Our dearest offering.

2 Into a world of toil
These little feet will roam,
Where sin its purity may soil,
Where care and grief may come.

3 O, then, let thy pure love,
With influence serene,
Come down, like water, from above,
To comfort and make clean!

364. S. M.

1 To Him who children blest,
And suffered them to come,
To Him who took them to his breast,
We bring these children home.

2 To thee, O God, whose face
Their spirits still behold,
We bring them, praying that thy grace
May keep, thine arms enfold.

3 And as this water falls
On each unconscious brow,
Thy holy spirit grant, O Lord,
To keep them pure as now!

365. L. M.

1 O Lord! encouraged by thy grace
We bring this infant to thy throne;
Give it within thy heart a place,
Let it be thine, and thine alone.

2 We ask not for it earthly bliss,
Or earthly honors, wealth, or fame:
The sum of our request is this,—
That it may love and fear thy name.

3 This infant we by faith commit
To thy kind love and guardian care;
We lay it at the Saviour's feet,
He will not let it perish there.

COMMUNION AT THE LORD'S SUPPER.

---

366. S. M.

1 Jesus, we look to thee,
Thy promised presence claim;
Thou in the midst of us shalt be,
Assembled in thy name.

2 Not in the name of pride
Or selfishness we meet;
From nature's paths we turn aside,
And worldly thoughts forget.

3 Present we know thou art;
But, O, thyself reveal!
Now, Lord, let every bounding heart,
The mighty comfort feel.

4 O, may thy quickening voice
The death of sin remove,
And bid our inmost souls rejoice,
In hope of perfect love.

367. C. M.

1 Ye followers of the Prince of Peace,
Who round his table draw!
Remember what his spirit was,
What his peculiar law.

2 The love which all his bosom filled
Did all his actions guide;
Inspired by love, he lived and taught,
Inspired by love he died.

3 Let all the sacred law fulfil;
Like his be every mind;
Be every temper formed by love,
And every action kind.

4 Let none who call themselves his friends
Disgrace the honored name;
But by a near resemblance prove
The title which they claim.

368. 8 & 7s. M.

1 From the table now retiring,
Which for us the Lord hath spread,
May our souls, refreshment finding,
Grow in all things like our Head.

2 His example by beholding,
May our lives his image bear;
Him our Lord and Master calling,
His commands may we revere.

3 Love to God and man displaying,
Walking steadfast in his way,
Joy attend us in believing!
Peace from God through endless day.

369. C. M.

1 O God, accept the sacred hour
Which we to thee have given;
And let this hallowed scene have power
To raise our souls to heaven.

2 Still let us hold, till life departs,
The precepts of thy Son,
Nor let our thoughtless, thankless hearts
Forget what he has done.

3 His true disciples may we live,
From all corruption free,
And humbly learn, like him, to give
Our powers, our wills, to thee.

370. C. M.

1 "O, not for these alone I pray,"
The dying Saviour said;
Though on his breast that moment lay
The loved disciple's head;—

2 Though to his eye that moment sprung
The kind, the pitying tear,
For those that eager round him hung,
His words of love to hear.

3 No, not for them alone he prayed,—
For all of mortal race,
Whene'er their fervent prayer is made,
Where'er their dwelling-place.

4 Sweet is the thought, when here we meet,
His feast of love to share;
And, 'mid the toils of life, how sweet
The memory of his prayer!

371. L. M.

1 When on the midnight of the East,
At the dead moment of repose,
Like Hope on Misery's darkened breast,
The planet of salvation rose,—

2 The shepherd, leaning o'er his flock,
Started, with broad and upward gaze,—
Kneeled,—while the star of Bethlehem broke
On music wakened into praise.

3 Shall we, for whom that star was hung
In the dark vault of frowning heaven,—
Shall we, for whom that strain was sung,
That song of peace and sin forgiven,—

4 Shall we, for whom the Saviour bled,
Careless his banquet's blessings see,
Nor heed the parting word that said,
"Do this in memory of me"?

372. L. M.

1 God, namèd Love, whose fount thou art,
Thy crownless Church before thee stands,
With too much hating in her heart,
And too much striving in her hands!

2 O loving Lord! O slain for love!
Thy blood upon thy garments came,—
Inwrap their folds our brows above,
Before we tell thee all our shame!

3 "Love as I loved you," was the sound
That on thy lips expiring sate!
Sweet words, in bitter strivings drowned!
We hated as the worldly hate.

4 Yet, Lord, thy wrongèd love fulfil!
Thy Church, though fallen, before thee stands,
Behold, the voice is Jacob's still,
Albeit the hands are Esau's hands!

5 O, move us — Thou hast power to move —
One in the one Beloved to be!
Teach us the heights and depths of love;
Give Thine, that we may love like thee!

373. C. M.

1 Beneath the shadow of the cross,
As earthly hopes remove,
His new commandment Jesus gives,
His blessed word of love.

2 O bond of union, strong and deep!
O bond of perfect peace!
Not even the lifted cross can harm,
If we but hold to this.

3 Then, Jesus, be thy spirit ours!
And swift our feet shall move
To deeds of pure self-sacrifice,
"And the sweet tasks of love."

374. 7s. M.

1 PEOPLE of the living God,
I have sought the world around,
Paths of sin and sorrow trod,
Peace and comfort nowhere found.

2 Now to you my spirit turns,—
Turns, a fugitive unblest;
Brethren, where your altar burns,
O, receive me into rest!

3 Lonely I no longer roam,
Like the cloud, the wind, the wave,
Where you dwell shall be my home,
Where you die shall be my grave.

4 Mine the God whom you adore;
Your Redeemer shall be mine;
Earth can fill my soul no more;
Every idol I resign.

375. 7s. M.

1 Glory of thy Father's face!
Fountain deep of love and grace!
Who, Lord, can repay thee thus,
As thou gav'st thyself for us?

2 What to thee shall we reply,
Who for us didst bleed and die,
When thou shalt the question make,
"What have ye done for my sake?"

3 Hard in heart, in action weak,
Lord, thy grace divine we seek:
Set us from our bondage free;
Draw us, and we follow thee.

376. 8 & 7s. M.

1 On the night of that last supper,
Seated with his chosen band,
Christ, as food to all his brethren,
Gives himself with his own hand.

2 He, as man with man conversing,
Stayed, the seeds of truth to sow;
Then he closed, in solemn order,
Wondrously, his life of woe.

3 Lo! o'er ancient forms departing
Newer rites of grace prevail;
Faith for all defects supplying,
Where the feeble senses fail.

4 To the Everlasting Father,
Through the Son who reigns on high,
Be salvation, honor, blessing,
Might, and endless majesty.

377. L. M.

1 The Word, descending from above,
Though with the Father still on high,
Went forth upon his work of love,
And soon to life's last eve drew nigh.

2 At birth, our brother he became;
Ever himself as food he gives;
To ransom us he died in shame;
As our reward, in bliss he lives.

3 O saving Leader! opening wide
The gate of heaven to man below!
Our foes press on from every side;
Thine aid supply, thy strength bestow.

378. C. M.

1 Ark of the Covenant! not that
Whence bondage came of old;
But that of pardon and of grace,
And mercies manifold!

2 Blest heart of Christ! in thy dear wound
The hidden depth we see
Of what were else unknown by us,—
His boundless charity.

3 O, who of his redeemed will him
Their mutual love refuse?
Who would not rather in that heart
Their home eternal choose?

379. C. M.

1 Ye hear how kindly he invites;
Ye hear his words so blest,—
"All ye that labor, come to me,
And I will give you rest."

2 What meeker than the Saviour's heart?
As on the cross he lay,
It did his murderers forgive,
And for their pardon pray.

3 Father! to each that mercy grant,
Which forth through him did flow;
New grace, new hope, inspire; a new
And better heart bestow.

380. C. M.

1 O, joy! to feel our Saviour's love,
To feel his presence near;
Yet loyal love his glory holds
A thousand times more dear.

2 Ah! never is our love so pure
As when refined by pain,
Or when God's glory upon earth
Finds in our loss its gain!

3 True love is worship: Saviour dear,
O, shed for us the light
To love, because the creature's love
Is the Creator's right!

381. L. M.

1 Now rest, my long-divided heart!
Fixed on this blissful centre, rest;
Here have I found a nobler part,
Here heavenly pleasures fill my breast.

2 High Heaven, that hears the solemn vow,
That vow renewed shall daily hear;
Till in life's latest hour I bow,
And bless in death a bond so dear.

382. C. M.

1 Let plenteous grace descend on those
Who, hoping in thy word,
This day have solemnly declared
That Jesus is their Lord.

2 With cheerful feet may they advance,
And run the Christian race,
And, through the troubles of the way,
Find all-sufficient grace.

3 Lord, plant us all into thy death,
That we thy life may prove, —
Partakers of thy cross beneath,
And of thy crown above.

383. 7s. M.

1 Bread of heaven! on thee we feed,
For thy flesh is meat indeed;
Ever let our souls be fed
With this true and living bread!

2 Vine of heaven! thy blood supplies
This blest cup of sacrifice;
Lord, thy wounds our healing give;
To thy cross we look and live.

3 Day by day with strength supplied,
Through the life of Him who died;
Lord of Life! O, let us be
Rooted, grafted, built on thee!

384. S. M.

1 Here, in the broken bread,
Here, in the cup we take,
His body and his blood behold,
Who suffered for our sake.

2 O Thou, who didst allow
Thy Son to suffer thus,
Father, what more couldst thou have done,
Than thou hast done for us?

3 We are persuaded now
That nothing can divide
Thy children from thy boundless love,
Displayed in Him who died;—

4 Who died to make us sure
Of mercy, truth, and peace,
And from the power and pains of sin
To bring a full release.

385. C. M.

1 If human kindness meets return,
And owns the grateful tie;
If tender thoughts within us burn
To feel that friends are nigh;—

2 O, shall not warmer accents tell
The gratitude we owe
To Him who died, our fears to quell,
And save from death and woe?

3 While yet in anguish he surveyed
Those pangs he would not flee,
What love his latest words displayed!
"Meet, and remember me."

4 Remember thee! thy death, thy shame,
Our sinful hearts to share!
O memory, leave no other name
But his recorded there!

386. 9 & 8s. M.

1 Bread of the world, in mercy broken,
Wine of the soul, in mercy shed!
By whom the words of life were spoken,
And in whose death our sins are dead!

2 Look on the heart by sorrow broken,
Look on the tears by sinners shed,
And be thy feast to us the token
That by thy grace our souls are fed.

387. C. M.

1 O, HERE, if ever, God of love!
Let strife and hatred cease;
And every thought harmonious move,
And every heart be peace.

2 Not here, where met to think on Him
Whose latest thoughts were ours,
Shall mortal passions come to dim
The prayer devotion pours.

3 "Thy kingdom come"; we watch, we wait,
To hear thy cheering call;
When heaven shall ope its glorious gate,
And God be all in all.

388. C. M.

1 GETHSEMANE can I forget?
Or there thy conflict see,
Thine agony and bloody sweat,
And not remember thee?

2 Thy body broken for my sake,
My bread from heaven shall be;
Thy testamental cup I take,
And thus remember thee.

3 When to the cross I turn mine eye,
And rest on Calvary,
O Lamb of God, my Sacrifice!
I must remember thee.

4 Remember thee, and all thy pains,
And all thy love to me;
Yea, while a breath, a pulse remains,
Will I remember thee.

389. 7s. M.

1 JESUS, we thy promise claim:
We are met in thy great name:
In the midst do thou appear,
Manifest thy presence here!

2 Sanctify us, Lord, and bless!
Breathe thy spirit, give thy peace;
Thou thyself within us move;
Make our feast a feast of love.

3 Plant in us thy humble mind,
Patient, pitiful, and kind;
Meek and lowly let us be,
Full of goodness, full of thee.

390. L. M.

1 DEAR Lord, may this communion prove
A never-failing bond of love;
Forgive my coldness, and supply
Mine every weak deficiency.

2 May thy best grace suffice for all,
And every wayward sense enthrall:
Such grace on every feeling pour,
As ne'er may leave thy servant more.

3 Each hope, each impulse, firmly bind
In grace to thee, my Saviour kind!
Such saving grace, dear Lord, be given,
As leads the happy soul to heaven.

391. C. M.

1 My God, accept my heart this day,
And make it always thine,
That I from thee no more may stray,
No more from thee decline.

2 Before the cross of Him who died,
Behold, I prostrate fall:
Let every sin be crucified, —
Let Christ be all in all!

3 Let every thought, and work, and word,
To thee be ever given;
Then life shall be thy service, Lord,
And death the gate of heaven!

392. L. M.

1 Light of the soul, O Saviour blest!
Soon as thy presence fills the breast,
Darkness and guilt are put to flight,
And all is sweetness and delight.

2 Son of the Father! Lord most high!
How glad is he who feels thee nigh!
Come in thy hidden majesty;
Fill us with love, fill us with thee.

3 Jesus is from the proud concealed,
But evermore to babes revealed,
Through him, unto the Father be
Glory and praise eternally.

393. C. M.

1 PLANTED in Christ, the living Vine,
This day, with one accord,
Ourselves, with humble faith and joy,
We yield to thee, O Lord!

2 Joined in one body may we be:
One inward life partake;
One be our heart, one heavenly hope
In every bosom wake.

3 In prayer, in effort, tears, and toils,
One Wisdom be our guide;
Taught by one Spirit from above,
In thee may we abide.

4 Then, when among the saints in light
Our joyful spirits shine,
Shall anthems of immortal praise,
O Lamb of God, be thine.

2 Son of the Father! Lord most high!
How glad is he who feels thee nigh!
Come in thy hidden majesty;
Fill us with love, fill us with thee.

3 Jesus is from the proud concealed,
But evermore to babes revealed,
Through him, unto the Father be
Glory and praise eternally.

393. C. M.

1 PLANTED in Christ, the living Vine,
This day, with one accord,
Ourselves, with humble faith and joy,
We yield to thee, O Lord!

2 Joined in one body may we be:
One inward life partake;
One be our heart, one heavenly hope
In every bosom wake.

3 In prayer, in effort, tears, and toils,
One Wisdom be our guide;
Taught by one Spirit from above,
In thee may we abide.

4 Then, when among the saints in light
Our joyful spirits shine,
Shall anthems of immortal praise,
O Lamb of God, be thine.

394. 7s. M.

1 Still, O Lord, our faith increase,
Give to us the fruits of peace,
Utterly abolish sin,
Write thy law of love within.

2 Hence may all our actions flow,
Love, the proof that Christ we know;
Mutual love the token be,
Lord, that we have walked with thee!

3 Love, thine image, love impart,
Stamp its impress on each heart;
Only love to us be given,
Lord, we ask no other heaven.

395. 7 & 6s. M.

1 O sacred Head, now wounded,
With grief and shame weighed down,
So scornfully surrounded,
With thorns thine only crown,
How art thou pale with anguish,
With sore abuse and scorn!
How do those features languish,
Which once were fair as morn!

2 What language shall I borrow
To thank thee, dearest Friend,
For this thy dying sorrow,
This love that knew no end?

2 One family, we dwell in him:
   One Church above, beneath;
 Though now divided by the stream,
   The narrow stream of death.

3 One army of the living God,
   To his command we bow;
 Part of the host have crossed the flood,
   And part are crossing now.

4 O God, be thou our constant guide!
   Then, when the word is given,
 Bid death's cold flood its waves divide,
   And land us safe in heaven.

398. L. M.

1 "Eat, drink, in memory of your Friend!"
   Such was our Master's last request;
 Who all the pangs of death endured,
   That we might live for ever blest.

2 Yes, we 'll record thy matchless love,
   Thou dearest, tenderest, best of friends!
 Thy dying love the noblest praise
   Of long eternity transcends.

3 'T is pleasure more than earth can give,
   Thy goodness through these veils to see;
 Thy table food celestial yields,
   And happy they who sit with thee!

399. L. M.

1 Our hearts, by dying love subdued,
Accept thine offered grace to-day;
Beneath the cross, with souls renewed,
We bow, and own thy gracious sway.

2 In thee we trust, — on thee rely;
Though we are feeble, thou art strong;
O, keep us till our spirits fly
To join the bright, immortal throng!

400. C. M.

1 Lord, may the spirit of this feast,
The earnest of thy love,
Maintain a dwelling in our breast,
Until we meet above.

2 The healing sense of pardoned sin, —
The hope that never tires, —
The strength a pilgrim's race to win, —
The joy that heaven inspires, —

3 Still may their light our duties trace,
In lines of hallowed flame,
Like that upon the prophet's face,
When from the mount he came.

401. 7s. M.

1 While to lips with praise that glow,
This communion cup we press,
Holy Father, let us grow
More like Him we here confess.

2 Reconcile us by thy Son,
In whose name on thee we call;
Make us perfect, all in one,
We in him, and thou in all.

3 While we here remember thee,
Who wast for our ransom slain,
Let thy love, thy purity,
Saviour, in our souls remain.

4 Father, while we break this bread,
And thy Christ remember thus,
Make us one with him, our Head,
Thou in him, and he in us.

FAMILY.—MORNING AND EVENING.

---

402. L. M.

1 O, TIMELY happy, timely wise,
Hearts that with rising morn arise!
Eyes that the beam celestial view,
Which evermore makes all things new!

2 New every morning is the love
Our wakening and uprising prove;
Through sleep and darkness safely brought,
Restored to life, and power, and thought.

3 New mercies, each returning day,
Hover around us while we pray;
New perils past, new sins forgiven,
New thoughts of God, new hopes of heaven.

4 If, on our daily course, our mind
Be set to hallow all we find,
New treasures still, of countless price,
God will provide for sacrifice.

5 Old friends, old scenes, will lovelier be,
As more of heaven in each we see;
Some softening gleams of love and prayer
Shall dawn on every cross and care.

403. L. M.

1 God of the morning, at whose voice
The cheerful sun makes haste to rise,
And, like a giant, doth rejoice
To run his journey through the skies:

2 O, like the sun may I fulfil
The appointed duties of the day;
With ready mind and active will
March on, and keep my heavenly way.

3 Lord, thy commands are clean and pure,
Enlightening our beclouded eyes;
Thy threatenings just, thy promise sure;
Thy Gospel makes the simple wise.

4 Give me thy counsel for my guide,
And then receive me to thy bliss;
All my desires and hopes beside
Are faint and cold, compared with this.

404. 11 & 10s. M.

1 Now, when the dusky shades of night, retreating
Before the sun's red banner, swiftly flee,
Now, when the terrors of the dark are fleeting,
O Lord! we lift our thankful hearts to thee.

2 To thee, whose word, the fount of light unsealing,
When hill and dale in thickest darkness lay,
Awoke bright rays across the dim earth stealing,
And bade the even and morn complete the day.

3 Look from the tower of heaven, and send to cheer us
Thy light and truth, to guide us onward still;
Still let thy mercy, as of old, be near us,
And lead us safely to thy holy hill.

4 In vain to labor, unless thou be with him,
Man goeth forth through all the weary day;
In vain his strife, in vain his toil unceasing,
Unless thy staff bring comfort on his way.

5 Thou, who hast made the north and south, watch o'er us;
Thou in whose name the lonely ones rejoice,
Still let thy cloudy pillar glide before us,
Still let us listen for thy warning voice.

6 So, when that morn of endless light is waking,
And shades of evil from its splendors flee,
Safe may we rise, the earth's dark breast forsaking,
Through all the long bright day to dwell with thee.

405. L. M.

1 Now with creation's early song,
Let us, the children of the day,
Cast off the darkness which so long
Has led our guilty souls astray.

2 O, may the morn so pure, so clear,
Its own sweet calm in us instil;
A guileless mind, a heart sincere,
Simplicity of word and will:

3 And ever, as the day glides by,
May we the busy senses rein;
Keep guard upon the hand and eye,
Nor let the body suffer stain.

4 Grant us the grace, for love of thee,
To scorn all vanities below;
Faith, to detect each falsity;
And knowledge, thee alone to know.

406. L. M.

1 True Sun! upon our souls arise,
Shining in beauty evermore;
And through each sense the quickening beam
Of the Eternal Spirit pour.

2 Confirm us in each good resolve;
The tempter's envious rage subdue;
Turn each misfortune to our good;
Direct us right in all we do.

3 May Christ himself be our true food,
And faith our daily cup supply;
While from the spirit's tranquil depth
We drink unfailing draughts of joy.

4 Still, ever with the peep of morn,
May saintly purity attend;

Faith sanctify the midday hours;
  Upon the soul no night descend.

5 Full breaks the day; — each whole in each,
  Come, Father blest! come, Son most high!
Shine in our souls, and be to them
  The dawn of immortality.

407. L. M.

1 FATHER, we know no sun but thee!
  Shine in our souls divinely bright!
We seek thee in simplicity;
  Through all our senses shed thy light.

2 Scatter our night, Eternal God!
  And kindle thy pure beam within;
Free us from guilt's oppressive load,
  And break the deadly bonds of sin.

3 A thousand objects all around
  In false, delusive colors shine;
To purge them clear, we ask, O Lord,
  But one immortal beam of thine.

408. L. M.

1 Now doth the sun ascend the sky,
  And wake creation with its ray;
Keep us from sin, O Lord, most high,
  Through all the actions of the day.

2 Curb thou for us th' unruly tongue;
Teach us the way of peace to prize;
And close our eyes against the throng
Of earth's absorbing vanities.

3 O, may our hearts be pure within!
No cherished madness vex the soul!
May abstinence the flesh restrain,
And its rebellious pride control.

4 So when the evening stars appear,
And in their train the darkness bring,
May we, O Lord, with conscience clear,
Our praise to thy pure glory sing.

409. L. M.

1 Where'er the Lord shall build my house,
An altar to his name I'll raise;
There, morn and evening, shall ascend
The sacrifice of prayer and praise.

2 With duteous mind, the social band
Shall search the records of thy law;
There learn thy will, and humbly bow
With filial reverence and awe.

3 Here may God fix his sacred seat,
And spread the banner of his love;
Till, ripened for a happier state,
We meet the family above.

410. L. M.

1 The dawn is sprinkling in the east
Its golden shower, as day flows in;
Fast mount the pointed shafts of light;—
Farewell to darkness and to sin!

2 Away, ye midnight phantoms all!
Away, despondence and despair!
Whatever guilt the night has brought,
Now let it vanish into air.

3 So, Lord, when that last morning breaks,
Which shrouds in darkness earth and skies,
May it on us, low bending here,
Arrayed in joyful light arise!

411. L. M.

1 Lord of eternal truth and might!
Ruler of nature's changing scheme!
Who dost bring forth the morning light,
And temper noon's effulgent beam:

2 Quench thou in us the flames of strife,
And bid the heat of passion cease;
From perils guard our feeble life,
And keep our souls in perfect peace.

412. S. M.

1 Behold, night's shadows fade,
And morn is in the skies!
To Him by whom all things were made
Our aspirations rise.

2 To break this deathly trance
Help us, our God, our stay!
Give the freed spirit utterance,
Its languors charm away!

3 So sin shall cease to reign,
So safety shall be nigh;
Rend, Spirit blest, the heavy chains
Of death, in victory!

413. L. M.

1 Awake, my soul! and with the sun
The daily stage of duty run;
Shake off dull sloth, and joyful rise
To pay thy morning sacrifice.

2 Thy precious time, misspent, redeem;
Each present day thy last esteem;
Improve thy talent with due care;
For the great day thyself prepare.

3 In conversation be sincere;
Keep conscience as the noontide clear;
Think how the all-seeing God thy ways
And all thy secret thoughts surveys.

4 Lord, I my vows to thee renew;
Scatter my sins like morning dew;
Guard my first springs of thought and will,
And with thyself my spirit fill.

5 Direct, control, suggest, this day,
All I design, or do, or say,
That all my powers, with all their might,
In thy sole glory may unite.

414. L. M.

1 New born, I bless the waking hour;
Once more, with awe, rejoice to be;
My conscious soul resumes her power,
And springs, my guardian God! to thee.

2 A deeper shade shall soon impend,
A deeper sleep my eyes oppress;
Yet then thy strength shall still defend,
Thy goodness still delight to bless.

3 That deeper shade shall break away,
That deeper sleep shall leave my eyes;
Thy light shall give eternal day,
Thy love, the rapture of the skies.

415. L. M.

1 As every day thy mercy spares,
Will bring its trials or its cares,
O Father, till my life shall end
Be thou my counsellor and friend;

Teach me thy statutes all divine,
And let thy will be always mine.

2 When each day's scenes and labors close,
And wearied nature seeks repose,
With pardoning mercy richly blest,
Guard me, my Father, while I rest;
And as each morning sun shall rise,
O, lead me onward to the skies!

3 And at my life's last setting sun,
My conflicts o'er, my labors done,
Father, thy heavenly radiance shed,
To cheer and bless my dying bed;
And from death's gloom my spirit raise,
To see thy face and sing thy praise.

416. C. M.

1 In mercy, Lord, remember me,
This instant passing night,
And grant to me most graciously
The safeguard of thy might.

2 With cheerful heart I close my eyes,
Since thou wilt not remove;
O, in the morning let me rise,
Rejoicing in thy love.

3 Or if this night should prove the last,
And end my transient days,
Lord, take me to thy promised rest,
Where I may sing thy praise.

4 Thus I am sure to live or die
To thee, the God of love;
In life and death I do rely
On thee, who reign'st above.

417. L. M.

1 Thus far the Lord has led me on,
Thus far his power prolongs my days!
And every evening shall make known
Some fresh memorial of his grace.

2 Much of my time has run to waste,
And I, perhaps, am near my home;
But he forgives my follies past,
He gives me strength for days to come.

3 I lay my body down to sleep;
Peace is the pillow for my head;
While well-appointed angels keep
Their watchful stations round my bed.

4 Faith in his name forbids my fear:
O, may thy presence ne'er depart!
And in the morning make me hear
Thy loving-kindness in my heart.

5 Thus, when the night of death shall come,
My flesh shall rest beneath the ground,
And wait thy voice to break the tomb,
With sweet salvation in the sound.

418. 7s. M.

1 Heavenly Father, gracious name!
Night and day his love the same!
Far be each suspicious thought,
Every anxious care forgot!

2 What if death my sleep invade?
Should I be of death afraid?
While encircled by thine arm,
Death may strike, but cannot harm.

3 With thy heavenly presence blest,
Death is life, and labor rest:
Welcome sleep or death to me,
Still secure, — for still with thee.

419. 7s. M.

1 Source of light and life divine!
Thou didst cause the light to shine;
Thou didst bring thy sunbeams forth
O'er thy new-created earth.

2 Shade of night, and morning ray,
Took from thee the name of day:
Now again the shades are nigh,
Listen to our mournful cry.

3 May we ne'er, by guilt depressed,
Lose the way to endless rest;
May no thoughts, corrupt and vain,
Draw our souls to earth again.

4 Rather lift them to the skies,
Where our much-loved treasure lies;
Help us in our daily strife,
Make us struggle into life.

420. 10s. M.

1 Abide with me! Fast falls the eventide,
The darkness deepens; Lord, with me abide!
When other helpers fail and comforts flee,
Help of the helpers, O, abide with me!

2 Swift to its close ebbs out life's little day;
Earth's joys grow dim, its glories pass away:
Change and decay in all around I see;
O Thou who changest not, abide with me!

3 I need thy presence every passing hour:
What but thy grace can foil the tempter's power?
Who like thyself my guide and stay can be?
On to the close, O Lord, abide with me!

421. L. M.

1 O thou true life of all that live!
Who dost, unmoved, all motion sway;
Who dost the morn and evening give,
And through its changes guide the day;—

2 Thy light upon our evening pour,—
So may our souls no sunset see;
But death to us an open door
To an eternal morning be.

422. C. M.

1 Father of lights, by whom each day
Is kindled out of night,
Who, when the heavens were made, didst lay
Their rudiments in light!

2 O God unchangeable and true,
Of all the life and power,
Dispensing light and silence through
Every successive hour!

3 Lord, brighten our declining day,
That it may never wane,
Till death, when all things round decay,
Brings back the morn again.

423. L. M.

1 O blest Creator of the light!
Who dost the dawn from darkness bring,
And, framing nature's depth and height,
Didst with the new-born light begin;—

2 Who gently blending eve with morn,
And morn with eve, didst call them day:—
Thick flows the flood of darkness down;
O, hear us as we weep and pray!

3 Keep thou our souls from schemes of crime;
Nor guilt remorseful let them know;
Nor, thinking but on things of time,
Into eternal darkness go.

4 Teach us to knock at heaven's high door;
Teach us the prize of life to win;
Teach us all evil to abhor,
And purify ourselves within.

424. L. M.

1 GLORY to thee, my God, this night,
For all the blessings of the light:
Keep me, O, keep me, King of kings,
Beneath thine own almighty wings.

2 Forgive me, Lord, through thy dear Son,
The ills which I this day have done;
That with the world, myself, and thee,
I, ere I sleep, at peace may be.

3 Teach me to live, that I may dread
The grave as little as my bed;
To die, that this vile body may
Rise glorious at the awful day.

4 O, may my soul on thee repose,
And with sweet sleep mine eyelids close!
Sleep that shall me more vigorous make
To serve my God when I awake.

425. L. M.

1 'T IS gone, that bright and orbèd blaze,
Fast fading from our wistful gaze;
Yon mantling cloud has hid from sight
The last faint pulse of quivering light.

2 Sun of my soul! thou Saviour dear,
It is not night if thou be near:
O, may no earth-born cloud arise
To hide thee from thy servant's eyes!

3 When the soft dews of kindly sleep
My wearied eyelids gently steep,
Be my last thought, how sweet to rest
For ever on my Saviour's breast!

4 Abide with me from morn till eve,
For without thee I cannot live;
Abide with me when night is nigh,
For without thee I dare not die.

426. P. M.

God, that madest earth and heaven,
Darkness and light,—
Who the day for toil hast given,
For rest the night,—
May thine angel guards defend us,
Slumber sweet thy mercy send us,
Holy dreams and hopes attend us,
This livelong night.

427. 7s. M.

1 Softly now the light of day
Fades upon my sight away;
Free from care, from labor free,
Lord, I will commune with thee

2 Thou, whose all-pervading eye
Naught escapes, without, within:
Pardon each infirmity,
Open fault, and secret sin.

3 Soon, for me, the light of day
Shall for ever pass away;
Then, from sin and sorrow free,
Take me, Lord, to dwell with thee.

428. 7s. M.

1 Slowly, by God's hand unfurled,
Down around the weary world
Falls the darkness; O, how still
Is the working of His will!

2 Mighty Spirit, ever nigh!
Work in me as silently;
Veil the day's distracting sights,
Show me heaven's eternal lights.

3 Living stars to view be brought
In the boundless realms of thought;
High and infinite desires,
Flaming like those upper fires!

4 Holy Truth, Eternal Right,
Let them break upon my sight;
Let them shine serene and still,
And with light my being fill.

429. L. M.

1 O'ER silent field and lonely lawn
Her dusky mantle night hath drawn;
At twilight's holy, heartfelt hour,
In man his better soul hath power.

2 The passions are at peace within,
And stilled each stormy thought of sin;
The yielding bosom, overawed,
Breathes love to man, and love to God.

430. 8 & 7s. M.

1 ON the dewy breath of even
Thousand odors mingling rise,
Borne like incense up to heaven, —
Nature's evening sacrifice.

2 With her favorite offerings blending,
Let our glad thanksgiving be,
To thy throne, O Lord, ascending,
Incense of our hearts to thee.

3 Thou, whose favors without number
All our days with gladness bless,
Let thine eye, that knows no slumber,
Guard our hours of helplessness.

4 Then, though conscious we are sleeping
In the outer courts of death,
Safe beneath a Father's keeping,
Calm we rest in perfect faith.

431. 7s. M.

1 O THOU holy God! come down,
God of spotless purity!
Claim and seize me for thy own,
Consecrate my heart to thee;
Under thy protection take;
Songs in the night season give;
Let me sleep to thee, and wake;
Let me die to thee, and live.

2 Loose me from the chains of sense,
Set me from the body free;
Draw with stronger influence
My unfettered soul to thee:
In me, Lord, thyself reveal;
Fill me with a sweet surprise;
Let me thee, when waking, feel,
Let me in thy image rise.

THANKSGIVING.

---

432. 6 & 4s. M.

1 The God of harvest praise;
In loud thanksgiving raise
Hand, heart, and voice;
The valleys smile and sing,
Forests and mountains ring,
The plains their tribute bring,
The streams rejoice.

2 Yea, bless his holy name,
And purest thanks proclaim
Through all the earth;
To glory in your lot
Is duty,—but be not
God's benefits forgot,
Amidst your mirth.

3 The God of harvest praise;
Hands, hearts, and voices raise,
With sweet accord;

From field to garner throng,
Bearing your sheaves along,
And in your harvest-song
  Bless ye the Lord.

433. 10s. M.

1 God of the changing year, whose arm of power
In safety leads through danger's darkest hour,
Here in thy temple bow thy creatures down,
To bless thy mercy, and thy might to own.

2 Thine are the beams that cheer us on our way,
And pour around the gladdening light of day;
Thine is the night, and the fair orbs that shine
To cheer its hours of darkness, — all are thine.

3 If round our path the thorns of sorrow grew,
And mortal friends were faithless, thou wert true;
Did sickness shake the frame, or anguish tear
The wounded spirit, thou wert present there.

4 Yet when our hearts review departed days,
How vast thy mercies! how remiss our praise!
Well may we dread thine awful eye to meet,
Bend at thy throne, and worship at thy feet.

5 O, lend thine ear, and lift our voice to thee;
Where'er we dwell, still let thy mercy be;
From year to year, still nearer to thy shrine
Draw our frail hearts, and make them wholly thine

434. 8 & 7s. M.

1 God of mercy, do thou never
From our offering turn away,
But command a blessing ever
On the memory of this day.

2 Light and peace do thou ordain it;
O'er it be no shadow flung,
Let no deadly darkness stain it,
And no clouds be o'er it hung.

3 May the song this people raises,
And its vows to thee addressed,
Mingle with the prayers and praises,
That thou hearest from the blest.

4 When the lips are cold that sing thee,
And the hearts that love thee dust,
Father, then our souls shall bring thee
Holier love and firmer trust.

435. L. M.

1 O holy Father, just and true
Are all thy works and words and ways,
And unto thee alone are due
Thanksgiving and eternal praise!
As children of thy gracious care,
We veil the eye, we bend the knee,
With broken words of praise and prayer,
Father and God, we come to thee.

2 For thou hast heard, O God of right,
The sighing of the hapless slave;
And stretched for him the arm of might,
Not shortened that it could not save.
The laborer sits beneath his vine,
The shackled soul and hand are free;—
Thanksgiving! for the work is thine!
Praise! for the blessing is of thee!

3 Speed on thy work, Lord God of hosts!
And when the bondsman's chain is riven,
And swells from all our country's coasts
The anthems of the free to heaven,
O, not to those whom thou hast led,
As with thy cloud and fire before,
But unto thee, in fear and dread,
Be praise and glory evermore.

436. L. M.

1 O God, beneath thy guiding hand,
Our exiled fathers crossed the sea,
And when they trod the wintry strand,
With prayer and psalm they worshipped thee.

2 Thou heard'st well pleased, the song, the prayer,—
Thy blessing came; and still its power
Shall onward through all ages bear
The memory of that holy hour.

3 Laws, freedom, truth, and faith in God
Came with those exiles o'er the waves;
And where their pilgrim feet have trod,
The God they trusted guards their graves.

4 And here thy name, O God of love,
  Their children's children shall adore,
Till these eternal hills remove,
  And spring adorns the earth no more.

437. L. M.

1 God of the rolling year! to thee
  Our songs shall rise, whose bounty pours
In many a goodly gift, with free
  And liberal hand, our autumn stores;
No firstlings of our flock we slay,
  No soaring clouds of incense rise,
But on thy hallowed shrine we lay
  Our grateful hearts in sacrifice.

2 Borne on thy breath, the lap of Spring
  Was heaped with many a blooming flower;
And smiling Summer joyed to bring
  The sunshine and the gentle shower;
And Autumn's rich luxuriance now,
  The ripening seed, the bursting shell,
The golden sheaf, and laden bough,
  The fulness of thy bounty tell.

3 And here shall rise our song to thee,
  Where lengthened vales and pastures lie,
And streams go singing, wild and free,
  Beneath a blue and smiling sky,
Where ne'er was reared a mortal throne,
  Where crowned oppressors never trod;
Here, at the throne of heaven alone,
  Shall man in reverence bow to God.

438. L. P. M.

1 With grateful hearts, with joyful tongues,
To God we raise united songs;
His power and mercy we proclaim;
This land through every age shall own
Jehovah here has fixed his throne,
And triumph in his mighty name.

2 Long as the moon her course shall run,
Or man behold the circling sun,
O, still may God amidst us reign,
Crown our just counsels with success,
With peace and joy our borders bless,
And all our sacred rights maintain.

439. 9 & 8s. M.

1 We come, our hearts with gladness glowing,
Thee, Lord of harvest, to adore,
For garners filled to overflowing
With treasured heaps and plenteous store;
To thank thee that thy Father hand
Has blest anew our happy land.

2 Our praise for this abundant blessing
With favor, gracious Father, hear,
More deeply on our minds impressing
Thy mercies, each successive year,
That so our thankful praise may be
A life devoted all to thee.

3 Since thou, on us compassion taking,
With daily bread our wants dost feed,
So, pity in our breasts awaking,
Make us to feel for others' need:
Thou rich and poor alike dost love,
Then let them both thy bounty prove.

4 Thy heavenly dews our seed have nourished,
And plenteous fruit our harvests yield;
But have the fruits of faith, too, flourished,
Within thy Son's own harvest-field?
And when his eye o'erlooks the ground,
Shall thriving plants therein be found?

440. L. M.

1 Great God! we sing thy mighty hand,
By which supported, still we stand:
The opening year thy mercy shows,
That mercy crowns it till it close.

2 By day, by night, at home, abroad,
Still we are guarded by our God;
By his incessant bounty fed,
By his unerring counsel led.

3 With grateful hearts the past we own;
The future, all to us unknown,
We to thy guardian care commit,
And, peaceful, leave before thy feet.

4 In scenes exalted or depressed,
Thou art our joy, and thou our rest;
Thy goodness all our hopes shall raise,
Adored through all our changing days.

441. 7s. M.

1 Thou who dwell'st enthroned above!
Thou in whom we live and move!
Thou who art most great, most high!
God from all eternity!

2 When the morning paints the skies,
When the stars of evening rise,
We thy praises will record,
Sovereign Ruler! mighty Lord!

3 Decks the spring with flowers the field?
Harvest rich doth autumn yield?
Giver of all good below!
Lord, from thee these blessings flow.

4 Sovereign Ruler! mighty Lord!
We thy praises will record:
Giver of these blessings! we
Pour the grateful song to thee.

442. C. M.

1 An offering to the shrine of power
Our hands shall never bring;
A garland on the car of pomp
Our hands shall never fling;
Applauding in the conqueror's path
Our voices ne'er shall be;
But we have hearts to honor those
Who bade the world go free!

444. 7s. M.

1 Come, ye thankful people, come,
Raise the song of Harvest-home!
All is safely gathered in,
Ere the winter storms begin:
God our Maker doth provide,
He our wants hath well supplied:
Come to God's own temple, come,
Raise the song of Harvest-home!

2 We ourselves are God's own field,
Fruit unto his praise to yield;
Wheat and tares together sown,
Unto joy or sorrow grown:
First the blade, and then the ear,
Then the full corn shall appear:
Grant, O harvest Lord! that we
Wholesome grain and pure may be.

3 Then, thou Church Triumphant, come,
Raise the song of Harvest-home!
All are safely gathered in,
Free from sorrow, free from sin;
There, for ever purified,
In God's garner to abide:
Come, ten thousand angels, come,
Raise the glorious Harvest-home!

444. 7s. M.

1 Come, ye thankful people, come,
Raise the song of Harvest-home!
All is safely gathered in,
Ere the winter storms begin:
God our Maker doth provide,
He our wants hath well supplied:
Come to God's own temple, come,
Raise the song of Harvest-home!

2 We ourselves are God's own field,
Fruit unto his praise to yield;
Wheat and tares together sown,
Unto joy or sorrow grown:
First the blade, and then the ear,
Then the full corn shall appear:
Grant, O harvest Lord! that we
Wholesome grain and pure may be.

3 Then, thou Church Triumphant, come,
Raise the song of Harvest-home!
All are safely gathered in,
Free from sorrow, free from sin;
There, for ever purified,
In God's garner to abide:
Come, ten thousand angels, come,
Raise the glorious Harvest-home!

FAST.

---

445. L. M.

1 Have mercy on me, O my God!
In loving kindness hear my prayer;
Withdraw the terror of thy rod;
Lord, in thy tender mercy, spare.

2 Offences rise where'er I look,
But I confess their guilt to thee;
Blot my transgressions from thy book;
Wash me from all iniquity.

3 Not streaming blood nor cleansing fire
Thy seeming anger can appease;
Burnt-offerings thou dost not require,
Or gladly I would render these.

4 The broken heart in sacrifice,
Alone, will thine acceptance meet;
My heart, O God, do not despise,
Abased and contrite at thy feet.

446. C. M.

1 ALMIGHTY Lord, before thy throne
Thy mourning people bend;
'T is on thy pardoning grace alone
Our dying hopes depend.

2 Dark judgments, from thy heavy hand,
Thy dreadful power display;
Yet mercy spares our guilty land,
And still we live to pray.

3 How changed, alas! are truths divine,
For error, guilt, and shame!
What impious numbers, bold in sin,
Disgrace the Christian name!

4 O, turn us, turn us, mighty Lord!
Convert us by thy grace;
Then shall our hearts obey thy word,
And see again thy face.

5 Then, should oppressing foes invade,
We will not yield to fear,
Secure of all-sufficient aid,
When thou, O God, art near.

447. 8 & 6s. M.

1 FROM foes that would the land devour;
From guilty pride, and lust of power;
From wild sedition's lawless hour;
From yoke of slavery;

From blinded zeal, by faction led;
From giddy change, by fancy bred;
From poisoned error's serpent head,
Good Lord, preserve us free!

2 Defend, O God, with guardian hand,
The laws and rulers of our land,
And grant thy churches grace to stand
In faith and unity!
Thy Spirit's help of thee we crave,
That thy Messiah, sent to save,
Returning to the world, might have
A people serving thee!

448. L. M.

1 WHY slumbereth, Lord, each promised sign?
Why worketh not the grace divine?
Why should the foe unchecked remain,
The holy name invoked in vain?

2 Thy chastening justice, Lord, we own;
On us be guilt and shame alone;
How can we hope those gifts to share
Which come by fasting and by prayer?

3 Weak in our faith, in duty weak,
Rather thy pitying love we seek;
Father, thine arm of vengeance stay;
Saviour, O, cast us not away!

449. S. M.

1 "Is this a fast for me?"
Thus saith the Lord our God;
"A day for man to vex his soul,
And feel affliction's rod?

2 "No; is not this alone
The sacred fast I choose,—
Oppression's yoke to burst in twain,
The bands of guilt unloose?

3 "To nakedness and want
Your food and raiment deal,
To dwell your kindred race among,
And all their sufferings heal?

4 "Then, like the morning ray,
Shall spring your health and light;
Before you, righteousness shall shine,
Behind, my glory bright!"

450. C. M.

1 O, COME not with thy tears alone,
Or outward form of prayer;
But let it in thy heart be known
That penitence is there.

2 Thy breast to beat, thy clothes to rend,
God asketh not of thee;
Thy stubborn soul he bids thee bend
In true humility.

3 O, let us, then, with heartfelt grief,
Draw near unto our God,
And pray to him to grant relief,
And stay the uplifted rod.

4 O righteous Judge! if thou wilt deign
To grant us all we need,
We pray for time to turn again,
And grace to turn indeed.

451. L. M.

1 Great Framer of unnumbered worlds!
And whom unnumbered worlds adore,
Whose goodness all thy creatures share,
While nature trembles at thy power!

2 Thine is the hand that moves the spheres,
That wakes the wind, and lifts the sea;
And man, who moves, the lord of earth,
Acts but the part assigned by thee.

3 While suppliant crowds implore thine aid,
To thee we raise the humble cry;
Thine altar is the contrite heart,
Thine incense, a repentant sigh.

4 O, may our land, in this her hour,
Confess thy hand and bless the rod;
By penitence make thee her friend,
And find in thee a guardian God.

452. C. M.

1 Daughter of sadness, from the dust
Exalt thy fallen head;
In thy Redeemer firmly trust;
He calls thee from the dead.

2 Awake, awake! put on thy strength,
Thy beautiful array;
The day of freedom dawns at length,
The Lord's appointed day.

3 Rebuild thy walls, — thy bounds enlarge,
And send thy heralds forth;
Say to the South, "Give up thy charge,
And keep not back, O North!"

453. 7s. M.

1 Lord! thou didst arise and say,
To the troubled waters, "Peace!"
And the tempest died away,
Down they sank, the foaming seas;
And a calm and heaving sleep
Spread o'er all the glassy deep;
All the azure lake serene
Like another heaven was seen!

2 Lord! thy gracious word repeat
To the billows of the proud;
Quell the tyrant's martial heat;
Quell the fierce and changing crowd;

Then the earth shall find repose
From oppressions and from woes;
And an imaged heaven appear
On our world of darkness here.

454. L. M.

1 Of old, O God, thine own right hand
A pleasant vine did plant and train;
Above the hills, o'er all the land,
It sought the sun, and drank the rain.

2 Lord God of hosts, thine ear incline,
Change into songs thy people's fears;
Return, and visit this thy vine,
Revive thy work amidst the years.

3 The plenteous and continual dew
Of thy rich blessing here descend;
So shall thy vine its leaf renew,
Till o'er the earth its branches bend.

4 Then shall it flourish wide and far,
While realms beneath its shadow rest;
The morning and the evening star
Shall mark its bounds from east to west.

THE NATION.

455. L. M.

1 Faith of our fathers! living still
  In spite of dungeon, fire, and sword:
O, how our hearts beat high with joy
  Whene'er we hear that glorious word!
Faith of our fathers! Holy Faith!
We will be true to thee till death!

2 Our fathers, chained in prisons dark,
  Were still in heart and conscience free:
How sweet would be their children's fate,
  If they, like them, could die for thee!
Faith of our fathers! Holy Faith!
We will be true to thee till death!

3 Faith of our fathers! Good men's prayers
  Shall win our country all to thee;
And through the truth that comes from God
  Our land shall then indeed be free.
Faith of our fathers! Holy Faith!
We will be true to thee till death!

4 Faith of our fathers! we will love
 Both friend and foe in all our strife:
And preach thee too, as love knows how,
 By kindly words and virtuous life:
Faith of our fathers! Holy Faith!
We will be true to thee till death!

456. 6 & 4s. M.

1 My country, 't is of thee,
Sweet land of liberty,
 Of thee I sing;
Land where my fathers died,
Land of the Pilgrims' pride,
From every mountain side
 Let freedom ring.

2 My native country, thee —
Land of the noble, free —
 Thy name — I love;
I love thy rocks and rills,
Thy woods and templed hills,
My heart with rapture thrills
 Like that above.

3 Our fathers' God! to thee,
Author of liberty,
 To thee we sing:
Long may our land be bright
With freedom's holy light;
Protect us by thy might,
 Great God, our King!

457. C. M.

1 O, GUARD our shores from every foe,
With peace our borders bless,
With prosperous times our cities crown,
Our fields with plenteousness.

2 Unite us in the sacred love
Of knowledge, truth, and thee;
And let our hills and valleys shout
The songs of liberty.

3 Here may religion pure and mild
Smile on our Sabbath hours;
And piety and virtue bless
The home of us and ours.

4 Lord of the nations! thus to thee
Our country we commend;
Be thou her refuge and her trust,
Her everlasting friend.

458. L. M.

1 IN pleasant lands have fallen the lines
That bound our goodly heritage,
And safe beneath our sheltering vines
Our youth is blest, and soothed our age.

2 What thanks, O God, to thee are due,
That thou didst plant our fathers here;
And watch and guard them as they grew,
A vineyard, to the planter dear.

3 The toils they bore, our ease have wrought;
They sowed in tears,—in joy we reap;
The birthright they so dearly bought
We 'll guard, till we with them shall sleep.

4 Thy kindness to our fathers shown
In weal and woe through all the past,
Their grateful sons, O God, shall own,
While here their name and race shall last.

459. L. M.

1 Like Israel's host to exile driven,
Across the flood the pilgrims fled;
Their hands bore up the ark of Heaven,
And Heaven their trusting footsteps led,
Till on these savage shores they trod,
And won the wilderness for God.

2 Then, when their weary ark found rest,
Another Zion proudly grew;
In more than Judah's glory dressed,
With light that Israel never knew,
From sea to sea her empire spread,
Her temple heaven, and Christ her head.

3 Then let the grateful Church to-day
Its ancient rite with gladness keep;
And still our fathers' God display
His kindness, though the fathers sleep.
O, bless, as thou hast blest the past,
While earth, and time, and heaven shall last!

460. 6 & 4s. M.

1 Gone are those great and good
Who here, in peril, stood
And raised their hymn.
Peace to the reverend dead!
The light, that on their head
Two hundred years have shed,
Shall ne'er grow dim.

2 Ye temples, that to God
Rise where our fathers trod,
Guard well your trust,—
The faith, that dared the sea,
The truth, that made them free,
Their cherished purity,
Their garnered dust.

3 Thou high and holy One,
Whose care for sire and son
All nature fills;
While day shall break and close,
While night her crescent shows,
O, let thy light repose
On these our hills!

461. L. M.

1 O Thou, at whose dread name we bend,
To whom our purest vows we pay,
God over all, in love descend,
And bless the labors of this day.

2 Our fathers here, a pilgrim band,
Fixed the proud empire of the free;
Art moved in gladness o'er the land,
And Faith her altars reared to thee.

3 Here, too, to guard, through every age,
The sacred rights their valor won,
They bade Instruction spread her page,
And send down truth from sire to son.

4 Here still, through all succeeding time,
Their stores may truth and learning bring,
And still the anthem-note sublime
To thee from children's children sing.

462. L. M.

1 When, driven by oppression's rod
Our fathers fled beyond the sea,
Their care was first to honor God,
And next to leave their children free.

2 Above the forest's gloomy shade
The altar and the school appeared;
On that the gifts of faith were laid,
In this their precious hopes were reared.

3 The altar and the school still stand,
The sacred pillars of our trust,
And freedom's sons shall fill the land
When we are sleeping in the dust.

4 Before thine altar, Lord, we bend,
With grateful song and fervent prayer,
For thou who wast our fathers' friend
Wilt make our offspring still thy care.

463. 6 & 4s. M.

1 God bless our native land!
Firm may she ever stand,
Through storm and night;
When the wild tempests rave,
Ruler of winds and wave,
Do thou our country save,
By thy great might.

2 For her our prayer shall rise
To God above the skies;
On him we wait;
Thou who hast heard each sigh,
Watching each weeping eye,
Be thou for ever nigh;—
God save the State!

464. P. M.

1 The breaking waves dashed high
On a stern and rock-bound coast,
And the woods against a stormy sky
Their giant branches tost;

2 And the heavy night hung dark,
The hills and waters o'er,
When a band of exiles moored their bark
On the wild New England shore.

3 Not as the flying come,
In silence and in fear;
They shook the depths of the desert's gloom
With their hymns of lofty cheer.

4 Amidst the storm they sang;
  And the stars heard, and the sea;
And the sounding aisles of the dim wood rang
  With the anthem of the free.

5 What sought they thus afar?
  Bright jewels of the mine?
The wealth of seas, the spoils of war?
  They sought a faith's pure shrine.

6 Ay, call it holy ground,
  The soil where first they trod;
They have left unstained what there they found,
  Freedom to worship God.

465. L. M.

1 O Thou, whose presence went before
Our fathers in their weary way,
As with thy chosen moved of yore
The fire by night, the cloud by day!

2 When, from each temple of the free,
A nation's song ascends to heaven,
Most holy Father, unto thee
Now let our humble prayer be given.

3 And grant, O Father, that the time
Of earth's deliverance may be near,
When every land, and tongue, and clime,
The message of thy love shall hear;—

4 When, smitten as with fire from heaven,
The captive's chain shall sink in dust,
And to his fettered soul be given
The glorious freedom of the just.

BROTHERHOOD.

---

466. L. M.

1 O FAIREST-BORN of Love and Light,
Yet bending brow and eye severe
On all which pains the holy sight,
Or wounds the pure and perfect ear, —

2 Beneath thy broad, impartial eye,
How fade the lines of caste and birth!
How equal in their sufferings lie
The groaning multitudes of earth!

3 Still to a stricken brother true,
Whatever clime hath nurtured him;
As stooped to heal the wounded Jew
The worshipper of Gerizim.

4 In holy words which cannot die,
In thoughts which angels leaned to know
Christ gave thy message from on high,
Thy mission to a world of woe.

5 That voice's echo hath not died;
From the blue lake of Galilee,
From Tabor's lonely mountain-side,
It calls a struggling world to thee.

467. S. M.

1 Hush the loud cannon's roar,
The frantic warrior's call!
Why should the earth be drenched with gore?
Are we not brothers all?

2 Want, from the wretch depart!
Chains, from the captive fall!
Sweet mercy, melt the oppressor's heart,—
Sufferers are brothers all.

3 Churches and sects, strike down
Each mean partition-wall!
Let love each harsher feeling drown,—
Christians are brothers all.

4 Let love and truth alone
Hold human hearts in thrall,
That heaven its work at length may own,
And men be brothers all.

468. C. M.

1 O pure Reformers! not in vain
Your trust in human kind;
The good which bloodshed could not gain,
Your peaceful zeal shall find.

2 The truths ye urge are borne abroad
By every wind and tide;
The voice of nature and of God
Speaks out upon your side.

3 The weapons which your hands have found
Are those which Heaven hath wrought,
Light, Truth, and Love, — your battle-ground,
The free, broad field of Thought.

4 O, may no selfish purpose break
The beauty of your plan,
Nor lie from throne or altar shake
Your steady faith in man.

5 Press on! and if we may not share
The glory of your fight,
We 'll ask at least, in earnest prayer,
God's blessing on the Right.

469. C. M.

1 O, HUSH, great God! the sounds of war,
And make thy children feel
That he, with thee, is noblest far,
Who toils for human weal; —

2 And though forgotten, he alone
Can be a Christian true
Who would his foes as brethren own,
And still their good pursue.

470. C. M.

1 Nay, tell us not of dangers dire
That lie in duty's path;
A warrior of the cross can feel
No fear of human wrath.

2 Where'er the Prince of Darkness holds
His earthly reign abhorred,
Sword of the spirit, thee we draw,
And battle for the Lord.

3 And still serene and fixed in faith,
We fear no earthly harm;
We know it is our Father's work,
We rest upon his arm.

471. C. M.

1 Make channels for the streams of love,
Where they may broadly run;
And love has overflowing streams,
To fill them every one.

2 But if at any time we cease
Such channels to provide,
The very founts of love for us
Will soon be parched and dried.

3 For we must share, if we would keep
That blessing from above;
Ceasing to give, we cease to have;—
Such is the law of love.

472. 7 & 6s. M.

1 Now, host with host assembling,
The victory we win;
Lo! on his throne sits trembling
That old and giant sin;
Like chaff by strong winds scattered,
His banded strength has gone,
His charmèd cup lies shattered,
And still the cry is, "On!"

2 Our fathers' God, our keeper!
Be thou our strength divine!
Thou sendest forth the reaper,
The harvest all is thine.
Roll on, roll on, this gladness,
Till, driven from every shore,
The drunkard's sin and madness
Shall smite the earth no more!

473. L. M.

1 All-seeing God! 't is thine to know
The springs whence wrong opinions flow;
To judge, from principles within,
When frailty errs, and when we sin.

2 Who among men, great Lord of all,
Thy servant to his bar shall call?
Judge him, for modes of faith, thy foe,
And doom him to the realms of woe?

3 Who with another's eye can read?
Or worship by another's creed?
Trusting thy grace, we form our own,
And bow to thy commands alone.

4 If wrong, correct; accept, if right;
While faithful, we improve our light,
Condemning none, but zealous still
To learn and follow all thy will.

474. L. M.

1 Had I the tongues of Greeks and Jews,
And nobler speech than angels use,
If love be absent, I am found,
Like tinkling brass, an empty sound.

2 Were I inspired to preach, and tell
All that is done in heaven and hell,
Or could my faith the world remove,
Still I am nothing without love.

3 Should I distribute all my store
To feed the cravings of the poor,
Or give my body to the flame,
To gain a martyr's glorious name,—

4 If love to God and love to men
Be absent, all my hopes are vain:
Nor tongues, nor gifts, nor fiery zeal,
The work of love can e'er fulfil.

475. C. M.

1 Defend the poor and desolate,
And rescue from the hands
Of wicked men the low estate
Of him that help demands.

2 Regard the weak and fatherless,
Despatch the poor man's cause,
And raise the man in deep distress
By just and equal laws.

3 Rise, God! judge thou the earth in might,
The oppressèd land redress;
For thou art he who shall by right
The nations all possess.

476. P. M.

Full of mercy, full of love,
Look upon us from above;
Let thy mercy teach one brother
To forgive and love another;
That, copying thy mercy here,
Thy goodness may hereafter rear
Our souls into thy glory, when
Our dust shalt cease to be with men.

477. C. M.

1 Lord, lead the way the Saviour went,
By lane and cell obscure,

And let our treasures still be spent,
Like his, upon the poor.

2 Like him, through scenes of deep distress,
Who bore the world's sad weight,
We, in their gloomy loneliness,
Would seek the desolate.

3 For thou hast placed us side by side
In this wide world of ill;
And that thy followers may be tried,
The poor are with us still.

4 Small are the offerings we can make;
Yet thou hast taught us, Lord,
If given for the Saviour's sake,
They lose not their reward.

478. 8, 6, & 7s. M.

1 Spirit of Charity! dispense
Thy grace to every heart;
Expel all other spirits hence;
Drive self from every part.
Charity divine! draw nigh;
Break the chains in which we lie.

2 All selfish souls, whate'er they feign,
Have still a slavish lot;
They boast of liberty in vain,
Of love, and feel it not.
He, whose bosom glows with thee,
He, and he alone, is free.

479. 6 & 4s. M.

1 The laws of Christian light,
These are our weapons bright,
Our mighty shield;
Christ is our leader high,
And the broad plains which lie
Beneath the blessèd sky,
Our battle-field.

2 On, then, in God's great name!
Let each pure spirit's flame
Burn bright and clear:
Stand firmly in your lot,
Cry ye aloud, "Doubt not!"
Be every fear forgot,
Christ leads us here.

3 So shall earth's distant lands
In happy, holy bands,
One brotherhood,
Together rise and sing,
And joyful offerings bring,
And heaven's Eternal King
Pronounce it good.

480. P. M.

1 Oppression shall not always reign;
There comes a brighter day,
When freedom, burst from every chain
Shall have triumphant way.

Then right shall over might prevail,
And truth, like hero armed in mail,
The hosts of tyrant wrong assail,
And hold eternal sway.

2 The hour of triumph comes apace,
The fated, promised hour,
When earth upon a ransomed race
Her bounteous gifts shall shower.
Ring, Liberty, thy glorious bell!
Bid high thy sacred banner swell!
Let trump on trump the triumph tell
Of Heaven's redeeming power.

481. C. M.

1 O'ER mountain tops, the mount of God,
In latter days, shall rise
Above the summits of the hills,
And draw the wondering eyes.

2 Nor war shall rage, nor hostile strife
Disturb those happy years;
To ploughshares men shall beat their swords,
To pruning-hooks their spears.

3 No longer host, encountering host,
Shall crowds of slain deplore;
They 'll lay the martial trumpet by,
And study war no more.

482. 7, 6, & 8s. M.

1 THINK gently of the erring!
Lord, let us not forget,
However darkly stained by sin,
He is our brother yet.
Heir of the same inheritance,
Child of the selfsame God,
He hath but stumbled in the path,
We have in weakness trod.

2 Speak gently to him, brother;
Thou yet mayst lead him back,
With holy words, and tones of love,
From misery's thorny track.
Forget not thou hast often sinned,
And sinful yet must be:
Deal gently with the erring one,
As God has dealt with thee.

483. S. M.

1 LORD Jesus, come! for here
Our path through wilds is laid;
We watch as for the day-spring near,
Amid the breaking shade.

2 Lord Jesus, come! for hosts
Meet on the battle plain:
The patriot mourns, the tyrant boasts,
And tears are shed like rain.

3 Lord Jesus, come! for chains
Are still upon the slave;
Bind up his wounds, relieve his pains,
The pining bondman save.

4 Hark! herald voices near
Lead on thy happier day:
Come, Lord, and our hosannas hear;
We wait to strew thy way.

5 Come, as in days of old,
With words of grace and power;
Gather us all within thy fold,
And let us stray no more.

484. C. M.

1 I MAY not scorn the meanest thing
That on the earth doth crawl;
The slave who would not burst his chain,
The tyrant in his hall.

2 The vile oppressor who hath made
The widowed mother mourn,
Though worthless, soulless, he may stand,
I cannot, dare not scorn.

3 The darkest night that shrouds the sky,
Of beauty hath a share:
The blackest heart hath sighs, to tell
That God still lingers there.

485. C. M.

1 This is the first and great command, —
To love thy God above:
And this the second, — as thyself
Thy neighbor thou shalt love.

2 Who is my neighbor? He who wants
The help which thou canst give;
And both the law and prophets say,
This do, and thou shalt live.

486. S. M.

1 Blest are the sons of peace,
Whose hearts and hopes are one;
Whose kind designs to serve and please
Through all their actions run.

2 Blest is the pious house
Where zeal and friendship meet;
Their songs of praise, their mingled vows,
Make their communion sweet.

3 Thus on the heavenly hills
The saints are blest above,
Where joy like morning dew distils,
And all the air is love.

487. C. M.

1 All men are equal in their birth,
Heirs of the earth and skies;
All men are equal when that earth
Fades from their dying eyes.

2 God meets the throngs who pay their vows
In courts that hands have made,
And hears the worshipper who bows
Beneath the plantain shade.

3 O, let man hasten to restore
To all their rights of love;
In power and wealth exult no more;
In wisdom lowly move.

4 Ye great, renounce your earth-born pride,
Ye low, your shame and fear;
Live, as ye worship, side by side;
Your brotherhood revere.

488. L. M.

1 When long the soul had slept in chains,
And man to man was stern and cold,
When love and worship were but strains
That swept the gifted chords of old,
By shady mount and peaceful lake,
A meek and lowly stranger came,
The weary drank the words he spake,
The poor and feeble blest his name.

2 He went where frenzy held its rule,
Where sickness breathed its spell of pain;
By famed Bethesda's mystic pool,
And by the darkened gate of Nain.
He soothed the mourner's troubled breast,
He raised the contrite sinner's head,
And on the loved ones' lowly rest
The light of better life he shed.

3 Father, the spirit Jesus knew
We humbly ask of thee to-night,
That we may be disciples, too,
Of him whose way was love and light.
Bright be the places where we tread
Amid earth's suffering and its poor,
Till we shall come where tears are shed
And broken sighs are heard no more.

489. C. M.

1 Who is thy neighbor? He whom thou
Hast power to aid or bless;
Whose aching heart or burning brow
Thy hand may soothe or press.

2 Thy neighbor? he who drinks the cup
When sorrow drowns the brim;
With words of high sustaining hope,
Go thou and comfort him.

3 Thy neighbor? 't is the weary slave,
Fettered in mind and limb;
He hath no hope this side the grave;
Go thou, and ransom him.

4 Thy neighbor? pass no mourner by;
Perhaps thou canst redeem
A breaking heart from misery;
Go, share thy lot with him.

490. C. M.

1 What shall we render, bounteous Lord,
For all the grace we see?
The goodness feeble man can yield
Extendeth not to thee.

2 To scenes of woe, to beds of pain,
We 'll cheerfully repair,
And, with the gifts thy hand bestows,
Relieve the sufferers there.

3 The widow's heart shall sing for joy;
The orphan shall be glad;
And hungering souls we 'll gladly point
To Christ, the living bread.

4 Thus what our Heavenly Father gave
Shall we as freely give;
Thus copy him who lived to save,
And died that we might live.

491. L. M.

1 O God of freedom! hear us pray
For steadfast hearts to toil as one,
Till thy pure law hath boundless sway,
Thy will in heaven and earth be done.

2 A piercing voice of grief and wrong
Goes upward from the groaning earth;
Most true and holy Lord! how long ?—
In majesty and might come forth!

492. 7s. M.

1 Lord! deliver; thou canst save;
Save from evil, mighty God!
Hear, O, hear the kneeling slave!
Break, O, break the oppressor's rod!

2 May the captive's pleading fill
All the earth, and all the sky;
Every other voice be still,
While he pleads with God on high.

3 From the tyranny within,
Save thy children, Lord! we pray;
Chains of iron, chains of sin,
Cast, for ever cast away.

4 Love to man, and love to God,
Are the weapons of our war;
These can break the oppressor's rod,
Burst the bonds that we abhor.

493. C. M.

1 Father of mercies! send thy grace
All-powerful from above,
To form in our obedient souls
The image of thy love.

2 O, may our sympathizing breasts
The generous pleasure know,
Kindly to share in others' joy,
And weep for others' woe.

494. 8s. M.

1 Lord, from whom all blessings flow,
Perfecting the Church below!
Steadfast may we cleave to thee;
Love the mystic union be.
Join our faithful spirits, join
Each to each, and all to thine:
Lead us through the paths of peace,
On to perfect holiness.

2 Sweetly may we all agree,
Touched with softest sympathy:
There is neither bond nor free,
Great nor servile, Lord, in thee;
Love, like death, hath all destroyed,
Rendered all distinctions void!
Names, and sects, and parties fall:
Thou, O Christ, art all in all!

495. L. M.

1 Assist us, Lord! to act, to be,
What nature and thy laws decree;
Worthy that intellectual flame,
Which from thy breathing spirit came.

2 May our expanded souls disclaim
The narrow view, the selfish aim;
But with a Christian zeal embrace,
Whate'er is friendly to our race.

3 O Father! grace and virtue grant;
No more we wish, no more we want:
To know, to serve thee, and to love,
Is peace below, is bliss above.

496. 7s. M.

1 MEN! whose boast it is, that ye
Come of fathers brave and free,
If there breathe on earth a slave,
Are ye truly free and brave?
If ye do not feel the chain
When it works a brother's pain,
Are ye not base slaves indeed,
Slaves unworthy to be freed?

2 Is true freedom but to break
Fetters for our own dear sake,
And with leathern hearts forget
That we owe mankind a debt?
No! true freedom is to share
All the chains our brothers wear,
And with heart and hand to be
Earnest to make others free.

3 They are slaves who fear to speak
For the fallen and the weak;
They are slaves, who will not choose
Hatred, scoffing, and abuse.

Rather than, in silence, shrink
From the truth they needs must think;
They are slaves, who dare not be
In the right with two or three.

497. 6 & 4s. M.

1 Lord, from thy blessed throne,
Sorrow look down upon!
God save the poor!
Teach them true liberty,
Make them from tyrants free,
Let their homes happy be!
God save the poor!

2 The arms of wicked men
Do thou with might restrain,—
God save the poor!
Raise thou their lowliness,
Succor thou their distress,
Thou whom the meanest bless!
God save the poor!

3 Give them stanch honesty,
Let their pride manly be,—
God save the poor!
Help them to hold the right,
Give them both truth and might,
Lord of all life and light!
God save the poor!

498. 11 & 10s. M.

1 Down the dark future, through long generations,
The sounds of war grow fainter, and then cease;
And like a bell with solemn, sweet vibrations,
I hear once more the voice of Christ say, "Peace!"

2 Peace! and no longer, from its brazen portals,
The blast of war's great organ shakes the skies;
But beautiful as songs of the immortals,
The holy melodies of love arise.

499. L. M.

1 Lord, when thine ancient people cried,
Oppressed and bound by Egypt's king,
Thou didst Arabia's sea divide,
And forth thy fainting Israel bring.

2 Lo, in these latter days, our land
Groans with the anguish of the slave:
Lord God of hosts! stretch forth thy hand,
Not shortened that it cannot save.

3 Roll back the swelling tide of sin,
The lust of gain, the lust of power;
The day of freedom usher in:
How long delays the appointed hour?

4 O, let thy smitten ones again
Take up the chorus of the free!
Praise ye the Lord! his power proclaim,
For he hath conquered gloriously!

500. L. M.

1 That stream of Truth — a silver thread,
Scarce known, save by its fountain-head —
Now onward pours, a mighty flood,
And fills the new-formed world with good.

2 Where'er that living fountain flows,
New life its healing wave bestows,
And man, from sin's corruptions free,
Inspires with its own purity.

3 A spirit breathed from Zion's hill
In holy hearts is living still, —
That Comforter from heaven above,
The presence of celestial love.

4 O, may this spirit ever be
Our bond of peace and unity!
Thus shall we teach, as Christ began,
Through love, the brotherhood of man.

SOCIAL WORSHIP.

---

501. C. M.

1 How good and pleasant is the sight,
How great the bliss they share,
When Christ's assembled flock unite
In acts of social prayer!
God thither, with paternal care,
His face benignant bends;
And Jesus, by his spirit, there
On faithful hearts descends.

2 To such, by hallowed lips expressed,
His grace confirms his word,
As once Cornelius' house it blest,
From holy Peter heard:
On prayer and praise, in faith preferred,
His heavenly dew is shed;
And he to all, who come prepared,
Dispenses heavenly bread.

3 To God, adored in ages past,
Enthroned in majesty, —
To God, whose worship aye shall last,
Throughout eternity, —
To thee, Great God, we bend the knee,
And in the Holy Ghost,
Through Christ, all glory give to thee,
With all thy heavenly host.

502. 7s. M.

1 As the sun's enlivening eye
Shines on every place the same;
So the Lord is always nigh
To the souls that love his name.

2 When they move at duty's call,
He is with them by the way;
He is ever with them all,
Those who go, and those who stay.

3 For a season called to part,
Let us then ourselves commend
To the gracious eye and heart
Of our ever-present Friend.

4 Father, hear our humble prayer!
Tender shepherd of thy sheep,
Let thy mercy and thy care
All our souls in safety keep.

503. 7s. M.

1 Let us join, as God commands,
Let us join our hearts and hands;
Help to gain our calling's hope;
Help to build each other up;
Carry on the Christian's strife;
Walk in holiness of life;
Faithfully our gifts improve
For the sake of him we love;—

2 Still forget the things behind;
Follow Christ in heart and mind;
Toward the mark unwearied press;
Seize the crown of righteousness,
While we walk with God in light,
God our hearts will still unite;
Dearest fellowship we prove,—
Fellowship in Jesus' love.

504. L. M.

1 Thy bounteous hand with food can bless
The bleak and barren wilderness,
And thou hast taught us, Lord, to pray
For daily bread from day to day.

2 And, O, when through the wilds we roam
That part us from our heavenly home;
When, lost in danger, want, and woe,
Our faithless tears begin to flow;—

3 Do thou thy gracious comfort give,
By which alone the soul can live;
And grant thy children, Lord, we pray,
The bread of life from day to day!

505. L. M.

1 THOU, Saviour, who thyself didst give,
That all the world might turn and live,
Who dost the careless sinner draw
With cords of love to thy pure law,
Who dost thy Church with fondness call,
And by thy grace receivest all; —

2 Behold us, Lord, before thy throne;
Inspire and make our hearts thine own;
Bind to thy cross our wandering will,
Each act with holy purpose fill;
Our weakness let thy strength defend,
Thou Author of our faith, and End!

506. 6 & 5s. M.

1 O THOU who hearest prayer,
Through his submission
Who did our sorrows bear,
Hear our petition:
Lead us in thine own way;
Grant us, we humbly pray,
For all our sins this day,
Holy contrition.

2 They shall lie down in peace,
Lord, whom thou keepest;
Thy mercies never cease;
Thou never sleepest:
Guard us till morning's ray
Bids us again essay
Who shall pour forth the lay
Loudest and deepest.

507. C. M.

1 THOU biddest, Lord, thy sons be bold,
Lord, thou hast set us free;
The dear adoption fast we hold, —
The glorious liberty!

2 We stand unto our God how near!
Nor priest, nor veil between,
Lord! full unto thine own appear;
We cast away each screen.

3 Thy truth is waiting to be seized;
Thou sweetly bid'st us dare;
We look, we seek, — and thou art pleased
To meet us everywhere.

4 Thy Spirit's fulness we embrace, —
Away with man's poor dole!
The sweetest visit of thy grace
Asks but an open soul.

5 Full feels our solemn privacy,
The sweet celestial air;

In humble joy we lay on thee
The loving clasp of prayer.

6 We mingle now our inmost fires,
A glowing spirit-throng!
All free and strong of wing, aspires
The passion of our song.

7 Thine own we are, Almighty One!
Thine own would ever be;
Endless thy dear dominion,
Our glorious liberty!

508. S. M.

1 Our Heavenly Father calls,
And Christ invites us near;
With both our friendship shall be sweet,
And our communion dear.

2 God pities all my griefs;
He pardons every day;
Almighty to protect my soul,
And wise to guide my way.

3 Jesus, my living Head,
I bless thy faithful care;
Mine advocate before the throne,
And my forerunner there.

4 Here fix my roving heart,
Here wait my warmest love,
Till the communion be complete
In nobler scenes above.

509. 7s. M.

1 Abba, Father, hear thy child,
Late in Jesus reconciled;
Hear, and all the graces shower,
All the joy, and peace, and power;
All my Saviour asks above,
All the life and heaven of love.

2 Heavenly Father, Life divine,
Change my nature into thine;
Move and spread throughout my soul,
Actuate and fill the whole:
Lord, I will not let thee go
Till the blessing thou bestow.

3 Holy Ghost, no more delay;
Come, and in thy temple stay:
Now thine inward witness bear,
Strong, and permanent, and clear:
Spring of life, thyself impart;
Rise eternal in my heart.

510. C. M.

1 Come, let us who in Christ believe
Our common Saviour praise:
To him, with joyful voices, give
The glory of his grace.

2 He now stands knocking at the door
Of every sinner's heart:
The worst need keep him out no more,
Or force him to depart.

3 Through grace we hearken to thy voice,
Yield to be saved from sin;
In sure and certain hope rejoice,
That thou wilt enter in.

4 Come quickly in, thou heavenly guest,
Nor ever hence remove;
But rest with us, and let the feast
Be everlasting love.

511. C. M.

1 FATHER, united by thy grace,
And each to each endeared,
With confidence we seek thy face,
And know our prayer is heard.

2 Make us into one spirit drink;
Baptize into one name;
And let us always kindly think
And sweetly speak the same.

512. 7s. M.

1 LET us for each other care;
Each the other's burden bear;
To thy Church the pattern give;
Show how true believers live.

2 Free from anger and from pride,
Let us thus in God abide;
All the depths of love express,
All the heights of holiness.

513. 7s. M.

1 Join us, in one spirit join,
Let us still receive of thine:
Still for more on thee we call,
Thou who fillest all in all!

2 Closer knit us to our Head;
Nourish us, in Christ, and feed;
Let us daily growth receive,
More and more in Jesus live.

3 Many are we now and one,
We who Jesus have put on:
There is neither bond nor free,
Neither great nor small, in thee.

4 Love, like death, hath all destroyed,
Rendered our distinctions void;
Names, and sects, and parties fall;
Thou, O God, art all in all!

514. 7s. M.

1 Centre of our hopes thou art;
End of our enlarged desires:
Stamp thine image on our heart;
Fill us now with heavenly fires:
Joined to thee by love divine,
Seal our souls for ever thine.

2 All our works in thee be wrought,—
Levelled at one common aim:

Every word and every thought
  Purge in the refining flame:
Lead us, through the paths of peace,
On to perfect holiness.

3 Let us all together rise,
  To thy glorious life restored;
Here regain our Paradise,
  Here prepare to meet our Lord;
Here enjoy the earnest given;
Travel hand in hand to heaven.

515. C. M.

1 THROUGH thee we now together came,
  In singleness of heart;
We met, O Jesus, in thy name,
  And in thy name we part.

2 Subsisteth in us all one soul,
  No power can make us twain;
And mountains rise, and oceans roll,
  To sever us, in vain.

3 We still in spirit present are,
  And intimately nigh,
While on the wings of faith and prayer
  We to each other fly.

4 Our life is hid with Christ in God;
  Our life shall soon appear,
And shed his glory all abroad,
  In all his members here.

516. C. M.

1 Try us, O God, and search the ground
Of every sinful heart:
Whate'er of sin in us is found,
O, bid it all depart!

2 Help us to help each other, Lord,
Each other's cross to bear;
Let each his friendly aid afford,
And feel his brother's care.

3 Help us to build each other up,
Our little stock improve;
Increase our faith, confirm our hope,
And perfect us in love.

4 Up into thee, our living Head,
Let us in all things grow,
Till thou hast made us free indeed,
And spotless here below.

517. C. M.

1 On the first Christian Sabbath eve,
When his disciples met,
O'er his lost fellowship to grieve,
Nor knew the Scripture yet,—

2 Lo, in their midst his form was seen,
The form in which he died;
Their Master's marred and wounded mien,
His hands, his feet, his side.

3 Be in our midst; let faith rejoice
Our risen Lord to view,
And make our spirits hear thy voice
Say, "Peace be unto you."

4 And while with thee in social hours
We commune through thy word,
May our hearts burn, and all our powers
Confess, "It is the Lord."

518. C. M.

1 We bow before thy gracious throne,
And think ourselves sincere;
But show us, Lord, is every one
Thy real worshipper?

2 Give us ourselves and thee to know,
In this our gracious day;
Repentance unto life bestow,
And take our sins away.

3 Impoverish, Lord, and then relieve,
And then enrich the poor;
The knowledge of our sickness give,
The knowledge of our cure.

4 O, that we all might now begin
Our foolishness to mourn,
And turn at once from every sin,
And to our Saviour turn.

THE FUTURE CHURCH.

---

519. S. M.

1 Come, kingdom of our God,
Sweet reign of light and love!
Shed peace, and hope, and joy abroad,
And wisdom from above.

2 Over our spirits first
Extend thy healing reign;
There raise and quench the sacred thirst,
That never pains again.

3 Come, kingdom of our God!
And make the broad earth thine;
Stretch o'er her lands and isles the rod
That flowers with grace divine.

4 Soon may all tribes be blest
With fruit from life's glad tree;
And in its shade like brothers rest,
Sons of one family.

520. C. M.

1 O, WHERE are kings and empires now
Of old that went and came?
But Holy Church is praying yet,
A thousand years the same.
Mark ye her holy battlements,
And her foundations strong;
And hear within, her solemn voice,
And her unending song.

2 For not like kingdoms of the world
The Holy Church of God!
Though earthquake shocks are rocking her,
And tempests are abroad;
Unshaken as eternal hills,
Immovable she stands,—
A mountain that shall fill the earth,
A fane unbuilt by hands.

521. 7 & 6s. M.

1 GOD comes, with succor speedy,
To those who suffer wrong;
To help the poor and needy,
And bid the weak be strong;
He comes to break oppression,
And set the captive free,
To take away transgression,
And rule in equity.

2 He shall come down, as showers
Upon the thirsty earth;
And joy and hope, like flowers,
Spring in his path to birth.
Before him, on the mountains,
Shall Peace, the herald, go,
And Righteousness, in fountains,
From hill to valley flow.

3 To him shall prayer unceasing,
And daily vows, ascend;
His kingdom still increasing,
A kingdom without end.
The tide of time shall never
His covenant remove;
His name shall stand for ever,
His great, best name of Love.

522. C. M.

1 Gone is the hollow, murky night,
With all its shadows dun;
O, shine upon us, heavenly Light,
As on the earth the sun!

2 Pour on our hearts thy heavenly beam,
In radiance sublime!
Retire before that ray supreme,
Ye sins of elder time!

3 Lo, on the morn that now is here
No night shall ever fall;
But faith shall burn, undimmed and clear,
Till God be all in all.

4 This is the dawn of infant faith;
The day will follow soon,
When hope shall breathe with freer breath,
And morn be lost in noon;

5 For to the seed that 's sown to-day
A harvest-time is given,
When charity, with faith to stay,
Shall make on earth a heaven.

523. 8 & 7s. M.

1 HEAR what God the Lord hath spoken:
O my people, faint and few,
Comfortless, afflicted, broken,
Fair abodes I build for you:
Scenes of heartfelt tribulation
Shall no more perplex your ways;
You shall name your walls salvation,
And your gates shall all be praise.

2 Ye, no more your suns descending,
Waning moons no more shall see;
But, your griefs for ever ending,
Find eternal noon in me:
God shall rise, and, shining o'er you,
Change to day the gloom of night;
He, the Lord, shall be your glory,
God your everlasting light.

524. 10s. M.

1 Rise, crowned with light, imperial Salem, rise!
Exalt thy towering head, and lift thine eyes;
See heaven its sparkling portals wide display,
And break upon thee in a flood of day.

2 See a long race thy spacious courts adorn;
See future sons and daughters yet unborn
In crowding ranks on every side arise,
Demanding life, impatient for the skies.

3 See barbarous nations at thy gates attend,
Walk in thy light, and in thy temple bend;
See thy bright altars, thronged with prostrate kings
While every land its joyous tribute brings.

4 The seas shall waste, the skies to smoke decay,
Rocks fall to dust, and mountains melt away;
But fixed his word, his saving power remains;
Thy realm shall last, thy own Messiah reigns.

525. 7 & 5s. M.

1 Onward speed thy conquering flight;
Angel, onward speed;
Cast abroad thy radiant light,
Bid the shades recede;
Tread the idols in the dust,
Heathen fanes destroy;
Spread the Gospel's holy trust,
Spread the Gospel's joy.

2 Onward speed thy conquering flight;
Angel, onward speed;
Morning bursts upon our sight,—
'T is the time decreed:
Jesus now his kingdom takes,
Thrones and empires fall;
And the joyous song awakes,
"God is all in all."

526. 7s. M.

1 WATCHMAN! tell us of the night,
What its signs of promise are.
Traveller! o'er yon mountain's height,
See that glory-beaming star.
Watchman! does its beauteous ray
Aught of joy or hope foretell?
Traveller! yes; it brings the day,
Promised day of Israel.

2 Watchman! tell us of the night;
Higher yet that star ascends.
Traveller! blessedness and light,
Peace and truth its course portends.
Watchman! will its beams alone
Gild the spot that gave them birth?
Traveller! ages are its own;
See, it bursts o'er all the earth.

3 Watchman! tell us of the night,
For the morning seems to dawn.
Traveller! darkness takes its flight;
Doubt and terror are withdrawn.

Watchman! let thy wanderings cease;
  Hie thee to thy quiet home.
Traveller! lo! the Prince of Peace,
  Lo! the Son of God, is come.

527. L. M.

1 O spirit of the living God,
  In all thy plentitude of grace,
Where'er the foot of man hath trod,
  Descend on our degenerate race!

2 Give tongues of fire and hearts of love,
  To preach the reconciling word;
Give power and unction from above,
  Where'er the joyful sound is heard.

3 Be darkness, at thy coming, light;
  Confusion, order, in thy path;
Souls without strength inspire with might;
  Bid mercy triumph over wrath.

4 Convert the nations; far and nigh,
  The triumphs of the cross record;
The name of Jesus glorify,
  Till every people call him Lord.

528. 7 & 6s. M.

1 When shall the voice of singing
  Flow joyfully along?
When hill and valley, ringing
  With one triumphant song,

Proclaim the contest ended,
  And Him who once was slain
Again to earth descended,
  In righteousness to reign?

2 Then from the craggy mountains
  The sacred shout shall fly,
And shady vales and fountains
  Shall echo the reply:
High tower and lowly dwelling
  Shall send the chorus round,
The hallelujah swelling
  In one eternal sound.

529. 10s. M.

1 Pour, blessed Gospel, glorious news for man!
  Thy stream of life o'er springless deserts roll:
Thy bond of peace the mighty earth can span,
  And make one brotherhood from pole to pole.

2 On, piercing Gospel, on! of every heart,
  In every latitude, thou own'st the key:
From their dull slumbers savage souls shall start,
  With all their treasures first unlocked by thee.

Spread, mighty Gospel, spread thy soaring wings!
  Gather thy scattered ones from every land:
Call home the wanderers to the King of kings;
  Proclaim them all thine own;—'t is Christ's command!

530. L. M.

1 Jesus shall reign where'er the sun
Does his successive journeys run;
His kingdom stretch from shore to shore,
Till moons shall wax and wane no more.

2 Blessings abound where'er he reigns;
The joyful prisoner bursts his chains;
The weary find eternal rest,
And all the sons of want are blest.

531. 8 & 7s. M.

1 O'er the gloomy hills of darkness,
Look, my soul, be still and gaze;
See the promises advancing
To a glorious day of grace.

2 Let the dark, benighted pagan,
Let the rude barbarian, see
That divine and glorious conquest
Once obtained on Calvary.

3 Kingdoms wide, that sit in darkness,
Grant them, Lord, the glorious light;
Now, from eastern coast to western,
May the morning chase the night.

4 Fly abroad, thou mighty Gospel;
Win and conquer, never cease:
May thy lasting, wide dominions
Multiply, and still increase.

532. 8, 7, & 4s. M.

1 On the mountain's top appearing,
Lo! the sacred herald stands,
Welcome news to Zion bearing, —
Zion, long in hostile lands:
Mourning captive,
God himself will loose thy bands.

2 Has thy night been long and mournful?
Have thy friends unfaithful proved?
Have thy foes been proud and scornful,
By thy sighs and tears unmoved?
Cease thy mourning;
Zion still is well beloved.

3 God, thy God, will now restore thee;
He himself appears thy friend;
All thy foes shall flee before thee;
Here their boasts and triumphs end:
Great deliverance
Zion's King will surely send.

4 Peace and joy shall now attend thee;
All thy warfare now be past;
God, thy Saviour, will defend thee;
Victory is thine at last:
All thy conflicts
End in everlasting rest.

533. 7s. M.

1 On thy Church, O Power Divine,
Cause thy glorious face to shine;
Till the nations from afar
Hail her as their guiding star;
Till her sons, from zone to zone,
Make thy great salvation known.

2 Then shall God, with lavish hand,
Scatter blessings o'er the land;
Earth shall yield her rich increase,
Every breeze shall whisper peace,
And the world's remotest bound
With the voice of praise resound.

534. C. M.

1 But who shall see the glorious day,
When, throned on Zion's brow,
The Lord shall rend the veil away
That hides the nations now!
When earth no more beneath the fear
Of his rebuke shall lie,
When pain shall cease, and every tear
Be wiped from every eye!

2 Then, Judah, thou no more shalt mourn
Beneath the heathen's chain;
Thy days of splendor shall return,
And all be new again.

The fount of life shall then be quaffed
In peace by all who come;
And every wind that blows shall waft
Some long-lost wanderer home.

535. P. M.

1 Daughter of Zion, awake from thy sadness!
Awake! for thy foes shall oppress thee no more;
Bright o'er thy hills dawns the day-star of gladness,
Arise! for the night of thy sorrow is o'er.

2 Strong were thy foes, but the arm that subdued them,
And scattered their legions, was mightier far;
They fled like the chaff from the scourge that pursued them,
Vain were their steeds and their chariots of war.

3 Daughter of Zion, the power that hath saved thee,
Extolled with the harp and the timbrel should be;
Shout! for the foe is destroyed that enslaved thee;
The oppressor is vanquished, and Zion is free.

536. 10s. M.

1 Restore, O Father! to our times restore
The peace which filled thine infant Church of yore;
Ere lust of power had sown the seeds of strife,
And quenched the new-born charities of life.

2 O, never more may differing judgments part
From kindly sympathy a brother's heart;
But, linked in one, believing thousands kneel,
And share with each the sacred joy they feel.

3 From soul to soul, quick as the sunbeam's ray,
Let concord spread one universal day;
And faith by love lead all mankind to thee,
Parent of peace, and fount of harmony!

537. C. M.

1 Pity the nations, O our God!
Constrain the earth to come;
Send thy victorious word abroad,
And bring the strangers home.

2 We long to see thy churches full,
That all thy faithful race
May, with one voice, and heart, and soul,
Sing thy redeeming grace.

538. 7 & 6s. M.

1 From Greenland's icy mountains,
From India's coral strand,
Where Afric's sunny fountains
Roll down their golden sand,
From many an ancient river,
From many a palmy plain,
They call us to deliver
Their land from error's chain.

2 What though the spicy breezes
Blow soft o'er Ceylon's isle;
Though every prospect pleases,
And only man is vile;
In vain with lavish kindness
The gifts of God are strown;
The heathen in his blindness
Bows down to wood and stone.

3 Shall we, whose souls are lighted
By wisdom from on high,
Shall we to men benighted
The lamp of life deny?
Salvation! O, salvation!
The joyful sound proclaim,
Till each remotest nation
Has learnt Messiah's name.

539. L. M.

1 Sovereign of worlds! display thy power;
Be this thy Zion's favored hour;
Bid the bright morning-star arise,
And point the nations to the skies.

2 Set up thy throne where Satan reigns,
On Afric's shore, on India's plains,
On lonely isles and lands unknown,
And make the nations all thine own.

3 Speak! and the world shall hear thy voice;
Speak! and the desert shall rejoice;
Scatter the gloom of heathen night,
And bid all nations hail the light.

540. 8 & 9s. M.

1 A LITTLE child, in bulrush ark,
Came floating on the Nile's broad water;
That child made Egypt's glory dark,
And freed his tribe from bonds and slaughter.

2 A little child for knowledge sought,
In Israel's temple, of its sages;
That child the world's religion brought,
And crushed the temples of past ages.

3 'Mid worst oppressions, if remain
Young hearts to freedom still aspiring;
If, nursed in superstition's chain,
The human mind be still inquiring,—

4 Then let not priest or tyrant dote
On dreams of long the world commanding;
The ark of Moses is afloat,
And Christ is in the temple standing.

VII.

THE HEART.

PENITENCE.

---

541. C. M.

1 O, WHEN the tide of graces set
So full upon my heart,
I know, dear Lord! how faithlessly
I did my little part.

2 And if some weariness should come,
A present from on high,
Teach me to find the hidden wealth
That in its depths may lie.

3 If I have served thee, Lord! for hire,
Hire which thy bounty showed,
Ah! I can serve thee now for naught,
And only as my God.

4 O, blessed be my darkness then,
The deep in which I lie,
And blessed be all things that teach
God's dread supremacy!

542. C. M.

1 Were not the sinful Mary's tears
An offering worthy heaven,
When o'er the faults of former years
She wept, and was forgiven?

2 When, bringing every balmy sweet
Her day of luxury stored,
She o'er her Saviour's hallowed feet
The precious perfume poured,—

3 Were not those sweets so humbly shed,
That hair, those weeping eyes,
And the sunk heart which inly bled,
Heaven's noblest sacrifice?

4 Thou that hast slept in error's sleep,
O, wouldst thou wake to heaven,
Like Mary kneel, like Mary weep;
"Love much," and be forgiven!

543. C. M.

1 This freezing heart, O Lord! this will
Dry as the desert sand,
Good thoughts that will not come, bad thoughts
That come without command,—

2 A faith that seems not faith, a hope
That cares not for its aim,
A love that none the warmer grows
At Jesus' blessed name,—

3 And if it hath been sin of mine,
O, show that sin to me,
Not to get back the sweetness lost,
But to make peace with thee.

544. C. M.

1 RETURN, O wanderer, now return,
And seek thy Father's face;
Those new desires which in thee burn
Were kindled by his grace.

2 Return, O wanderer, now return,
And wipe the falling tear;
Thy Father calls, — no longer mourn;
'T is Love invites thee near.

545. 7s. M.

1 HAST thou wasted all the powers
God for noble uses gave?
Squandered life's most golden hours?
Turn thee, brother, God can save!

2 Is a mighty famine now
In thy heart and in thy soul?
Discontent upon thy brow?
Turn thee, God will make thee whole!

3 Fall before him on the ground,
Pour thy sorrow in his ear,
Seek him while he may be found,
Call upon him while he 's near.

546. C. M.

1 Long have I seemed to serve thee, Lord,
With unavailing pain:
Fasted and prayed, and read thy word,
And heard it preached in vain.

2 Oft did I with the assembly join,
And near thine altar drew;
A form of godliness was mine,
The power I never knew.

3 I rested in the outward law;
Nor knew its deep design:
The length and breadth I never saw,
And height, of love divine.

4 Where am I now, or what my hope?
What can my weakness do?
Father, to thee my soul looks up:
'T is thou must make it new.

547. L. M.

1 Come, now, ye wanderers, to your God,
Through love, to purity restored;
The proffered benefit embrace,
The plenitude of heavenly grace;—

2 The seeing eye, the feeling sense,
The mystic joys of penitence;
The tears that tell your sins forgiven;
The sighs that waft your souls to heaven;—

3 The guiltless shame, the sweet distress,
The unutterable tenderness;
The genuine meek humility,
The wonder, "Why such love to me?" —

4 The o'erwhelming power of saving grace,
The sight that veils the seraph's face;
The speechless awe that dares not move,
And all the silent heaven of love.

548. L. M.

1 Loosed from my God, and far removed,
Long have I wandered to and fro;
O'er earth in endless circles roved,
Nor found whereon to rest below:
But now, my God, to thee I fly,
For, oh! estranged from thee, I die.

2 Selfish pursuits, and nature's maze,
The things of sense, for thee I leave:
Put forth thy hand, thy hand of grace;
Into the ark of love receive;
Take my poor, fluttering soul to rest,
And lodge it, Father, in thy breast.

3 Endow me with my Saviour's peace,
Confirm and keep my longing heart;
In thee may all my wanderings cease;
From thee may I no more depart:
Then shall the joy within me prove
The fulness of my Father's love!

549. C. M.

1 Back to the world we've faithless turned,
And far along the wild,
With labor lost, and sorrow earned,
Our steps have been beguiled.

2 Yet full before us, all the while,
The guiding pillar stays;
The living waters brightly smile,
Th' eternal turrets blaze.

3 O Father, of long-suffering grace,
Thou who in love dost stay,
Pleading with sinners face to face,
Through all their devious way,—

4 Thy guardian fire, thy guiding cloud,
Be round us as our wall;
Nor be our erring hearts allowed
Again to faint or fall.

550. L. M.

1 O Father, full of truth and grace,
More full of grace than man of sin,
Yet once again we seek thy face;
Open thine arms and take us in,
And freely our backslidings heal,
And love thy faithless children still.

2 Ah, give me, Lord, the tender heart,
That trembles at the approach of sin:

A godly fear of sin impart;
Implant and root it deep within:
The errors of my soul repair,
And make my heart a house of prayer.

3 Give to mine eyes refreshing tears,
And kindle my relentings now;
Fill my whole soul with filial fears;
To thy sweet yoke my spirit bow,
That I may know thy Spirit's power,
And never dare to grieve thee more.

551. S. M.

1 My Father bids me come,
O, why do I delay?
He calls the wandering spirit home,
And yet from him I stay!

2 Father, the hindrance show,
Which I have failed to see;
And let me now consent to know
What keeps me far from thee.

3 Searcher of hearts, in mine
Thy trying power display;
Into its darkest corners shine,
Take every veil away.

4 In me the hindrance lies;
The fatal bar remove:
And let me see, in sweet surprise,
Thy full redeeming love.

552. C. M.

1 Weak and irresolute is man:
The purpose of to-day,
Woven with pains into his plan,
To-morrow rends away.

2 Some foe to his upright intent
Finds out his weaker part;
Virtue engages his assent,
But pleasure wins his heart.

3 Bound on a voyage of fearful length,
Through dangers little known,
A stranger to superior strength,
Man vainly trusts his own.

4 But oars alone can ne'er prevail
To reach the distant coast;
The breath of heaven must swell the sail,
Or all the toil is lost.

553. C. M.

1 Unworthy to be called thy son,
I come with shame to thee,
Father! O, more than Father, thou
Hast always been to me!

2 Help me to break the heavy chains
The world has round me thrown,
And know the glorious liberty
Of an obedient son.

3 That I may henceforth heed whate'er
Thy voice within me saith,
Fix deeply in my heart of hearts
A principle of faith, —

4 Faith that, like armor to my soul,
Shall keep all evil out,
More mighty than an angel host,
Encamping round about.

554. 7s. M.

1 SINNERS, turn! why will ye die?
God, your Maker, asks you why;
God who did your being give,
Made you with himself to live.

2 Sinners, turn! why will ye die?
Christ, your Saviour, asks you why;
Christ, who did your souls retrieve,
Died himself, that ye might live.

3 Will ye not his grace receive?
Will ye still refuse to live?
Why, you long-sought sinners, why
Will you grieve your God, and die?

555. C. M.

1 How long shall dreams of earthly bliss
Our flattering hopes employ,
And mock our fond, deluded eyes
With visionary joy?

2 Why from the mountains and the hills
  Is our salvation sought,
While our eternal Rock 's forsook,
  And Israel's God forgot?

3 The living spring neglected flows
  Full in our daily view;
Yet we, with anxious, fruitless toil,
  Our broken cisterns hew.

4 These fatal errors, gracious God,
  With gentle pity see;
To thee our roving eyes direct,
  And fix our souls on thee.

556. 8, 7, & 4s. M.

1 COME, ye sinners, poor and needy,
  Weak and wounded, sick and sore,
Jesus ready stands to save you,
  Full of pity, love, and power;
    He is able,
  He is willing, doubt no more.

2 Let not conscience make you linger,
  Nor of fitness idly dream;
All the fitness he requireth
  Is to feel your need of him;
    This he gives you,
  'T is the spirit's struggling beam.

3 Agonizing in the garden,
  Blessed Jesus prostrate lies;

On the bloody cross behold him!
Hear him cry before he dies,
"It is finished!"
Sinner, will not this suffice?

4 Saints and angels, joined in concert,
Sing the praises of the Lamb;
While the blissful seats of heaven
Sweetly echo with his name, —
Hallelujah!
Sinners here may do the same.

557. C. M.

1 Deepen the wound thy hands have made
In this weak, helpless soul,
Till mercy, with its balmy aid,
Descend to make me whole.

2 I see the exceeding broad command,
Which all contains in one:
Enlarge my heart to understand
The mystery unknown.

3 O that, with all thy saints, I might
By sweet experience prove
What is the length, and breadth, and height,
And depth, of perfect love!

558. C. M.

1 O for that tenderness of heart
Which bows before the Lord,

That owns how just and good thou art,
  And trembles at thy word!

2 O for those humble, contrite tears,
  Which from repentance flow,
That sense of guilt, which, trembling, fears
  The long-suspended blow!

3 O Lord, to me in pity give,
  For sin the deep distress,
The pledge thou wilt at last receive,
  And bid me die in peace.

4 O, fill my soul with faith and love,
  And strength to do thy will;
Raise my desires and hopes above;
  Thyself to me reveal.

559. 7s. M.

1 Lord, have mercy when we pray
Strength to seek a better way;
When our wakening thoughts begin
First to loathe their cherished sin;
Sigh for death, yet fear it still,
From the dread of future ill;
When the dim, advancing gloom
Tells us that our hour is come.

2 Lord, have mercy, when we know
First how vain this world below;
When its darker thoughts oppress,
Doubts perplex, and fears distress;

When the earliest gleam is given
Of the bright but distant heaven;
Then thy fostering grace afford;
Then, O, then, have mercy, Lord!

560. L. M.

1 The wandering star and fleeting wind
Are emblems of the fickle mind;
The morning cloud and early dew
Bring our inconstancy to view.

2 But cloud and wind and dew and star
Only a faint resemblance bear;
Nor can there aught in nature be
So changeable and frail as we.

3 Our outward walk and inward frame
Are scarcely through an hour the same;
We vow, and straight our vows forget,
And then those very vows repeat.

4 With contrite hearts, Lord, we confess
Our folly and unsteadfastness:
When shall these hearts more stable be,
Fixed by thy grace alone on thee?

561. C. M.

1 Times without number have I prayed,
"This only once forgive";
Relapsing when thy hand was stayed,
And suffered me to live.

2 Yet now the kingdom of thy peace,
Lord, to my heart restore;
Forgive my vain repentances,
And bid me sin no more.

562. L. M.

1 My soul before thee prostrate lies;
To thee, her source, my spirit flies;
My wants I mourn, my chains I see;
O, let thy presence set me free!

2 In life's short day, let me yet more
Of thy enlivening power implore;
My mind must deeper sink in thee,
My foot stand firm, from wandering free.

3 Take full possession of my heart;
The lowly mind of Christ impart;
I still will wait, O Lord, on thee,
Till, in thy light, the light I see.

RENEWAL.

---

563. S. M.

1 How blest is man, O God!
When first with single eye
He views the lustre of thy word,
The day-spring from on high!

2 Through storms that veil the skies,
And frown on earthly things,
The Sun of Righteousness breaks forth,
With healing on his wings.

3 Struck by that light, his heart,
A barren soil no more,
Sends shoots of righteousness abroad,
Where follies sprung before.

4 The soul so dreary once,
Once misery's dark domain,
Feels happiness unknown before,
And owns a heavenly reign.

564. C. M.

1 Give us ourselves and thee to know,
In this our gracious day;
Repentance unto life bestow,
And take our sins away.

2 Impoverish, Lord, and then relieve,
And then enrich the poor;
The knowledge of our sickness give,
The knowledge of our cure.

3 Convince us of our unbelief,
And freely then release;
Fill every soul with sacred grief,
And then with sacred peace.

565. S. M.

1 Thou must be born again!
Such was the solemn word
To him who came, not all in vain,
By night to seek his Lord.

2 Thou must be born again!
But not the birth of clay;
The immortal seed must thence obtain
Deliverance unto day.

3 Thou canst not choose but trace
The steps the Master trod,
If once thou feel his truth and grace,
A conscious child of God.

4 The mortal's birth is past;
The immortal's birth must be;
Seek well, and thou shalt find at last
That blest nativity.

566. S. M.

1 How glorious is the hour
When first our souls awake,
And through thy spirit's quickening power
Of the new life partake!

2 With richer beauty glows
The world, before so fair;
Her holy light religion throws,
Reflected everywhere.

3 Amid repentant tears
We feel sweet peace within;
We know the God of mercy hears,
And pardons every sin.

4 Born of thy spirit, Lord,
Thy spirit may we share;
Deep in our hearts inscribe thy word,
And place thine image there.

567. 7 & 6s. M.

1 A THOUSAND years have fleeted,
And, Saviour, still we see
Thy deed of love repeated
On all who come to thee.

As he who sat benighted,
  Afflicted, poor, and blind,
So now — thy word is plighted —
  Joy, light, and peace I find.

2 I came with steps that faltered,
  Thy course I felt thee check;
Then straight my mind was altered,
  And bowed my stubborn neck:
Thou saidst, "What art thou seeking?"
  "O Lord! that I might see."
O, then I heard thee speaking,
  "Believe, and it shall be!"

3 Our hope, Lord, faileth never,
  When thou thy word dost plight;
My fears then ceased for ever,
  And all my soul was light.
Thou gavest me thy blessing;
  From former guilt set free,
Now heavenly joy possessing,
  O Lord! I follow thee.

568. 8, 8, & 7s. M.

1 One thing first and only knowing,
Elsewhere not a thought bestowing,
  Now I quit the paths I trod;
Stranger to the world's vain pleasure,
Here I've no abiding treasure,
  Hid my life with Christ in God.

2 Let me now in thee inherit;
O, let heart and soul and spirit
  To thy service, Lord, be bowed!

Thine henceforth, O blessed Saviour!
May I, in my whole behaviour,
Practise what my lips have vowed.

3 No fatigue or pain declining,
All my heart to thee resigning,
I will go where thou dost lead;
If my every word and action
In thy sight give satisfaction,
Nothing more I then can need.

PRAYER.

---

569. S. M.

1 Our Heavenly Father, hear
The prayer we offer now:—
Thy name be hallowed far and near;
To thee all nations bow.

2 Thy kingdom come; thy will
On earth be done in love,
As saints and seraphim fulfil
Thy perfect law above.

3 Our daily bread supply,
While by thy word we live;
The guilt of our iniquity
Forgive, as we forgive.

4 From dark temptation's power
Our feeble hearts defend;
Deliver in the evil hour,
And guide us to the end.

5 Thine, then, for ever be
Glory and power divine;
The sceptre, throne, and majesty
Of heaven and earth are thine.

570. C. M.

1 Far from the world, O Lord! I flee,
From strife and tumult far;
From scenes, where Satan wages still
His most successful war.

2 The calm retreat, the silent shade,
With prayer and praise agree;
And seem, by thy sweet bounty, made
For those who follow thee.

3 There, if thy spirit touch the soul,
And grace her mean abode,
O, with what peace, and joy, and love,
She communes with her God!

4 Author and Guardian of my life,
Sweet Source of light divine,
And all harmonious names in one,
My Father,—thou art mine!

571. C. M.

1 Prayer is the soul's sincere desire,
Uttered or unexpressed;
The motion of a hidden fire
That trembles in the breast.

2 Prayer is the burden of a sigh,
  The falling of a tear;
The upward glancing of an eye,
  When none but God is near.

3 Prayer is the simplest form of speech
  That infant lips can try;
Prayer, the sublimest strains that reach
  The Majesty on high.

4 O thou, by whom we come to God,
  The Life, the Truth, the Way,
The path of prayer thyself hast trod;
  Lord, teach us how to pray!

572. L. M.

1 PRAYER is to God the soul's sure way;
  So flows the grace he waits to give;
Long as they live should Christians pray;
  They learn to pray when first they live.

2 If pain afflict or wrongs oppress,
  If cares distract or fears dismay,
If guilt deject, if sin distress,
  In every need still watch and pray.

3 'T is prayer supports the soul that 's weak,
  Though poor and broken be its word;
Pray if thou canst, or canst not, speak:
  The breathings of the soul are heard.

4 Depend on Him; thou shalt prevail;
  Make all thy wants and wishes known;
Fear not, his mercy will not fail;
  Ask but in faith, it shall be done.

573. 8 & 6s. M.

1 Meek hearts are by sweet manna fed,—
The Spirit and the Word;
Grace falls like dew upon the head
Of him whose sins are daily spread
In grief before the Lord.

2 My Saviour! see a suppliant bend,
Imploring thee to come,
And with the Spirit condescend
To sup with me, as friend with friend,
My honored heart thy home.

3 The prayer of faith grows wondrous bold,—
Vouchsafe, O God! to give;
Enlarge my heart with grace to hold
More than the highest heavens enfold,—
The God of Christ, and live.

574. P. M.

1 To prayer! for the day that God hath blest
Comes tranquilly on with its welcome rest.
It speaks of creation's early bloom;
It speaks of the Prince who burst the tomb.
Then summon the spirit's exalted powers,
And devote to Heaven the hallowed hours.

2 To prayer, to prayer! when the morning breaks,
And earth in her Maker's smile awakes;
His light is on all below and above,—
The light of gladness, of life, and of love,

O, then, on the breath of the early air,
Send up the incense of grateful prayer!

3 To prayer! when the glorious sun is gone,
And the gathering darkness of night comes on:
Like a curtain from God's kind hand it flows,
To shade the couch where his children repose.
Then kneel, while the watching stars are bright,
And give your last thoughts to the Guardian of
night.

575. C. M.

1 HAD I, dear Lord! no pleasure found
But in the thought of thee,
Prayer would have come unsought, and been
A truer liberty.

2 Yet thou art oft most present, Lord!
In weak, distracted prayer;
A sinner out of heart with self
Most often finds thee there.

3 And prayer that humbles sets the soul
From all illusions free,
And teaches it how utterly,
Dear Lord! it hangs on thee.

4 These surface troubles come and go,
Like rufflings of the sea;
The deeper depth is out of reach
To all, my God, but thee!

576. C. M.

1 Prayer is the spirit of our God
Returning whence it came;
Love is the sacred fire within,
And prayer the rising flame.

2 It gives the burdened soul repose,
And soothes the wounded breast;
Yields comfort to the mourner here,
And to the weary rest.

3 Prayer is the contrite sinner's voice,
Returning from his ways;
While angels in their songs rejoice,
And cry, "Behold, he prays!"

4 Prayer is the Christian's vital breath,
The Christian's native air,
His watchword at the gates of death;
He enters heaven with prayer.

577. C. M.

1 Lord, teach us how to pray aright,
With reverence and with fear:
Though dust and ashes in thy sight,
We may, we must, draw near.

2 Give deep humility; the sense
Of godly sorrow give;
A strong desiring confidence,
To hear thy voice and live; —

3 Patience, to watch, and wait, and weep,
Though mercy long delay;
Courage, our fainting souls to keep,
And trust thee, though thou slay.

4 Give these,—and then thy will be done;
Thus, strengthened with all might,
We, by thy Spirit and thy Son,
Shall pray, and pray aright.

578. L. M.

1 Prayer makes the darkened cloud withdraw;
Prayer climbs the ladder Jacob saw,
Gives exercise to faith and love,
Brings every blessing from above.

2 Have you no words? Ah! think again;
Words flow apace when you complain,
And fill your fellow-creature's ear
With the sad tale of all your care.

3 Were half the breath thus vainly spent
To Heaven in supplication sent,
Your cheerful song would oftener be,
"Hear what the Lord has done for me."

579. L. M.

1 O God, thou sovereign Lord of all,
The same through one eternal day,
Attend thy feeble children's call,
And, O, instruct us how to pray!

Pour out the supplicating grace,
And win the heart to seek thy face.

2 We shall not think a gracious thought,
We shall not feel a pure desire,
Till thou, who call'st a world from naught,
The power into our hearts inspire:
And then we in thy spirit come,
And then we give thee back thine own.

3 Come, in thy pleading spirit, down
To us, who for thy coming stay;
Of all thy gifts we ask but one,
We ask the constant power to pray;
O, grant us, Lord, this great request,
Thou canst not then deny the rest.

580. S. M.

1 THE praying spirit breathe,
The watching power impart,
From all entanglements beneath
Call off my peaceful heart:
My feeble mind sustain,
By worldly thoughts oppressed;
Appear, and bid me turn again
To my eternal rest.

2 Swift to my rescue come,
Thy own this moment seize;
Gather my wandering spirit home,
And keep in perfect peace:

Suffered no more to rove
O'er all the earth abroad,
Arrest the prisoner of thy love,
And shut me up in God.

581. S. M.

1 Come to the morning prayer,
Come, let us kneel and pray,—
Prayer is the Christian pilgrim's staff,
To walk with God all day.

2 At noon, beneath the Rock
Of Ages, rest and pray;
Sweet is that shelter from the heat,
When the sun smiles by day.

3 At evening, shut thy door,
Round the home altar pray;
And finding there the house of God,
At heaven's gate close the day.

4 When midnight veils our eyes,
O, it is sweet to say,
I sleep, but my heart waketh, Lord,
With thee to watch and pray!

ASPIRATION.

---

582. 7 & 6s. M.

1 Rise, my soul, and stretch thy wings;
Thy better portion trace;
Rise, from transitory things,
Towards heaven, thy native place:
Sun, and moon, and stars decay,
Time shall soon this earth remove;
Rise, my soul, and haste away
To seats prepared above.

2 Rivers to the ocean run,
Nor stay in all their course;
Fire ascending seeks the sun,—
Both speed them to their source:
So a soul that 's born of God
Pants to view his glorious face,
Upward tends to his abode,
To rest in his embrace.

583. C. M.

1 The bird let loose in Eastern skies,
Returning fondly home,
Ne'er stoops to earth her wing, nor flies
Where idler warblers roam.

2 But high she shoots through air and light,
Above all low delay,
Where nothing earthly bounds her flight,
Nor shadow dims her way.

3 So grant me, Lord, from every snare
Of sinful passion free,
Aloft through faith's serener air
To hold my course to thee.

4 No sin to cloud, no lure to stay
My soul, as home she springs;
Thy sunshine on her joyful way,
Thy freedom in her wings.

584. L. P. M.

1 Spring up, my soul, with ardent flight,
Nor let this earth delude thy sight
With glittering trifles gay and vain:
Wisdom divine directs thy view
To objects ever grand and new,
And faith displays the shining train.

2 Be dead, my hopes, to all below;
Nor let unbounded torrents flow,
When mourning o'er my withered joys:

So this deceitful world is known;
Possessed, I call it not my own,
Nor glory in its painted toys.

3 The empty pageant rolls along;
The giddy, inexperienced throng
Pursue it with enchanted eyes;
It passeth in swift march away;
Still more and more its charms decay,
Till the last gaudy color dies.

4 My God, to thee my soul shall turn;
For thee my noblest passions burn,
And drink in bliss from thee alone;
I fix on that unchanging home,
Where never-fading pleasures bloom,
Fresh springing round thy radiant throne.

585. S. M.

1 The fountain in its source
No drought of summer fears;
The farther it pursues its course,
The nobler it appears.

2 But shallow cisterns yield
A scanty, short supply;
The morning sees them amply filled,
At evening they are dry.

3 The cisterns I forsake,
O Fount of bliss, for thee!
My thirst with living waters slake,
And drink eternity.

586. 7s. M.

1 WHAT is this? and whither, whence,
This consuming secret sense,
Longing for its rest and food,
In some hidden, untried good?

2 'T is the soul, mysterious name!
God it seeks, from God it came;
While I muse I feel the fire,
Burning on, and mounting higher.

3 Onward, upward, to thy throne,
O thou Infinite, Unknown,
Still it presseth, till it see
Thee in all, and all in thee.

587. 6s. M.

1 I FEEL within a want
For ever burning there;
What I so thirst for, grant,
O Thou who hearest prayer!

2 This is the thing I crave,
A likeness to thy Son;
This would I rather have
Than call the world my own.

3 'T is my most fervent prayer;
Be it more fervent still,
Be it my highest care,
Be it my settled will.

588. 8 & 7s. M.

1 Hath the immortal spirit freedom,
Mated with its mortal clod?
Lo! it soars, and, faith-supported,
Claims affinity with God.

2 Proudly it disclaims the shackles
Of the frame to which it clings,
And would fly to heights celestial
Upon love's angelic wings.

3 But the hand of Law restrains it;
Narrow is the widest span,
Measured by the deeds or efforts
Of the aspiring soul of man.

4 Yet, O soul! there 's freedom for thee;
Thou mayst win it;—not below;
Not on earth, with mortal vesture,
Where to love, to feel, to know,

5 Is to suffer; but, unfettered,
Thou mayst spring to riper life,
Purified from hate and evil,
And mortality and strife.

6 Be thou meek to exaltation,—
Death shall give thee wings to soar;
Loving God, and knowing all things,
Upward springing evermore.

589. 10 & 6s. M.

1 Dear, beauteous Death; the jewel of the just!
Shining nowhere but in the dark;
What mysteries do lie beyond thy dust,
Could man outlook that mark!

2 O holy hope! and high humility!
High as the heavens above!
These are your walks, and you have showed them me
To kindle my cold love.

3 And yet, as angels in some brighter dreams
Call to the soul, where man doth sleep,
So some strange thoughts transcend our wonted themes,
And into glory peep.

4 O Father of eternal life, and all
Created glories under thee!
Resume thy spirit from this world of thrall
Into true liberty!

590. L. M.

1 O Love, of pure and heavenly birth!
O simple Truth, scarce known on earth!
Whom men resist with stubborn will,
And, more perverse and daring still,
Smother and quench with reasonings vain,
While error and deception reign;—

2 Whence comes it, that, your power the same
As His on high, from whom you came,
Ye rarely find a listening ear,
Or heart, that makes you welcome here?
Because ye bring reproach and pain,
Where'er ye visit, in your train.

3 Then let the price be what it may,
Though poor, I am prepared to pay:
Come shame, come sorrow; spite of tears,
Weakness, and heart-oppressing fears;
One soul, at least, shall not repine
To give you room;— come, reign in mine!

591. 7s. M.

1 King of mercy, King of love,
In whom I live, in whom I move,
Perfect what thou hast begun,
Let no night put out the sun.

2 Grant I may, my chief Desire,
Long for thee, to thee aspire!
Let my youth, my bloom of days,
Be my comfort and thy praise;

3 That hereafter, when I look
O'er the sullied, sinful book,
I may find thy hand therein
Wiping out my shame and sin.

592. 10s. M.

1 Unseen, yet not unfelt! — if any thought
Has raised our mind from earth, — a pure desire,
A glorious act, a noble purpose brought, —
It is thy breath, O Lord, which fans the fire.

2 To me, the meanest of thy creatures, kneeling,
Conscious of weakness, ignorance, sin, and shame,
Give such a force of holy thought and feeling,
That I may live to glorify thy name.

3 I am unworthy; — yet for their dear sake
I ask, whose roots in me are planted found;
For precious vines are propped by rudest stake,
And heavenly roses fed in darkest ground.

4 And let not all the pains and toil be wasted,
Spent on my youth by saints now gone to rest,
Nor that deep sorrow my Redeemer tasted,
When on his soul the guilt of man was pressed.

5 Let all this goodness by my soul be seen,
Let all this mercy on my heart be sealed;
Lord, if thou wilt, thy power can make me clean;
O, speak the word, thy servant shall be healed!

593. 7s. M.

1 Lord! we sit and cry to thee,
Like the blind beside the way:

Make our darkened souls to see
  The glory of thy perfect day:
Lord! rebuke our sullen night,
And give thyself unto our sight.

2 Lord! we do not ask to gaze
  On our dim and earthly sun;
But the light that still shall blaze
  When every star its course hath run,
The glory of thy blest abode,
The uncreated light of God.

594. L. M.

1 LORD, thou wouldst have us like to thee;
  Lord, thou wouldst lift us to thy Son:
Thou biddest us aspirants be,—
  Put all divine ambition on!

2 We cannot be too richly blest,—
  We cannot be too strong of wing:
Thyself, thyself, thou offerest
  To our sublime endeavoring.

3 Thou Sovereign Lord Almighty, lo!
  On, on to thee the weaklings press,
From strength to strength our souls would go,
  Up-climbing thine Almightiness.

4 All-holy One! we give not o'er;
  We sinners would be one with thee!
Yes, all-prevailingly explore,
  Depth after depth, thy purity.

5 Alas our wrath! alas our pride!
Yet shall they not at last be gone?
O, may we not each day abide
Still nearer the All-loving One?

6 Father of lights! our darkness dares
Hope into something bright to rise,
Each well-won truth our souls declares
Of closer kin to thee, All-Wise.

7 Would we not grow divinely bright?
Take sweetness in, put glory on,—
Yes, wax more worthy to delight
In thee, First Fair, All-glorious One?

595. 10s. M.

1 Father divine! this deadening power control,
Which to the senses binds the immortal soul;
O, break this bondage, Lord! I would be free,
And in my soul would find my heaven in thee.

2 My heaven in thee! O God, no other heaven
To the immortal soul can e'er be given;
O, let thy kingdom now within me come,
And as above, so here, thy will be done!

3 My heaven in thee, O Father, let me find,
My heaven in thee, within a heart resigned;
No more, of heaven and bliss, my soul, despair;
For where my God is found, my heaven is there.

596. 7s. M.

1 As the hart, with eager looks,
Panteth for the water-brooks,
So my soul, athirst for thee,
Pants the living God to see;
When, O, when, with filial fear,
Lord, shall I to thee draw near?

2 Why art thou cast down, my soul?
God, thy God, shall make thee whole:
Why art thou disquieted?
God shall lift thy fallen head,
And his countenance benign
Be the saving health of thine.

597. L. M.

1 O, DRAW me, Father, after thee,
So shall I run, and never tire;
With gracious words still comfort me;
Be thou my hope, my sole desire;
Free me from every weight; nor fear
Nor sin can come, if thou art here.

2 From all eternity, with love
Unchangeable thou hast me viewed;
Ere knew this beating heart to move,
Thy tender mercies me pursued;
Ever with me may they abide,
And close me in on every side.

3 In suffering be thy love my peace,
In weakness be thy love my power;
And when the strength of life shall cease,
My God! in that important hour,
In death as life be thou my Guide,
And bear me through death's whelming tide.

598. L. M.

1 O THAT my heart was right with thee,
And loved thee with a perfect love!
O that my Lord would dwell in me,
And never from his seat remove!

2 Father, I dwell in mournful night,
Till thou dost in my heart appear;
Arise, propitious sun! and light
An everlasting morning there.

3 O, let my prayer acceptance find,
And bring the mighty blessing down;
Eyesight impart, for I am blind;
And seal me thine adopted son.

599. C. M.

1 BE thou, O God, by night, by day,
My Guide, my Guard from sin,
My Life, my Trust, my Light Divine,
To keep me pure within;—

2 Pure as the air, when day's first light
A cloudless sky illumes;

And active as the lark, that soars
  Till heaven shines round its plumes.

3 So may my soul, upon the wings
  Of faith, unwearied rise,
Till at the gate of heaven it sings,
  Midst light from paradise.

600. P. M.

1 NEARER, my God, to thee,
  Nearer to thee!
E'en though it be a cross
  That raiseth me:
Still all my song would be,
Nearer, my God, to thee, —
  Nearer to thee!

2 Though like the wanderer,
  The sun gone down,
Darkness be over me,
  My rest a stone;
Yet in my dreams I'd be,
Nearer, my God, to thee, —
  Nearer to thee!

3 There let the way appear
  Steps unto heaven;
All that thou sendest me
  In mercy given;
Angels to beckon me
Nearer, my God, to thee, —
  Nearer to thee!

4 Then with my waking thoughts
  Bright with thy praise,
Out of my stony griefs
  Bethel I 'll raise:
So by my woes to be
Nearer, my God, to thee,—
  Nearer to thee!

5 Or if on joyful wing
  Cleaving the sky,
Sun, moon, and stars forgot,
  Upwards I fly,
Still all my song shall be,
Nearer my God to thee,—
  Nearer to thee!

CONSECRATION.

---

601. L. M.

1 O Lord, thy heavenly grace impart,
And fix my frail, inconstant heart;
Henceforth my chief desire shall be
To dedicate myself to thee.

2 Whate'er pursuits my time employ,
One thought shall fill my soul with joy;
That silent, secret thought shall be,
That all my hopes are fixed on thee.

3 Thy glorious eye pervadeth space;
Thy presence, Lord, fills every place;
And, wheresoe'er my lot may be,
Still shall my spirit cleave to thee.

4 Renouncing every worldly thing,
And safe beneath thy sheltering wing,
My sweetest thought henceforth shall be,
That all I want I find in thee.

602. L. M.

1 Behold! the servant of the Lord,
I wait thy guiding hand to feel;
To hear and keep thy every word,—
To prove and do thy perfect will:
Joyful from my own works to cease,
Glad to fulfil all righteousness.

2 My every weak, though good design,
O'errule or change, as seemeth meet
Jesus, let all my work be thine!
Thy work, O Lord, is all complete,
And pleasing in thy Father's sight;
Thou only hast done all things right.

3 Here, then, to thee thine own I leave;
Mould as thou wilt thy passive clay;
But let me all thy stamp receive,—
But let me all thy words obey:
Serve with a single heart and eye,
And to thy glory live and die.

603. C. M.

1 Father, I know that all my life
Is portioned out to me,
The changes that must surely come,
I do not fear to see;
I ask thee for the present mind,
Intent on pleasing thee.

2 I ask thee for a thankful love,
Through constant watching wise,
To meet the glad with cheerful smile,
And wipe the weeping eyes;
A heart at leisure from itself,
To soothe and sympathize.

3 I would not have the restless will,
That hurries to and fro,
Seeking for some great thing to do,
Or secret thing to know;
I would be dealt with as a child,
And guided where to go.

4 Wherever in the world I am,
In whatsoe'er estate,
I would have fellowship with hearts
To keep and cultivate;
A work of holy love to do,
For Him on whom I wait.

604. 7s. M.

1 As earth's pageant passes by,
Let reflection turn thine eye
Inward, and observe thy breast;
There alone dwells solid rest.

2 That 's a close-immurèd tower,
Which can mock all hostile power;
To thyself a tenant be,
And inhabit safe and free.

3 Say not that this house is small,
Girt up in a narrow wall;
In a cleanly, sober mind,
Heaven itself full room doth find.

4 The Infinite Creator can
Dwell in it; and may not man?
Here, content, make thy abode
With thyself and with thy God.

605. S. M.

1 Behold what wondrous grace
The Father has bestowed
On sinners of a mortal race,
To call them sons of God!

2 Nor doth it yet appear
How great we must be made;
But when we see our Saviour here,
We shall be like our Head.

3 We would no longer lie
Like slaves beneath the throne;
My faith shall Abba, Father, cry,
And thou the kindred own.

606. L. M.

1 'T is not the skill of human art,
Which gives me power my God to know;
The sacred lessons of the heart
Come not from instruments below.

2 Love is my teacher; he can tell
The wonders that he learnt above:
No other master knows so well;—
'T is Love alone can tell of Love.

3 Love is my master; when it breaks,
The morning light, with rising ray,
To thee, O God! my spirit wakes,
And Love instructs it all the day.

4 And when the gleams of day retire,
And midnight spreads its dark control,
Love's secret whispers still inspire
Their holy lessons in the soul.

607. 8 & 7s. M.

1 Know, my soul, thy full salvation;
Rise o'er sin, and fear, and care;
Joy to find, in every station,
Something still to do or bear:
Think what spirit dwells within thee;
Think what Father's smiles are thine;
Think what Jesus did to win thee:
Child of heaven, canst thou repine?

2 Haste thee on from grace to glory,
Armed by faith and winged by prayer;
Heaven's eternal day 's before thee;
God's own hand shall guide thee there:
Soon shall close thy earthly mission;
Soon shall pass thy pilgrim days;
Hope shall change to glad fruition,
Faith to sight, and prayer to praise.

608. P. M.

1 As, down in the sunless retreats of the ocean,
Sweet flowers are springing no mortal can see,
So, deep in my heart, the still prayer of devotion,
Unheard by the world, rises, silent, to thee,
My God! silent, to thee,—
Pure, warm, silent, to thee.

2 As still to the star of its worship, though clouded,
The needle points faithfully o'er the dim sea,
So, dark as I roam, thro' this wintry world shrouded,
The hope of my spirit turns, trembling, to thee,
My God! trembling, to thee,—
True, fond, trembling, to thee.

609. C. M.

1 O LOVE! O true and fadeless light!
And shall it ever be,
That after all our toils and tears
Thy Sabbath we shall see?

2 'Mid thousand fears and dangers now
We sow our seed with prayer,
But know that joyful hands shall reap
The shining harvests there.

3 O God of justice, God of power!
Our faith and hope increase,
And crown them, in the future years,
With endless love and peace.

610. L. M.

1 Thou hidden love of God, whose height,
Whose depth unfathomed, no man knows;
I see from far thy beauteous light,
Inly I sigh for thy repose.
My heart is pained; nor can it be
At rest, till it find rest in thee.

2 'T is mercy all, that thou hast brought
My mind to seek her peace in thee:
Yet, while I seek, but find thee not,
No peace my wandering soul shall see.
O, when shall all my wanderings end,
And all my steps to thee-ward tend!

3 Is there a thing beneath the sun,
That strives with thee my heart to share?
Ah! tear it thence, and reign alone,
The Lord of every motion there!
Then shall my heart from earth be free,
When it hath found repose in thee.

611. 8 & 7s. M.

1 Take my heart, O Father, take it,
Make and keep it all thine own;
Let thy Spirit melt and break it, —
This proud heart of sin and stone.

2 Father! make it pure and lowly,
Fond of peace and far from strife,

Turning from the paths unholy
  Of this vain and sinful life.

3 Ever let thy grace surround it,
  Strengthen it with power divine,
Till thy cords of love have bound it
  Make it to be wholly thine.

4 May the blood of Jesus heal it,
  And its sins be all forgiven;
Holy Spirit, take and seal it,—
  Guide it in the path to heaven.

612. C. M.

1 Unite, my roving thoughts, unite
  In silence soft and sweet:
And thou, my soul, sit gently down
  At thy great Sovereign's feet.

2 Jehovah's awful voice is heard,
  Yet gladly I attend;
For lo! the everlasting God
  Proclaims himself my friend.

3 Harmonious accents to my soul
  The sound of peace convey;
The tempest at his word subsides,
  And winds and seas obey.

4 By all its joys I charge my heart
  To grieve his love no more;
But, charmed by melody divine,
  To give its follies o'er.

613. 10s. M.

1 FATHER, there is no change to live with thee,
Save that in Christ I grow from day to day;
In each new word I hear, each thing I see,
I but rejoicing hasten on my way.

2 The morning comes, with blushes overspread,
And I, new wakened, find a morn within,
And in its modest dawn around me shed,
Thou hear'st the prayer and the ascending hymn.

3 Hour follows hour, the lengthening shades descend;
Yet they could never reach as far as me,
Did not thy love its kind protection lend,
That I, thy child, might sleep in peace with thee.

614. L. M.

1 THOU hidden source of calm repose,
Thou all-sufficient love divine,
My help and refuge from my foes,
Secure I am, if thou art mine!
And, lo! from sin, and grief, and shame
I hide me, Father, in thy name.

2 Father, my all in all thou art,
My rest in toil, my ease in pain;
The healing of my broken heart;
In strife, my peace; in loss, my gain;
My smile beneath the tyrant's frown;
In shame, my glory and my crown;—

3 In want, my plentiful supply;
 In weakness, my almighty power;
In bonds, my perfect liberty;
 My light in evil's darkest hour;
In grief, my joy unspeakable;
My life in death, my all in all.

615. S. M.

1 When shall thy love constrain,
 And force me to thy breast?
When shall my soul return again
 To God, her only rest!

2 Ah! what avails my strife,
 My wandering to and fro!
Thou giv'st the words of endless life:
 Ah! whither should I go?

3 Thy condescending grace
 To me did freely move;
It calls me still to seek thy face,
 And stoops to ask my love.

4 Here at thy feet I fall,
 I long to be made free;
I fain would now obey the call,
 And give up all for thee.

616. C. P. M.

1 How happy are the new-born race,
Partakers of adopting grace!
 How pure the bliss they share!

Hid from the world and all its eyes,
Within their heart the blessing lies,
And conscience feels it there.

2 The moment we believe, 't is ours;
And if we love with all our powers
The God from whom it came,
And if we serve with hearts sincere,
'T is still discernible and clear,
An undisputed claim.

3 O messenger of dear delight!
Whose voice dispels the deepest night,
Sweet, peace-proclaiming Dove!
With thee at hand to soothe our pains,
No wish unsatisfied remains,
No task but that of love.

617. C. M.

1 She loved her Saviour, and to him
Her costliest present brought;
To crown his head, or grace his name,
No gift too rare she thought.

2 So let the Saviour be adored,
And not the poor despised,
Give to the hungry from your hoard,
But all, give all to Christ.

3 Go, clothe the naked, lead the blind,
Give to the weary rest;
For sorrow's children comfort find,
And help for all distressed; —

4 But give to Christ alone thy heart,
Thy faith, thy love supreme;
Then for his sake thine alms impart,
And so give all to him.

618. L. M.

1 O HUMAN heart! thou hast a song
For all that to the earth belong,
Whene'er the golden chain of love
Hath linked thee to the heaven above.

2 O human heart! what deed of thine
Could gain a kingdom so divine?
'T was asked but this, in accents mild,
The gentle spirit of a child.

3 O human heart! that singest still,
Through chastening good, misreckoned ill,
Thou mind'st Bethesda's fount to feel,
The angel troubles but to heal.

4 O human heart! thou hast a song
For all that to the earth belong,
Whene'er the golden chain of love
Hath linked thee to the heaven above.

619. C. M.

1 ALAS the outer emptiness!
What life has it to give?
O, shall it God's own fire oppress?
Soul, wilt thou slightly live?

2 Some joy of thine own seeking win;
To thine own strength repair:
Breathe, breathe the awful life within, —
Feel all the glory there!

3 Thyself amidst the silence clear,
The world far off and dim,
Thy vision free, the Bright One near,
Thyself alone with Him.

4 The silence throngèd gloriously
With business how divine!
God's glory passing unto thee, —
All heaven becoming thine.

5 The rapture, mighty, measureless,
In each eternal thing, —
The mingling with Almightiness, —
The dwelling by Life's Spring!

6 Thus sweetly live, thus greatly watch, —
Soul, be but inly bright!
All outer things must smile, must catch
Thy strong, transcendent light.

7 Near thee no darkness dares abide,
Thou makest all things shine;
Soul, whom the Lord has glorified,
Is not all glory thine?

620. S. M.

1 The thing my God doth hate
That I no more may do,
Thy creature, Lord, again create,
And all my soul renew:

My soul shall then, like thine,
Abhor the thing unclean,
And, sanctified by love divine,
For ever cease from sin.

2 That blessed law of thine,
Father, to me impart;
The Spirit's law of life divine,
O, write it in my heart!
Implant it deep within,
Whence it may ne'er remove,
The law of liberty from sin,
The perfect law of love.

3 Thy nature be my law,
Thy spotless sanctity,
And sweetly every moment draw
My happy soul to thee.
Soul of my soul remain!
Who didst for all fulfil,
In me, O Lord, fulfil again
My Heavenly Father's will.

621. L. M.

1 O Thou, who hast at thy command
The hearts of all men in thy hand!
Our wayward, erring hearts incline
To have no other will but thine.

2 Our wishes, our desires, control;
Mould every purpose of the soul;
O'er all may we victorious be
That stands between ourselves and thee.

3 Thrice blest will all our blessings be,
When we can look through them to thee,
When each glad heart its tribute pays
Of love, and gratitude, and praise.

4 And while we to thy glory live,
May we to thee all glory give,
Until the final summons come,
That calls thy willing servants home.

622. S. M.

1 Our heaven is everywhere,
If we but love the Lord,
Unswerving tread the narrow way,
And ever shun the broad.

2 'T is where the trusting heart
Bows meekly to its grief,
Still looking up with earnest faith
For comfort and relief;—

3 Where guileless infancy
In happiness doth dwell,
And where the aged one can say,
"He hath done all things well."

4 Wherever truth abides,
Sweet peace is ever there;
If we but love and serve the Lord,
Our heaven is everywhere.

623. C. M.

1 I WANT a principle within
Of jealous, godly fear;
A sensibility of sin,
A pain to find it near.

2 I want the first approach to feel
Of pride or fond desire;
To catch the wandering of my will,
And quench the kindling fire.

3 From thee that I no more may part,
No more thy goodness grieve,
The filial awe, the fleshly heart,
The tender conscience, give.

4 Quick as the apple of the eye,
O God, my conscience make!
Awake my soul when sin is nigh,
And keep it still awake.

624. C. M.

1 O FOR a closer walk with God!
A calm and heavenly frame!
A light to shine upon the road
That leads me to the Lamb!

2 What peaceful hours I once enjoyed!
How sweet their memory still!
But now I find an aching void
The world can never fill.

3 Return, O holy Dove! return,
Sweet messenger of rest!
I hate the sins that made thee mourn,
And drove thee from my breast.

4 The dearest idol I have known,
Whate'er that idol be,
Help me to tear it from thy throne,
And worship only thee.

625. C. M.

1 LET Him, to whom we now belong,
His sovereign right assert,
And take up every thankful song,
And every loving heart.

2 He justly claims us for his own,
Who bought us with a price;
The Christian lives to God alone,
To God alone he dies!

3 Father, thine own at last receive;
Fulfil our hearts' desire,
And let us to thy glory live,
And in thy cause expire.

4 Our souls and bodies we resign;
With joy we render thee
Our all, no longer ours, but thine
To all eternity.

626. 7s. M.

1 Father, they who thee receive,
And in thee begin to live,
Day and night they cry to thee,
As thou art, so let us be.

2 Fix, O, fix my wavering mind!
To the cross my spirit bind:
Earthly passions far remove;
Fill the soul with perfect love.

3 Who in heart on thee believes,
He the promise now receives;
He with joy beholds thy face,
Triumphs in thy pardoning grace.

4 Boundless wisdom, power divine,
Love unspeakable, are thine:
Praise by all to thee be given,
Sons of earth, and hosts of heaven.

627. S. M.

1 Father, my lifted eye
Be fixed on thee alone;
Thy name be praised on earth, on high;
Thy will by all be done.

2 Spirit of faith, inspire
My consecrated heart;
Fill me with pure celestial fire,
With all thou hast and art.

628. C. P. M.

1 Father! on me the grace bestow,
Which all that feel shall surely know,
Their sins on earth forgiven;
Give me to prove the kingdom mine,
And taste, in holiness divine,
The happiness of heaven.

2 Come, and thy crowning grace impart!
Bless me with purity of heart!
That, now beholding thee,
I soon may view thy open face,
On all thy glorious beauties gaze,
And God for ever see.

629. S. M.

1 Teach me, my God and King,
In all things thee to see;
And what I do in any thing,
To do it as for thee!

2 To scorn the senses' sway,
While still to thee I tend;
In all I do, be thou the way;
In all, be thou the end.

3 All may of thee partake:
Nothing so small can be,
But draws, when acted for thy sake,
Greatness and worth from thee.

4 If done beneath thy laws,
E'en servile labors shine;
Hallowed is toil, if this the cause,
The meanest work divine.

630. L. M.

1 Great God! my Father and my Friend,
On whom I cast my constant care,
On whom for all things I depend!
To thee I raise my humble prayer.

2 Endue me with a holy fear;
The frailty of my heart reveal;
Sin and its snares are always near,
Thee may I always nearer feel.

3 O that to thee my constant mind
May with a steady flame aspire;
Pride in its earliest motions find,
And check the rise of wrong desire!

4 O that my watchful soul may fly
The first perceived approach of sin;
Look up to thee when danger 's nigh,
And feel thy fear control within!

GENTLENESS AND HUMILITY.

---

631. C. M.

1 Thy home is with the humble, Lord!
The simplest are the best;
Thy lodging is in child-like hearts;
Thou makest there thy rest.

2 Dear Comforter! Eternal Love!
If thou wilt stay with me,
Of lowly thoughts and simple ways
I'll build a house for thee.

3 Who made this beating heart of mine
But thou, my heavenly Guest?
Let no one have it, then, but thee,
And let it be thy rest.

632. C. M.

1 He that is down need fear no fall,
He that is low no pride;
He that is humble ever shall
Have God to be his guide.

2 Fulness to such a burden is,
That go on pilgrimage;
Here little, and hereafter bliss,
Is best from age to age.

633. L. M.

1 The bird that soars on highest wing
Builds on the ground her lowly nest;
And she that doth most sweetly sing
Sings in the shade when all things rest:—
In lark and nightingale we see
What honor hath humility.

2 When Mary chose the better part,
She meekly sat at Jesus' feet;
And Lydia's gently opened heart
Was made for God's own temple meet:—
Fairest and best adorned is she
Whose clothing is humility.

3 The saint that wears heaven's brightest crown
In deepest adoration bends;
The weight of glory bows him down,
Then most when most his soul ascends:—
Nearest the throne itself must be
The footstool of humility.

634. L. M.

1 Blest are the humble souls that see
Their emptiness and poverty;
Treasures of grace to them are given,
And crowns of joy laid up in heaven.

2 Blest are the meek, who stand afar
From rage and passion, noise and war;
God will secure their happy state,
And plead their cause against the great.

3 Blest are the pure, whose hearts are clean
From the defiling powers of sin;
With endless pleasure they shall see
A God of spotless purity.

635. 7s. M.

1 Lord, that I may learn of thee,
Give me true simplicity;
Wean my soul, and keep it low,
Willing thee alone to know.

2 Let me cast my reeds aside,
All that feeds my knowing pride;
Not to man, but God, submit,
Lay my reasonings at thy feet;—

3 Of my boasted wisdom spoiled,
Docile, helpless as a child;
Only seeing in thy light,
Only walking in thy might.

4 Then infuse the teaching grace,
Spirit of true righteousness;
Knowledge, love divine, impart,
Life eternal to my heart.

636. L. M.

1 WHEREFORE should man, frail child of clay,
Who, from the cradle to the shroud,
Lives but the insect of a day,—
O, why should mortal man be proud?

2 By doubt perplexed, in error lost,
With trembling step he seeks his way:
How vain of wisdom's gift the boast!
Of reason's lamp, how faint the ray!

3 Follies and sins, a countless sum,
Are crowded in life's little span:
How ill, alas! does pride become
That erring, guilty creature, man!

4 God of my life! Father divine!
Give me a meek and lowly mind:
In modest worth, O, let me shine,
And peace in humble virtue find.

637. P. M.

1 SOUL! couldst thou while on earth remaining
A childlike frame be still retaining,
With thee e'en here, I know full well,
God and his paradise would dwell.

2 O childhood! well beloved of Heaven,
Whose mind to Christ alone is given,
How longs my heart to feel like thee!
O Jesus, form thyself in me!

3 Lord! let me, while on earth remaining,
Such childlike frame be still retaining;
With me then here, I know full well,
God and his paradise will dwell.

638. L. M.

1 AND is the Gospel peace and love?
So let our conversation be;
The serpent blended with the dove,
Wisdom and meek simplicity.

2 Whene'er the angry passions rise,
And tempt our thoughts or tongues to strife,
On Jesus let us fix our eyes,
Bright pattern of the Christian life!

3 O, how benevolent and kind!
How mild! how ready to forgive!
Be this the temper of our mind,
And his the rules by which we live.

639. S. M.

1 O, ARM me with the mind,
Saviour, that was in thee!
And let my fervid zeal be joined
With perfect charity.

2 Control my every thought;
My whole of sin remove;
Let all my works in thee be wrought;
Let all be wrought in love.

3 O, may I learn the art,
With meekness to reprove!
To hate the sin with all my heart,
But still the sinner love.

640. C. M.

1 SPEAK gently, — it is better far
To rule by love than fear;
Speak gently, — let no harsh word mar
The good we may do here.

2 Speak gently to the young, — for they
Will have enough to bear;
Pass through this life as best they may,
'T is full of anxious care.

3 Speak gently to the aged one,
Grieve not the careworn heart;
The sands of life are nearly run,
Let them in peace depart.

4 Speak gently to the erring ones, —
They must have toiled in vain;
Perchance unkindness made them so;
O, win them back again!

5 Speak gently, — 't is a little thing,
Dropped in the heart's deep well;
The good, the joy, that it may bring,
Eternity shall tell.

641. 7s. M.

1 LORD, if thou thy grace impart,
Poor in spirit, meek in heart,

We shall, as our Master, be
Rooted in humility;—

2 Simple, teachable, and mild,
Like unto a little child;
Pleased with all the Lord provides;
Weaned from all the world besides.

3 Father, fix our souls on thee;
Every evil let us flee;
Nothing want, beneath, above,
Happy in thy precious love.

4 O, that all may seek and find
Every good in Jesus joined!
Him let every soul adore,
Trust him, praise him, evermore.

642. C. M.

1 Father, whate'er of earthly bliss
Thy sovereign will denies,
Accepted at thy throne, let this,
My humble prayer, arise:—

2 Give me a calm and thankful heart,
From every murmur free;
The blessings of thy grace impart,
And make me live to thee;—

3 Let the sweet hope that thou art mine
My life and death attend,
Thy presence through my journey shine,
And bless my journey's end.

GRATITUDE.

---

643. L. M.

1 My soul! what hast thou done for God?
Look o'er thy misspent years and see;
Sum up what thou hast done for God,
And then what God hath done for thee.

2 He made thee when he might have made
A soul that would have loved him more;
He rescued thee from nothingness,
And set thee on life's happy shore.

3 He gave thee rights thou couldst not claim;
He gave his love no Sabbath rest,
Still plotting happiness for men,
And new designs to make them blest.

4 The Son hath come; and maddened sin
The world's Redeemer crucified;
The Spirit comes, and stays, while men
His presence doubt, his gifts deride.

5 Yet still the sun is fair by day,
The moon still beautiful by night;
The world goes round, and joy with it,
And life, free life, is men's delight.

6 And now the Father keeps himself,
In patient and forbearing love,
To be his creature's heritage
In that undying life above.

644. L. M.

1 If all our hopes and all our fears
Were prisoned in life's narrow bound;
If, travellers through this vale of tears,
We saw no better world beyond;—

2 O, who could check the rising sigh?
What earthly thing could pleasure give?
O, who would venture then to die?
O, who could then endure to live?

3 And such were life, without the ray
From our divine religion given;
'T is this that makes our darkness day;
'T is this that makes our earth a heaven.

4 Bright is the golden sun above,
And beautiful the flowers that bloom;
And all is joy, and all is love,
Reflected from a world to come.

645. 8 & 7s. M.

1 Lord, with fervor I would praise thee,
For the bliss thy love bestows,
For the pardoning grace that saves me,
And the peace that from it flows:
Help, O God, my weak endeavor;
This dull soul to rapture raise;
Thou must light the flame, or never
Can my love be warmed to praise.

2 Praise, my soul, the God that sought thee,
Wretched wanderer, far astray,
Found thee lost, and kindly brought thee
From the paths of death away;
Praise, with love's devoutest feeling,
Him who saw thy guilt-born fear,
And, the light of hope revealing,
Bade the blood-stained cross appear.

3 Lord, this bosom's ardent feeling
Vainly would my lips express;
Low before thy footstool kneeling,
Deign thy suppliant's prayer to bless.
Let thy grace, my soul's chief treasure,
Love's pure flame within me raise,
And, since words can never measure,
Let my life show forth thy praise

CONFIDENCE AND JOY.

---

646. S. M.

1 Give to the winds thy fears;
Hope and be undismayed;
God hears thy sighs, God counts thy tears;
God shall lift up thy head.

2 Through waves, through clouds and storms,
He gently clears thy way;
Wait thou his time; so shall the night
Soon end in joyous day.

3 He everywhere hath rule,
And all things serve his might;
His every act pure blessing is,
His path unsullied light.

4 Let us, in life or death,
Boldly thy truth declare;
And publish, with our latest breath,
Thy love and guardian care.

647. C. M.

1 Mere human powers shall fast decay,
And youthful vigor cease;
But those who wait upon the Lord
In strength shall still increase.

2 They with unwearied feet shall tread
The path of life divine;
With growing ardor onward move,
With growing brightness shine.

648. L. M.

1 How rich the blessings, O my God,
Which teach this grateful heart to glow!
How kindly poured, and free bestowed,
The rivers of thy mercy flow.

2 How calmly rolls the sea of life!
Secure in thine immortal trust,
The soul has hushed her secret strife,
Nor longer shudders at the dust.

3 Though sorrow's cloud awhile o'ercast
The dawn of earthly hope and joy,
She knows that it must soon be past,
And will unveil eternity.

4 Then virtue's humble toil and prayer
Shall stand acknowledged at thy throne,
Triumphant over earthly care,
And the blest record thou wilt own.

649. 7 & 6s. M.

1 Sometimes a light surprises
The Christian while he sings;
It is the Lord, who rises
With healing in his wings:
When comforts are declining,
He grants the soul again
A season of clear shining,
To cheer it after rain.

2 In holy contemplation,
We sweetly then pursue
The theme of God's salvation,
And find it ever new:
Set free from present sorrow,
We cheerfully can say,
"E'en let the unknown morrow
Bring with it what it may."

3 It can bring with it nothing,
But he will bear us through;
Who gives the lilies clothing,
Will clothe his people too:
Beneath the spreading heavens,
No creature but is fed;
And he who feeds the ravens
Will give his children bread.

650. 7s. M.

1 Hope, though slow she be, and late,
Yet outruns swift time and fate;

And aforehand loves to be
With remote futurity.

2 Hope is comfort in distress;
Hope is in misfortune bliss;
Hope, in sorrow, is delight;
Hope is day in darkest night.

3 Hope casts anchor upward, where
Storms durst never domineer;
Trust, and Hope will welcome thee
From storms to full security.

651. C. M.

1 The world may change from old to new,
From new to old again;
Yet hope and heaven, for ever true,
Within man's heart remain.
The dreams that bless the weary soul,
The struggles of the strong,
Are steps towards some happy goal,
The story of hope's song.

2 Hope leads the child to plant the flower,
The man to sow the seed;
Nor leaves fulfilment to her hour,
But prompts again to deed.
And ere upon the old man's dust
The grass is seen to wave,
We look through falling tears, — to trust
Hope's sunshine on the grave.

652. 7s. M.

1 All before us lies the way,
Give the past unto the wind;
All before us is the day,
Night and darkness are behind.

2 Eden, with its angels bold,
Love and flowers and coolest sea,
Is less ancient story told,
Than a glowing prophecy.

3 In the spirit's perfect air,
In the passions tame and kind,
Innocence from selfish care,
The real Eden we shall find.

4 When the soul to sin hath died,
True and beautiful and sound,
Then all earth is sanctified,
Upsprings paradise around.

5 From this spirit-land afar,
All disturbing force shall flee;
Stir, nor toil, nor hope, shall mar
Its immortal unity.

653. 7 & 6s. M.

1 God is my strong salvation;
What foe have I to fear?
In darkness and temptation,
My Light, my Help, is near:

Though hosts encamp around me,
Firm in the fight I stand;
What terror can confound me,
With God at my right hand?

2 Place on the Lord reliance;
My soul, with courage wait;
His truth be thine affiance,
When faint and desolate;
His might thy heart shall strengthen,
His love thy joy increase;
Mercy thy days shall lengthen;
The Lord will give thee peace.

654. L. M.

1 Thy happy ones a strain begin:
Dost thou not, Lord, glad souls possess?
Thy cheerful spirit dwells within;
We feel thee in our joyfulness.

2 Our mirth is not afraid of thee;
Our life rejoices to be bright;
We would not from our gladness flee,
But give full welcome to delight.

3 Thou wilt not, Lord, our smiles deny:
Dost thou not deem them of rich worth?
Our cheer flows on beneath thine eye;
We feel accepted in our mirth.

4 We turn to thee a smiling face,
Thou sendest us the smile again;
Our joy, the richness of thy grace,—
Thine own, the cheer of this glad strain.

655. C. H. M.

1 WHEN I can trust my all with God,
In trial's fearful hour,
Bow, all resigned, beneath his rod,
And bless his sparing power,
A joy springs up amid distress,
A fountain in the wilderness.

2 O, blessèd be the hand that gave,
Still blessèd when it takes;
Blessèd be he who smites to save,
Who heals the heart he breaks:
Perfect and true are all his ways,
Whom heaven adores and death obeys.

FAITH AND SUBMISSION.

---

656. C. P. M.

1 "FATHER, thy will, not mine, be done!"
So prayed on earth thy suffering Son,
So, in his name, I pray;
The spirit faints, the flesh is weak,
Thy help in agony I seek;
O, take this cup away!

2 If such be not thy sovereign will,
Thy wiser purpose then fulfil;
My wishes I resign,
Into thy hands my soul commend,
On thee for life or death depend;
Thy will be done, not mine!

657. C. M.

1 THY path, like most by mortals trod,
Will have its thorns and flowers,
Its stony steps, its velvet sod,
Its sunshine and its showers.

2 Through smooth and rough, o'er flower and thorn,
Beneath whatever sky,
Still bear thee as a being born
For immortality!

3 And be thy choicest treasure stored
Where Faith may hold the key;
For "where our treasure is," our Lord
Hath said, "the heart shall be."

658. L. M.

1 To weary hearts, to mourning homes,
God's meekest angel gently comes;
No power hath he to banish pain,
Or give us back our lost again,
And yet, in tenderest love, our dear
And Heavenly Father sends him here.

2 Angel of patience! sent to calm
Our feverish brows with cooling balm,
To lay with hope the storms of fear,
And reconcile life's smile and tear,
The throbs of wounded pride to still,
And make our own our Father's will!

3 O thou who mournest on thy way,
With longings for the close of day,
He walks with thee, that angel kind,
And gently whispers, "Be resigned!
Bear up, bear on, the end shall tell,
The dear Lord ordereth all things well."

659. C. M.

1 Beneath thine hammer, Lord, I lie
With contrite spirit prone;
O, mould me till to self I die,
And live to thee alone!

2 With frequent disappointments sore
And many a bitter pain,
Thou laborest at my being's core
Till I be formed again.

3 Smite, Lord! thine hammer's needful wound
My baffled hopes confess;
Thine anvil is the sense profound
Of mine own nothingness.

4 Smite, till, from all its idols free,
And filled with love divine,
My heart shall know no good but thee,
And have no will but thine.

660. C. M.

1 I cannot call affliction sweet;
And yet 't was good to bear:
Affliction brought me to thy feet,
And I found comfort there.

2 My wearied soul was all resigned
To thy most gracious will:
O had I kept that better mind,
Or been afflicted still!

3 Where are the vows which then I vowed?
The joys which then I knew?
Those vanished like the morning cloud,
These like the early dew.

4 Lord, grant me grace for every day,
Whate'er my state may be,
Through life, in death, with truth to say,
"My God is all to me!"

661. C. M.

1 God moves in a mysterious way,
His wonders to perform;
He plants his footsteps in the sea,
And rides upon the storm.

2 Deep in unfathomable mines
Of never-failing skill,
He treasures up his vast designs,
And works his sovereign will.

3 Ye fearful saints! fresh courage take:
The clouds ye so much dread
Are big with mercy, and will break
In blessings on your head.

4 Blind unbelief is sure to err,
And scan his work in vain:
God is his own interpreter,
And he will make it plain.

662. L. M.

1 When darkness long has veiled my mind,
And smiling day once more appears,
Then, O my Father, then I find
The folly of my doubts and fears.

2 Ah! let me then again be taught
What I am still so slow to learn,
That God is love, and changes not,
Nor knows the shadow of a turn.

3 Sweet truth, and easy to repeat!
But when my faith is sharply tried,
I find myself a learner yet,
Unskilful, weak, and apt to slide.

4 But, O my God! one look from thee
Subdues the disobedient will,
Drives doubt and discontent away,
And thy rebellious child is still.

663. L. M.

1 Eternal and immortal King!
Thy peerless splendors none can bear,
But darkness veils seraphic eyes,
When God with all his glory 's there.

2 Yet faith can pierce the awful gloom;
The great Invisible can see;
And with its tremblings mingle joy,
In fixed regards, great God! on thee.

3 O, ever conscious to my heart,
Witness to its supreme desire!
Behold it presseth on to thee,
For it hath caught the heavenly fire.

4 This one petition would it urge,—
To bear thee ever in its sight;
In life, in death, in worlds unknown,
Its only portion and delight.

664. 7s. M.

1 QUIET, Lord, my froward heart;
Make me teachable and mild,
Upright, simple, free from art;
Make me as a little child;
From distrust and envy free,
Pleased with all that pleases thee.

2 What thou shalt to-day provide,
Let me as a child receive;
What to-morrow may betide,
Calmly to thy wisdom leave;
'T is enough that thou wilt care;
Why should I the burden bear?

3 As a little child relies
On a care beyond his own,
Knows he 's neither strong nor wise,
Fears to stir a step alone,
Let me thus with thee abide,
As my Father, Guard, and Guide.

665. L. M.

1 Spirit of God, immortal Love!
Whom we, that have not seen thy face,
By faith, and faith alone, embrace,
Believing where we cannot prove:

2 Thou wilt not leave us in the dust:
Thou madest man, he knows not why;
He thinks he was not made to die;
And thou hast made him: thou art just.

3 Our little systems have their day;
They have their day, and cease to be;
They are but broken lights of thee,
And thou, O Lord, art more than they.

4 We have but faith; we cannot know;
For knowledge is of things we see;
And yet we trust it comes from thee,
A beam in darkness: let it grow.

5 Let knowledge grow from more to more,
But more of reverence in us dwell;
That mind and soul, according well,
May make one music, as before: —

6 But vaster: we are fools and slight;
We mock thee when we do not fear:
But help thy foolish ones to bear;
Help thy vain world to bear thy light.

666. C. P. M.

1 Long plunged in sorrow, I resign
My soul to that dear hand of thine,
Without reserve or fear;
That hand shall wipe my streaming eyes,
Or into smiles of glad surprise
Transform the falling tear.

2 My sole possession is thy love;
In earth beneath or heaven above,
I have no other store;
And though with fervent suit I pray,
And importune thee night and day,
I ask thee nothing more.

3 By thy command, where'er I stray,
Sorrow attends me all my way,
A never-failing friend;
And if my sufferings may augment
Thy praise, behold me well content,
Let sorrow still attend!

667. L. M.

1 When adverse winds and waves arise,
And in my heart despondence sighs,
When life her throng of cares reveals,
And weakness o'er my spirit steals,
Grateful I hear the kind decree,
That "as my day, my strength shall be."

2 When, with sad footsteps, memory roves
'Mid smitten joys and buried loves,
When sleep my tearful pillow flies,
And dewy morning drinks my sighs,
Still to thy promise, Lord, I flee,
That "as my day, my strength shall be."

3 One trial more must yet be past,
One pang, — the keenest and the last;
And when, with brow convulsed and pale,
My feeble, quivering heart-strings fail,
Redeemer, grant my soul to see
That "as her day, her strength shall be."

668. C. M.

1 A TRUSTING heart, a yearning eye,
Can win their way above;
If mountains can be moved by faith,
Is there less power in love?

2 How little of that road, my soul!
How little hast thou gone!
Take heart, and let the thought of God
Allure thee further on.

3 The freedom from all wilful sin,
The Christian's daily task, —
O, these are graces far below
What longing love would ask!

4 Dole not thy duties out to God,
But let thy hand be free:
Look long at Jesus; his sweet blood,
How was it dealt to thee?

5 Be docile to thine unseen Guide,
Love him as he loves thee;
Time and obedience are enough,
And thou a saint shalt be!

669. L. M.

1 'Tis by the faith of joys to come
We walk through deserts dark as night:
Till we arrive at heaven, our home,
Faith is our guide, and faith our light.

2 The want of sight she well supplies;
She makes the pearly gates appear;
Far into distant worlds she pries,
And brings eternal glories near.

3 Cheerful we tread the desert through,
While faith inspires a heavenly ray;
Though lions roar, and tempests blow,
And rocks and dangers fill the way.

4 So Abraham, by divine command,
Left his own house to walk with God;
His faith beheld the promised land,
And fired his zeal along the road.

670. C. M.

1 Blest is the man who fears the Lord!
His well-established mind,
In every varying scene of life
Shall true composure find.

2 Oft through the deep and stormy sea
The heavenly footsteps lie;
But on a glorious world beyond
His faith can fix its eye.

3 Though dark his present prospects be,
And sorrows round him dwell,
Yet hope can whisper to his soul,
That all shall issue well.

4 Full in the presence of his God,
Through every scene he goes;
And, fearing him, no other fear
His steadfast bosom knows.

671. C. M.

1 All nature feels attractive power,
A strong, embracing force;
The drops that sparkle in the shower,
The planets in their course.

2 Thus, in the universe of mind,
Is felt the law of love;
The charity both strong and kind,
For all that live and move.

3 More perfect bond, the Christian plan
Attaches soul to soul;
Our neighbor is the suffering man,
Though at the farthest pole.

4 To earth below, from heaven above,
The faith in Christ professed
More clearly shows that God is love,
And whom he loves is blest.

672. S. M.

1 To keep the lamp alive,
With oil we fill the bowl;
'T is water makes the willow thrive,
And grace that feeds the soul.

2 The Lord's unsparing hand
Supplies the living stream;
It is not at our own command,
But still derived from him.

3 Man's wisdom is to seek
His strength in God alone;
And e'en an angel would be weak,
Who trusted in his own.

4 In God is all our store;
Grace issues from his throne;
Whoever says, "I want no more,"
Confesses he has none.

673. C. M.

1 Lord! I believe; thy power I own,
Thy word I would obey;
I wander comfortless and lone,
When from thy truth I stray.

2 Lord! I believe; but gloomy fears
Sometimes bedim my sight;
I look to thee with prayers and tears,
And cry for strength and light.

3 Lord! I believe; but oft, I know,
My faith is cold and weak;
Strengthen my weakness, and bestow
The confidence I seek!

4 Yes, I believe; and only thou
Canst give my soul relief;
Lord! to thy truth my spirit bow,
Help thou my unbelief!

674. L. M.

1 The darkened sky, how thick it lowers,
Troubled with storms, and big with showers!
No cheerful gleam of light appears,
And nature pours forth all her tears.

2 But seeds of ecstasy unknown
Are in these watered furrows sown:
See the green blades, how thick they rise,
And with fresh verdure bless our eyes!

3 In secret foldings they contain
Unnumbered ears of golden grain:
And heaven shall pour its beams around,
Till the ripe harvest load the ground.

4 Then shall the trembling mourner come,
And bind his sheaves and bear them home;
The voice long broke with sighs shall sing,
Till heaven with hallelujahs ring.

675. 7s. M.

1 WHY, thou never-setting Light,
Is thy brightness veiled from me?
Why does this unwonted night
Cloud thy blest benignity?

2 I am lost without thy ray;
Guide my wandering footsteps, Lord!
Light my dark and erring way
To the noontide of thy word.

676. 7s. M.

1 HEAVENLY Father! to whose eye
Future things unfolded lie;
Through the desert when I stray
Let thy counsels guide my way.

2 Should thy wisdom, Lord, decree
Trials long and sore for me,
Pain or sorrow, care or shame,
Father! glorify thy name.

3 Let me neither faint nor fear,
Feeling still that thou art near;
In the course my Saviour trod,
Tending home to thee, my God.

677. C. M.

1 Mistaken souls, that dream of heaven,
And make their empty boast
Of inward joys, and sins forgiven,
While they are slaves to lust!

2 Vain are our fancy's airy flights,
If faith be cold and dead;
None but a living power unites
To Christ, the living Head.

3 'T is faith that changes all the heart;
'T is faith that works by love,
That bids all sinful joys depart,
And lifts the thoughts above.

4 'T is faith that conquers earth and hell
By a celestial power;
This is the grace that shall prevail
In the decisive hour.

678. 7s. M.

1 Day by day the manna fell:
O to learn this lesson well!
Still by constant mercy fed,
Give me, Lord, my daily bread.

2 "Day by day," the promise reads;
Daily strength for daily needs:
Cast foreboding fears away;
Take the manna of to-day.

3 Lord! my times are in thy hand:
All my sanguine hopes have planned
To thy wisdom I resign,
And would make thy purpose mine.

4 Thou my daily task shalt give:
Day by day to thee I live;
So shall added years fulfil,
Not my own, my Father's will.

679. L. M.

1 Glory to thee, whose powerful word
Bids the tempestuous wind arise;
Glory to thee, the sovereign Lord
Of air and earth and seas and skies!

2 Let air and earth and skies obey,
And seas thine awful will perform;
From them we learn to own thy sway,
And shout to meet the gathering storm.

3 What though the floods lift up their voice,
Thou hearest, Lord, our louder cry;
They cannot damp thy children's joys,
Or shake the soul when God is nigh.

4 Roar on, ye waves! our souls defy
Your roaring to disturb our rest;
In vain to impair the calm ye try,
The calm in a believer's breast.

680. C. M.

1 Father, I know thy ways are just,
Although to me unknown;
O, grant me grace thy love to trust,
And cry, "Thy will be done!"

2 If thou shouldst hedge with thorns my path,
Should wealth and friends be gone,
Still with a firm and lively faith
I 'll cry, "Thy will be done!"

3 Although thy steps I cannot trace,
Thy sovereign right I 'll own;
And, as instructed by thy grace,
I 'll cry, "Thy will be done!"

681. L. M.

1 My God, I thank thee! may no thought
E'er deem thy chastisements severe;
But may this heart, by sorrow taught,
Calm each wild wish, each idle fear.

2 Thy mercy bids all nature bloom;
The sun shines bright, and man is gay;
Thine equal mercy spreads the gloom,
That darkens o'er his little day.

3 Full many a throb of grief and pain
Thy frail and erring child must know;
But not one prayer is breathed in vain,
Nor does one tear unheeded flow.

4 Thy various messengers employ;
Thy purposes of love fulfil;
And 'mid the wreck of human joy,
Let kneeling faith adore thy will.

682. C. M.

1 One prayer I have, all prayers in one,
When I am wholly thine:
Thy will, my God, thy will be done,
And let that will be mine.

2 All-wise, Almighty, and all-good,
In thee I firmly trust;
Thy ways, unknown or understood,
Are merciful and just.

3 Thy gifts are only then enjoyed,
When used as talents lent;
Those talents only well employed,
When in thy service spent.

4 And though thy wisdom takes away,
Shall I arraign thy will?
No, let me bless thy name, and say,
"The Lord is gracious still."

683. C. M.

1 O Lord! my best desires fulfil,
And help me to resign
Life, health, and comfort to thy will,
And make thy pleasure mine.

2 Why should I shrink at thy command,
Whose love forbids my fears;
Or tremble at the gracious hand
That wipes away my tears?

3 No! let me rather freely yield
What most I prize, to thee,
Who never hast a good withheld,
Nor wilt withhold, from me.

4 But ah! my inward spirit cries,
Still bind me to thy sway;
Else the next cloud that veils the skies
Drives all these thoughts away.

684. P. M.

1 Thy will be done! In devious way
The hurrying stream of life may run;
Yet still our grateful hearts shall say,
Thy will be done!

2 Thy will be done! If o'er us shine
A gladdening and a prosperous sun,
This prayer shall make it more divine: —
Thy will be done!

3 Thy will be done! Though shrouded o'er
Our path with gloom, one comfort, one,
Is ours, — to breathe, while we adore,
Thy will be done!

685. L. M.

1 Thy will be done! I will not fear
The fate provided by thy love;
Though clouds and darkness shroud me here,
I know that all is bright above.

2 The stars of heaven are shining on,
Though these frail eyes are dimmed with tears,
And though the hopes of earth be gone,
Yet are not ours the immortal years?

3 Father! forgive the heart that clings,
Thus trembling, to the things of time;
And bid the soul, on angel wings,
Ascend into a purer clime.

4 There shall no doubts disturb its trust,
No sorrows dim celestial love;
But these afflictions of the dust,
Like shadows of the night, remove.

686. P. M.

1 I cannot always trace the way
Where thou, Almighty One, dost move,
But I can always, always say,
That God is love.

2 When fear her chilling mantle throws
O'er earth, my soul to heaven above,
As to her native home, upsprings,
For God is love.

3 When mystery clouds my darkened path,
I 'll check my dread, my doubts reprove;
In this my soul sweet comfort hath,
That God is love.

4 Yes, God is love; — a thought like this
Can every gloomy thought remove,
And turn all tears, all woes, to bliss,
For God is love.

687. 8 & 6s. M.

1 My God, my Father, while I stray
Far from my home on life's rough way,
O, teach me from my heart to say,
"Thy will, my God, be done!"

2 What though in lonely grief I sigh
For friends beloved no longer nigh;
Submissive still would I reply,
"Thy will, my God, be done!"

3 If thou shouldst call me to resign
What most I prize, — it ne'er was mine, —
I only yield thee what is thine;
"Thy will, my God, be done!"

4 Renew my will from day to day,
Blend it with thine, and take away
Whate'er now makes it hard to say,
"Thy will, my God, be done!"

688. C. M.

1 The Lord, — how tender is his love!
His justice how august!
Hence all her fears my soul derives,
There anchors all her trust.

2 His power directs the rushing wind,
Or tips the bolt with flame;
His goodness breathes in every breeze,
And warms in every beam.

3 For me, O Lord! whatever lot
The hours commissioned bring, —
Do all my withering blessings die,
Or fairer clusters spring, —

4 O, grant that still, with grateful heart,
My years resigned may run!
'T is thine to give, or to resume,
And may thy will be done!

689. 6 & 4s. M.

1 Father, O, hear me now!
Father divine!
Thou, only thou, canst see
The heart's deep agony, —
Help me to say to thee,
Thy will, not mine!

2 O God! be thou my stay,
In this dark hour;

Kindly each sorrow hear,
Hush every troubled fear,
And let me still revere
And own thy power.

3 In thee alone I trust,
The Holy One!
Humbly to thee I pray,
That, through each troubled day
Of life, I still may say,
Thy will be done!

690. 8 & 6s. M.

1 I ASK not now for gold to gild,
With mocking shine, an aching frame;
The yearning of the mind is stilled,—
I ask not now for fame.

2 But, bowed in lowliness of mind,
I make my humble wishes known;
I only ask a will resigned,
O Father, to thine own.

3 In vain I task my aching brain,
In vain the sage's thoughts I scan;
I only feel how weak I am,
How poor and blind is man.

4 And now my spirit sighs for home,
And longs for light whereby to see,
And like a weary child would come,
O Father, unto thee.

691. L. M.

1 He sendeth sun, he sendeth shower,
Alike they 're needful to the flower,
And joys and tears alike are sent
To give the soul fit nourishment.
As comes to me or cloud or sun,
Father, thy will, not mine, be done!

2 Can loving children e'er reprove
With murmurs whom they trust and love?
Creator, I would ever be
A trusting, loving child to thee.
As comes to me or cloud or sun,
Father, thy will, not mine, be done!

3 O, ne'er will I at life repine!
Enough that thou hast made it mine.
When falls the shadow cold of death,
I yet will sing, with parting breath,
As comes to me or cloud or sun,
Father, thy will, not mine, be done!

692. C. M.

1 I worship thee, sweet Will of God!
And all thy ways adore,
And every day I live, I long
To love thee more and more.

2 Man's weakness waiting upon God
Its end can never miss,

For men on earth no work can do
More angel-like than this.

3 He always wins who sides with God,
To him no chance is lost;
God's will is sweetest to him when
It triumphs at his cost.

4 Ill that God blesses is our good,
And unblest good is ill;
And all is right that seems most wrong,
If it be his dear will!

5 When obstacles and trials seem
Like prison-walls to be,
I do the little I can do,
And leave the rest to thee.

6 I have no cares, O blessed Will!
For all my cares are thine;
I live in triumph, Lord! for thou
Hast made thy triumphs mine.

CONSOLATION.

---

693. H. M.

1 Thou, infinite in love!
Guide this bewildered mind,
Which, like the trembling dove,
No resting-place can find
On the wild waters, God of light,
Through the thick darkness lead me right!

2 Bid the fierce conflict cease,
And fear and anguish fly;
Let there again be peace,
As in the days gone by:
In Jesus' name I cry to thee,
Remembering Gethsemane.

3 Though through the future shade
Pale phantoms I descry,
Let me not shrink dismayed,
But ever feel thee nigh;
There may be grief, and pain, and care,
But, O my Father! thou art there.

694. 11 & 4s. M.

1 WITH silence only as their benediction,
God's angels come
Where, in the shadow of a great affliction,
The soul sits dumb.

2 Yet would we say, what every heart approveth,—
Our Father's will,
Calling to him the dear ones whom he loveth,
Is mercy still.

3 Not upon us or ours the solemn angel
Hath evil wrought;
The funeral anthem is a glad evangel;
The good die not!

4 God calls our loved ones, but we lose not wholly
What he has given;
They live on earth in thought and deed, as truly
As in his heaven.

695. L. M.

1 THE mourners came, at break of day,
Unto the garden sepulchre,
With saddened hearts, to weep and pray
For him, the loved one, buried there.
What radiant light dispels the gloom?
An angel sits beside the tomb.

2 The earth doth mourn her treasures lost,
All sepulchred beneath the snow,

When wintry winds and chilling frost
Have laid her summer glories low;
The spring returns, the flowerets bloom, —
An angel sits beside the tomb.

3 Then mourn we not belovèd dead,
E'en while we come to weep and pray;
The happy spirit hath but fled
To brighter realms of heavenly day;
Immortal hope dispels the gloom, —
An angel sits beside the tomb.

696. C. M.

1 Bright were the mornings first impearled
O'er earth and sea and air;
The birthdays of a rising world, —
For power divine was there.

2 But fairer shone the Saviour's tears,
For Lazarus, o'er his grave;
While love divine renewed the years
Of one he sought to save.

3 Sweet drops of grace, the pledges given
Of Mercy's mighty plan, —
That he, who was the Prince of heaven,
Had pity upon man!

4 Let us thy dear example, Lord,
Fixed in our memories keep, —
That we, obedient to thy word,
May weep with those that weep.

697. L. M.

1 The waters of Bethesda's pool
Were to the outward eye as clear,
And to the outward touch as cool,
Before the visitant drew near.

2 But while untroubled, they possessed
No healing virtue; — gentle friend,
Is there no fount within the breast
To which an angel may descend?

3 O, while the soul unruffled lies,
Its mirror only can display,
However beautiful their dyes,
The forms of things that pass away.

4 But when its troubled waters own
A Saviour's presence, in the wave
The healing power of grace is known,
And found omnipotent to save.

5 A glimpse of glories far more bright
Than earth can give is mirrored there;
And perfect purity and light
The presence of its God declare.

698. L. M.

1 The energies too stern for mirth,
The reach of thought, the strength of will,
'Mid cloud and tempest have their birth,
Through blight and blast their course fulfil

2 And yet 't is when it mourns and fears,
The loaded spirit feels forgiven;
And through the mist of falling tears
We catch the clearest glimpse of heaven.

699. C. M.

1 Where is the tree the prophet threw
Into the bitter wave,
Left it no scion where it grew,
The thirsting soul to save?

2 Hath nature lost the hidden power
Its precious foliage shed?
Is there no distant eastern bower
With such sweet leaves o'erspread?

3 Nay, wherefore ask? since gifts are ours
Which yet may well imbue
Earth's many troubled founts with showers
Of heaven's own balmy dew.

4 O, mingled with the cup of grief
Let faith's deep spirit be,
And every prayer shall win a leaf
From that blest healing tree!

700. L. M.

1 Is there a lone and dreary hour,
When worldly pleasures lose their power?
My Father! let me turn to thee,
And set each thought of darkness free.

2 Is there a time of racking grief,
Which scorns the prospect of relief?
My Father! break the cheerless gloom,
And bid my heart its calm resume.

3 Is there an hour of peace and joy,
When hope is all my soul's employ?
My Father! still my hopes will roam,
Until they rest with thee, their home.

4 The noontide blaze, the midnight scene,
The dawn, or twilight's sweet serene,
The glow of life, the dying hour,
Shall own my Father's grace and power.

701. L. M.

1 PEACE, troubled soul! whose plaintive moan
Hath taught these rocks the notes of woe;
Cease thy complaint, suppress thy groan,
And let thy tears forget to flow:
Behold, the precious balm is found,
Which lulls thy pain, which heals thy wound.

2 Come, freely come, by sin oppressed,
Unburden here the weighty load;
Here find thy refuge and thy rest,
And trust the mercy of thy God:
Thy God 's thy Father,—glorious word!
For ever love and praise the Lord.

702. S. M.

1 What though the stream be dead,
Its banks all still and dry!
It murmureth o'er a lovelier bed,
In air-groves of the sky.

2 What though our bird of light
Lie mute, with plumage dim;
In heaven I see her glancing bright,
I hear her angel hymn.

3 True that our beauteous doe
Hath left her still retreat,
But purer now, in heavenly snow,
She lies at Jesus' feet.

4 O star untimely set!
Why should we weep for thee?
Thy bright and dewy coronet
Is rising o'er the sea.

703. 11 & 10s. M.

1 Come, ye disconsolate, where'er ye languish;
Come, at the mercy-seat fervently kneel:
Here bring your wounded hearts, here tell your anguish;
Earth has no sorrow that heaven cannot heal.

2 Joy of the desolate, light of the straying,
Hope of the penitent, fadeless and pure,
Here speaks the Comforter, tenderly saying,
Earth has no sorrow that heaven cannot cure.

704. C. M.

1 O Thou who driest the mourner's tear,
How dark this world would be
If, when deceived and wounded here,
We could not fly to thee!

2 But thou wilt heal the broken heart,
Which, like the plants that throw
Their fragrance from the wounded part,
Breathes sweetness out of woe.

3 O, who would bear life's stormy doom,
Did not thy wing of love
Come, brightly wafting through the gloom
Our peace-branch from above?

4 Then sorrow touched by thee grows bright
With more than rapture's ray,
As darkness shows us worlds of light
We never saw by day.

705. L. M.

1 When Power Divine, in mortal form,
Hushed with a word the raging storm,
In soothing accents Jesus said,
"Lo, it is I!— be not afraid."

2 So, when in silence nature sleeps,
And his lone watch the mourner keeps,
One thought shall every pang remove,—
Trust, feeble man, thy Maker's love

3 God calms the tumult and the storm;
He rules the seraph and the worm:
No creature is by him forgot,
Of those who know, or know him not.

4 Blest be the voice that breathes from heaven,
To every heart in sunder riven,
When love and joy and hope are fled,
"Lo, it is I! — be not afraid."

706. 8 & 7s. M.

1 Cease, ye mourners, cease to languish
O'er the grave of those you love;
Pain, and death, and night, and anguish,
Enter not the world above.

2 While our silent steps are straying,
Lonely, through night's deepening shade,
Glory's brightest beams are playing
Round the happy Christian's head.

3 Endless pleasure pain excluding,
Sickness there no more can come;
There no fear of woe intruding
Sheds o'er heaven a moment's gloom.

707. 8, 7, & 4s. M.

1 Gently, Lord, O, gently lead us
Through these scenes of joy and tears,

And, O Lord, in mercy give us
  Thy rich grace in all our fears:
    O, refresh us,
  O, refresh us by thy grace!

2 Though ten thousand ills beset us,
  From without and from within,
God hath said, he 'll ne'er forget us,
  But will save from every sin.
    Therefore praise him,
  Praise thy great Redeemer's name.

3 Though distresses now attend thee,
  And thou tread'st the thorny way,
His right hand shall still defend thee,
  And his love shall be thy stay;
    Therefore praise him,
  Praise thy great Redeemer's name.

708. 8 & 4s. M.

1 There is a calm for those who weep,
  A rest for weary pilgrims found:
And while the mouldering ashes sleep
    Low in the ground,

2 The soul, of origin divine,
  God's glorious image, freed from clay,
In heaven's eternal sphere shall shine,
    A star of day!

3 Now, traveller 'mid these flying years
  To realms of everlasting light!
Through heavy clouds, or boding fears,
    Pursue thy flight.

4 The sun is but a spark of fire,
A transient meteor in the sky;
The soul, immortal as its Sire,
Shall never die!

709. L. M.

1 Deem not that they are blest alone,
Whose days a peaceful tenor keep;
The God who loves our race has shown
A blessing for the eyes that weep.

2 The light of smiles shall beam again
From lids that now o'erflow with tears,
And weary hours of woe and pain
Are earnests of serener years.

3 O, there are days of hope and rest
For every dark and troubled night,
And grief may bide, an evening guest,
But joy shall come with morning light

4 And ye, who o'er a friend's low bier
Now shed the bitter drops like rain,
Hope that a brighter, happier sphere
Will give him to your arms again.

710. 6 & 5s. M.

1 Where the mourner weeping
Sheds the secret tear,
God his watch is keeping,
Though none else is near.

2 God will never leave thee,
  All thy wants he knows,
Feels the pains that grieve thee,
  Sees thy cares and woes.

3 Raise thine eyes to heaven
  When thy spirits quail,
When, by tempests driven,
  Heart and courage fail.

4 All thy woe and sadness
  In this world below
Balance not the gladness
  Thou in heaven shalt know.

5 When thy gracious Saviour
  In the realms above,
Crowns thee with his favor,
  Fills thee with his love.

VIII.

LIFE.

EARLY RELIGION.

---

711. C. M.

1 How shall the young secure their hearts,
And guard their lives, from sin?
Thy word the choicest rules imparts
To keep the conscience clean.

2 'T is, like the sun, a heavenly light,
That guides us all the day,
And, through the dangers of the night,
A lamp to lead our way.

3 Thy word is everlasting truth:
How pure is every page!
That holy book shall guide our youth,
And well support our age.

712. C. M.

1 By cool Siloam's shady rill
How sweet the lily grows!

How sweet the breath beneath the hill
Of Sharon's dewy rose!

2 Lo, such the child whose early feet
The paths of peace have trod;
Whose secret heart, with influence sweet,
Is upward drawn to God.

3 O Thou who giv'st us life and breath,
We seek thy grace alone,
In childhood, manhood, age, and death,
To keep us still thine own.

713. C. M.

1 O, SAY not, think not, heavenly notes
To childish ears are vain;
That the young mind at random floats,
And cannot reach the strain.

2 Was not our Lord, a little child,
Taught by degrees to pray,
By father dear and mother mild
Instructed day by day?

3 And though some tones be weak and low,
What are all prayers beneath,
But cries of babes, that cannot know
Half the deep thought they breathe?

4 In his own words we Christ adore;
But angels, as we speak,
Higher above our meaning soar,
Than we o'er children weak.

714. L. M.

1 In Israel's fane, by silent night,
The lamp of God was burning bright;
And there, by viewless angels kept,
Samuel, the child, securely slept.

2 A voice unknown the stillness broke;
"Samuel!" it called, and thrice it spoke;
He rose; he asked whence came the word;
From Eli? No, — it was the Lord.

3 Thus early called to serve his God,
In paths of righteousness he trod;
Prophetic visions fired his breast,
And all the chosen tribes were blest.

4 Speak, Lord! and, from our earliest days,
Incline our hearts to love thy ways;
Thy wakening voice hath reached our ear:
Speak, Lord, to us; thy servants hear.

715. 6 & 4s. M.

1 Shepherd of tender youth,
Guiding, in love and truth,
Through devious ways!
Christ, our triumphant King!
We come thy name to sing,
And here our children bring,
To shout thy praise.

2 Thou art our holy Lord!
The all-subduing Word!
Healer of strife!
Thou didst thyself abase,
That from sin's deep disgrace
Thou mightest save our race,
And give us life.

3 Thou art our soul's High-Priest!
Thou hast prepared the feast
Of holy love,
And in our mortal pain
None calls on thee in vain,
Help thou dost not disdain,—
Help from above.

4 Ever be thou our guide,
Our Shepherd and our pride,—
Our staff and song!
Jesus! thou Christ of God!
By thy perennial word
Lead us where thou hast trod,
Make our faith strong.

5 So now, and till we die,
Sound we thy praises high,
And joyful sing;
Infants, and the glad throng
Who to thy Church belong
Unite and swell the song
To Christ our King.

CHOICE.

---

716. L. M.

1 Ah wretched souls, who strive in vain,
Slaves to the world, and slaves to sin!
A nobler toil may I sustain,
A nobler satisfaction win.

2 May I resolve, with all my heart,
With all my powers, to serve the Lord;
Nor from his precepts e'er depart,
Whose service is a rich reward.

3 Be this the purpose of my soul,
My solemn, my determined choice,
To yield to his supreme control,
And in his kind commands rejoice.

4 O, may I never faint nor tire,
Nor, wandering, leave his sacred ways!
Great God! accept my soul's desire,
And give me strength to live thy praise.

717. L. M.

1 Why do we waste in trifling cares
The lives divine compassion spares,
While, through the various range of thought,
The one thing needful is forgot?

2 Our Father calls us from above;
Our Saviour pleads his dying love;
Awakened conscience gives us pain:
Shall all these pleas unite in vain?

3 Not so our dying eyes will view
The objects which we now pursue;
Not so eternity appear,
When death's decisive hour is near.

4 Then wake, my soul; thy way prepare,
And lose in this each meaner care;
With steady step that path be trod,
Which through the grave conducts to God.

718. L. M.

1 Beset with snares on every hand,
In life's uncertain path I stand:
Father divine! diffuse thy light
To guide my doubtful footsteps right.

2 Engage this roving, treacherous heart,
Wisely to choose the better part;
To scorn the trifles of a day,
For joys that none can take away.

3 Then let the wildest storms arise,
Let tempests mingle earth with skies,
No fatal shipwreck shall I fear,
But all my treasures with me bear.

4 If thou, my Saviour, still be nigh,
Cheerful I live, and joyful die;
Secure, when mortal comforts flee,
To find ten thousand worlds in thee.

ACTION.

---

719. S. M.

1 Sow in the morn thy seed,
At eve hold not thy hand;
To doubt and fear give thou no heed,
Broadcast it o'er the land!
Beside all waters sow,
The highway furrows stock,
Drop it where thorns and thistles grow,
Drop it upon the rock!

2 The good, the fruitful ground,
Expect not here nor there;
O'er hill and dale and plain 't is found;
Go forth, then, everywhere!
And duly shall appear,
In verdure, beauty, strength,
The tender blade, the stalk, the ear,
And the full corn at length.

3 Thou canst not toil in vain;
Cold, heat, and moist and dry,
Shall foster and mature the grain
For garners in the sky;

Then, when the glorious end,
The day of God, shall come,
The angel-reapers shall descend,
At heaven's great harvest-home.

720. S. M.

1 My soul, be on thy guard;
Ten thousand foes arise;
The hosts of sin are pressing hard
To draw thee from the skies.

2 O, watch, and strive, and pray;
The battle ne'er give o'er;
Renew it boldly every day,
And help divine implore.

3 Ne'er think the victory won,
Nor lay thine armor down:
Thy arduous work will not be done
Till thou obtain thy crown.

4 Fight on, my soul, till death
Shall bring thee to thy God;
He 'll take thee, at thy parting breath,
To His divine abode.

721. L. M.

1 So let our lips and lives express
The holy Gospel we profess,
So let our works and virtues shine,
To prove the doctrine all divine.

2 Thus shall we best proclaim abroad
The honors of our Saviour, God,
When the salvation reigns within,
And grace subdues the power of sin.

3 Our flesh and sense must be denied,
Passion and envy, lust and pride,
While justice, temperance, truth, and love
Our inward piety approve.

4 Religion bears our spirits up,
While we expect that blessed hope,
The bright appearance of the Lord,
And faith stands leaning on his word.

722. S. M.

1 My God, my strength, my hope,
On thee I cast my care,
With humble confidence look up,
And know thou hear'st my prayer.
Give me on thee to wait,
Till I can all things do;
On thee, almighty to create,
Almighty to renew.

2 I want a godly fear,
A quick-discerning eye,
That ever watches unto prayer,
And sees the tempter fly;
A soul inured to pain,
To hardship, grief, and loss,
Bold to take up, firm to sustain,
The consecrated cross.

3 I rest upon thy word;
The promise is for me;
My succor and salvation, Lord,
Shall surely come from thee:
But let me still abide,
Nor from my hope remove,
Till thou my patient spirit guide
Into thy perfect love.

723. S. M.

1 A CHARGE to keep I have,
A God to glorify;
A never-dying soul to save,
And fit it for the sky;
To serve the present age,
My calling to fulfil:
O, may it all my powers engage
To do my Master's will!

2 Arm me with jealous care,
As in thy sight to live;
And, O, thy servant, Lord, prepare
The strict account to give!
Help me to watch and pray,
And on thyself rely:
Assured, if I my trust betray,
I shall forsaken die.

724. S. M.

1 YE servants of the Lord!
Each in your office wait,

Observant of his heavenly word,
And watchful at his gate.

2 Let all your lamps be bright,
And trim the golden flame:
Gird up your loins, as in his sight,
For awful is his name.

3 Watch! 't is your Lord's command;
And while we speak, he 's near;
Mark the first signal of his hand,
And ready all appear.

4 O happy servant he,
In such a posture found!
He shall his Lord with rapture see,
And be with honor crowned.

725. S. M.

1 Soldiers of Christ, arise,
And gird your armor on,
Strong in the strength which God supplies,
Through his eternal Son.

2 From strength to strength go on;
Wrestle, and fight, and pray;
Tread all the powers of darkness down,
And win the well-fought day.

3 Still let the Spirit cry,
In all his soldiers, "Come,"
Till Christ the Lord descends from high,
And takes the conquerors home.

726. C. M.

1 Our God! our God! thou shinest here;
Thine own this latter day;
To us thy radiant steps appear, —
Here goes thy glorious way.

2 We shine not only with the light
Thou sheddest down of yore;
On us thou streamest strong and bright, —
Thy comings are not o'er.

3 The fathers had not all of thee;
New births are in thy grace;
All open to our souls shall be
Thy glory's hiding-place.

4 We gaze on thy outgoings bright;
Down cometh thy full power;
We the glad bearers of thy light, —
This, this thy saving hour!

5 On us thy spirit hast thou poured,
To us thy word has come:
We feel, we thank thy quickening, Lord!
Thou shalt not find us dumb.

6 Thou comest near, — thou standest by, —
Our work begins to shine:
Thou dwellest with us mightily;
On come the years divine.

727. 7 & 5s. M.

1 WORK, — and thou wilt bless the day
Ere the toil be done;
They that work not cannot play,
Cannot feel the sun.
God is living, working still;
All things work and move;
Work, wouldst thou their beauty feel,
And thy Maker's love.

2 All the rolling planets glow
Bright as burning gold!
Should they pause, how soon they 'd grow
Colorless and cold!
Joy and beauty, — where were they
If the world stood still?
Like the world, thy law obey,
And thy calling fill.

3 Wouldst thou know the joy of health?
Wouldst thou feel thy powers?
Industry alone is wealth,
What we do is ours.
Load the passive hours with thought,
While they stay with thee;
Then despatch them, richly fraught,
To eternity.

728. 7s. M.

1 MAN'S life is the holy land,
We, Lord, thy crusader band;

Shrived by thee from pagan sin,
Shrine of God man's heart would win.

2 On our shield thy cross we bear,
By our side thy sword we wear;
Shield of faith, so stout, so strong!
Sword of truth, so bright, so long!

3 Courage, Lord, we seek from thee,
From the foe we would not flee,
Manful quit us in the fight,
Toil from dawning until night.

4 Gift us with the conqueror's crown,
At thy feet we lay it down,
Deeply feeling, not our own —
Thine the glory, thine alone.

729. P. M.

1 Hast thou, 'midst life's empty noises,
Heard the solemn steps of time,
And the low, mysterious voices
Of another clime?

2 Early hath life's mighty question
Thrilled within thy heart of youth,
With a deep and strong beseeching, —
What, and where, is truth?

3 Not to ease and aimless quiet
Doth the inward answer tend;
But to works of love and duty,
As our being's end.

4 Earnest toil and strong endeavor
Of a spirit which within
Wrestles with familiar evil
And besetting sin,

5 And without, with tireless vigor,
Steady heart, and purpose strong,
In the power of truth assaileth
Every form of wrong.

730. 8 & 7s. M.

1 Tell me not, in mournful numbers,
Life is but an empty dream;
For the soul is dead that slumbers,
And things are not what they seem.

2 Life is real! life is earnest!
And the grave is not its goal;
Dust thou art, to dust returnest,
Was not spoken of the soul.

3 Not enjoyment, and not sorrow,
Is our destined end and way;
But to act, that each to-morrow
Find us further than to-day.

4 Let us, then, be up and doing,
With a heart for any fate;
Still achieving, still pursuing,
Learn to labor and to wait.

731. 8 & 7s. M.

1 Cheek grow pale, but heart be vigorous!
Body fall, but soul have peace!
Welcome, pain! thou searcher rigorous!
Slay me, but my faith increase.

2 Sin, o'er sense so softly stealing;
Doubt, that would my strength impair;
Hence at once from life and feeling!
Now my cross I gladly bear.

3 Up, my soul! with clear sedateness
Read heaven's law, writ bright and broad,
Up! a sacrifice to greatness,
Truth, and goodness, — up to God!

4 Up to labor! from thee shaking
Off the bonds of sloth, be brave!
Give thyself to prayer and waking;
Toil some fainting heart to save!

732. L. M.

1 Awake, our souls! away, our fears!
Let every trembling thought be gone!
Awake, and run the heavenly race,
And put a cheerful courage on.

2 True, 't is a strait and thorny road,
And mortal spirits tire and faint;
But they forget the mighty God,
That feeds the strength of every saint; —

3 The mighty God, whose matchless power
Is ever new and ever young,
And firm endures, while endless years
Their everlasting circles run.

4 Swift as an eagle cuts the air,
We 'll mount aloft to thine abode;
On wings of love our souls shall fly,
Nor tire amidst the heavenly road.

733. L. M.

1 Awake, my soul! lift up thine eyes;
See where thy foes against thee rise,
In long array, a numerous host;
Awake, my soul! or thou art lost.

2 Thou treadst upon enchanted ground;
Perils and snares beset thee round;
Beware of all; guard every part,
But most, the traitor in thy heart.

3 Come then, my soul! now learn to wield
The weight of thine immortal shield;
Put on the armor from above
Of heavenly truth and heavenly love.

4 The terror and the charm repel,
And powers of earth, and powers of hell;
The man of Calvary triumphed here;—
Why should his faithful followers fear?

734. L. M.

1 How happy is he born or taught,
Who serveth not another's will;
Whose armor is his honest thought,
And simple truth his utmost skill;

2 Whose passions not his masters are;
Whose soul is still prepared for death,
Not tied unto the world with care
Of prince's ear or vulgar breath;

3 Who God doth late and early pray
More of his grace than goods to lend,
And walks with man, from day to day,
As with a brother and a friend!

4 This man is freed from servile bands
Of hope to rise, or fear to fall;
Lord of himself, though not of lands,
And having nothing, yet hath all.

735. L. M.

1 O Israel, to thy tents repair!
Why thus secure on hostile ground?
Thy Lord commands thee to beware,
For many foes thy camp surround.

2 O, sleep not thou, as others do;
Awake, be vigilant, be brave;
The coward and the sluggard too
Must wear the fetters of the slave.

3 A nobler lot is cast for thee;
A crown awaits thee in the skies:
With such a hope shall Israel flee,
And yield through weariness the prize?

4 No; let a careless world repose,
And slumber on through life's short day,
While Israel to the conflict goes,
And bears the glorious prize away.

736. 10s. M.

1 O, WHAT is man, great Maker of mankind!
That thou to him so great respect dost bear!
That thou adorn'st him with so bright a mind,
Mak'st him a king, and e'en an angel's peer?

2 O, what a lively life, what heavenly power,
What spreading virtue, what a sparkling fire,
How great, how plentiful, how rich a dower,
Dost thou within this dying flesh inspire!

3 Nor hast thou given these blessings for a day,
Nor made them on the body's life depend:
The soul, though made in time, survives for aye;
And though it hath beginning, sees no end.

737. L. M.

1 GOD's law demands one living faith,
Not a gaunt crowd of lifeless creeds:
Its warrant is a firm "God saith," —
Its claim, not words, but loving deeds.

2 Yet, Lord, forgive! thy simple law
Grows tarnished in our earthly grasp;
Pure in itself, without a flaw,
It dims in our too worldly clasp.

3 We handle it with unwashed hands,
We stain it with unhallowed breath,
We gloss it with device of man's,
And hide thine image underneath.

4 Forgive the sacrilege, and take
From off our souls the unworthy stain;
And show us, for thy Son's dear sake,
Thy pure and perfect law again.

738. C. M.

1 The world throws wide its brazen gates;
With thee we enter in;
O, grant us, in our humble sphere,
To free that world from sin!

2 We have one mind in Christ our Lord
To stand and point above;
To hurl rebuke at social wrong;
But all, O God, in love.

3 The star is resting in the sky;
To worship Christ we came;
The moments haste; O, touch our tongues
With thy celestial flame!

4 The truest worship is a life;
All dreaming we resign;
We lay our offerings at thy feet,—
Our lives, O Christ, are thine!

739. C. M.

1 A soldier's course, from battles won
To new-commencing strife;
A pilgrim's, restless as the sun;—
Behold the Christian's life!

2 The hosts of darkness pant for spoil,—
How can our warfare close?
Lonely we tread a foreign soil,—
How can we hope repose?

3 O, let us seek our heavenly home,
Revealed in sacred lore;
The land whence pilgrims never roam,
Where soldiers war no more;

4 Where they who meet shall never part;
Where grace achieves its plan;
And God, uniting every heart,
Dwells face to face with man.

740. C. M.

1 Awake, my soul! stretch every nerve,
And press with vigor on:
A heavenly race demands thy zeal,
And an immortal crown.

2 A cloud of witnesses around
Hold thee in full survey:
Forget the steps already trod,
And onward urge thy way.

3 'T is God's all-animating voice
That calls thee from on high;
'T is his own hand presents the prize
To thine aspiring eye;—

4 That prize with peerless glories bright,
Which shall new lustre boast,
When victors' wreaths and monarchs' gems
Shall blend in common dust.

741. S. M.

1 LABORERS of Christ, arise,
And gird you for the toil;
The dew of promise from the skies
Already cheers the soil.

2 Go where the sick recline,
Where mourning hearts deplore;
And where the sons of sorrow pine,
Dispense your hallowed lore.

3 Urge, with a tender zeal,
The erring child along,
Where peaceful congregations kneel,
And pious teachers throng.

4 So shall you share the wealth,
That earth may ne'er despoil,
And the blest Gospel's saving health
Repay your arduous toil.

742. C. M.

1 O, SPEED thee, Christian, on thy way,
And to thy armor cling;
With girded loins the call obey
That grace and mercy bring.

2 There is a battle to be fought,
An upward race to run,
A crown of glory to be sought,
A victory to be won.

3 O, faint not, Christian! for thy sighs
Are heard before His throne;
The race must come before the prize,
The cross before the crown.

743. L. M.

1 THE Christian warrior, see him stand
In the whole armor of his God,
The spirit's sword is in his hand,
His feet are with the Gospel shod.

2 In panoply of truth complete,
Salvation's helmet on his head,
With righteousness, a breastplate meet,
And faith's broad shield before him spread,—

3 With this omnipotence he moves;
From this the alien armies flee;
Till more than conqueror he proves,
Through Christ, who gives him victory.

4 Thus strong in his Redeemer's strength,
Sin, death, and hell he tramples down,
Fights the good fight, and wins at length,
Through mercy, an immortal crown.

744. C. M.

1 Am I a soldier of the cross,
A follower of the Lamb?
And shall I fear to own his cause,
Or blush to speak his name?

2 Must I be carried to the skies
On flowery beds of ease,
While others fought to win the prize,
And sailed through bloody seas?

3 Sure I must fight, if I would reign;
Increase my courage, Lord!
I 'll bear the toil, endure the pain,
Supported by thy word.

4 Thy saints, in all this glorious war,
Shall conquer, though they 're slain:
They see the triumph from afar,
And soon with Christ shall reign.

5 When that illustrious day shall rise,
And all thy armies shine
In robes of victory through the skies,
The glory shall be thine.

745. C. M.

1 Walk in the light! so shalt thou know
That fellowship of love
His spirit only can bestow,
Who reigns in light above.

2 Walk in the light! and thou shalt own
Thy darkness passed away,
Because that light hath on thee shone
In which is perfect day.

3 Walk in the light! and e'en the tomb
No fearful shade shall wear;
Glory shall chase away its gloom,
For Christ hath conquered there!

4 Walk in the light! and thine shall be
A path, though thorny, bright:
For God, by grace, shall dwell in thee,
And God himself is light!

746. L. M.

1 As body when the soul has fled,
As barren trees, decayed and dead,
Is faith; a hopeless, lifeless thing,
If not of righteous deeds the spring.

2 One cup of healing oil and wine,
One tear-drop shed on mercy's shrine,
Is thrice more grateful, Lord, to thee,
Than lifted eye or bended knee.

3 In true and genuine faith we trace
The source of every Christian grace;
Within the pious heart it plays,
A living fount of joy and praise.

4 Kind deeds of peace and love betray
Where'er the stream has found its way;
But where these spring not rich and fair,
The stream has never wandered there.

747. C. M.

1 Scorn not the slightest word or deed,
Nor deem it void of power;
There's fruit in each wind-wafted seed,
Waiting its natal hour.

2 A whispered word may touch the heart,
And call it back to life;
A look of love bid sin depart,
And still unholy strife.

3 No act falls fruitless; none can tell
How vast its power may be;
Nor what results enfolded dwell
Within it, silently.

4 Work, and despair not: bring thy mite,
Nor care how small it be;
God is with all that serve the right,
The holy, true, and free.

748. L. M.

1 The Lord receives his highest praise
From humble minds and hearts sincere;
While all the loud professor says
Offends the righteous Judge's ear.

2 To walk as children of the day,
To mark the precepts' holy light,
To wage the warfare, watch and pray,
Show who are pleasing in his sight.

3 Easy indeed it were to reach
A mansion in the courts above,
If swelling words and fluent speech
Might serve instead of faith and love.

4 But none shall gain the blissful place,
Or God's unclouded glory see,
Who talks of free and sovereign grace,
Unless that grace has made him free.

749. L. M.

1 Life is the time to serve the Lord,
The time to insure the great reward;
And while the lamp holds out to burn,
The vilest sinner may return.

2 Life is the season God has given
To fit us for the joys of heaven;
That day of grace fleets fast away,
And none its rapid course can stay.

3 Then what our thoughts design to do,
Let us with all our might pursue;
And wisely every hour employ,
That faith and hope may turn to joy.

750. L. M.

1 The God of glory walks his round,
From day to day, from year to year,
And warns us each, with awful sound,
"No longer stand ye idle here!

2 "Ye, whose young cheeks are rosy-bright,
Whose hands are strong, whose hearts are clear,
Waste not of hope the morning light!
Ah, fools, why stand ye idle here?

3 "And ye, whose locks of scanty gray
Foretell your latest travail near,
How swiftly fades your worthless day!
And stand ye yet so idle here?"

4 O Thou, by all thy works adored,
To whom the sinner's soul is dear,
Recall us to thy vineyard, Lord,
And grant us grace to please thee here!

751. 8 & 5s. M.

1 Every day hath toil and trouble,
Every heart hath care;
Meekly bear thine own full measure,
And thy brother's share.

Fear not, shrink not, though the burden
Heavy to thee prove;
God shall fill thy mouth with gladness,
And thy heart with love.

2 Patiently enduring, ever
Let thy spirit be
Bound, by links that cannot sever,
To humanity.
Labor! wait! thy Master perished
Ere his task was done:
Count not lost thy fleeting moments,
Life hath but begun.

3 Labor! wait! though midnight shadows
Gather round thee here,
And the storm above thee lowering
Fill thy heart with fear, —
Wait in hope! the morning dawneth
When the night is gone,
And a peaceful rest awaits thee
When thy work is done.

752. C. M.

1 Workman of God! O, lose not heart,
But learn what God is like;
And in the darkest battle-field
Thou shalt know where to strike.

2 O, blest is he to whom is given
The instinct that can tell
That God is on the field, when he
Is most invisible!

3 And blest is he who can divine
Where real right doth lie,
And dares to take the side that seems
Wrong to man's blindfold eye!

4 O, learn to scorn the praise of men!
O, learn to lose with God!
For Jesus won the world through shame,
And beckons thee his road.

PASSAGE OF TIME.

---

753. L. M.

1 The glories of our birth and state
Are shadows, not substantial things;
There is no armor against fate;
Death lays his icy hands on kings.

2 Princes and magistrates must fall,
And in the dust be equal made,
The high and mighty with the small,
Sceptre and crown with scythe and spade.

3 The laurel withers on our brow;
Then boast no more your mighty deeds:
Upon death's purple altar now
See where the victor victim bleeds!

4 All heads must come to the cold tomb;
Only the actions of the just
Preserve in death a rich perfume,
Smell sweet and blossom in the dust.

754. L. M.

1 God of eternity! from thee
Did infant time his being draw:
Moments and days, and months and years,
Revolve by thine unvaried law.

2 Silent, but swift, they glide away;
Steady and strong the current flows,
Lost in eternity's wide sea,
The boundless gulf from which it rose.

3 Yet while the shore, on either side,
Presents a gaudy, flattering show,
We gaze, in fond amusement lost,
Nor think to what a world we go.

4 Great Source of wisdom! teach our hearts
To know the worth of every hour;
That time may bear us on to joys
Beyond its measure and its power.

755. L. M.

1 Like shadows gliding o'er the plain,
Or clouds that roll successive on,
Man's busy generations pass,
And while we gaze, their forms are gone.

2 "He lived,—he died"; behold the sum,
The abstract of the historian's page!
Alike in God's all-seeing eye
The infant's day, the patriarch's age.

3 O Father, in whose mighty hand
The boundless years and ages lie!
Teach us thy boon of life to prize,
And use the moments as they fly;

4 To crowd the narrow span of life
With wise designs and virtuous deeds:
So shall we wake from death's dark night,
To share the glory that succeeds.

756. C. M.

1 Our God, our help in ages past,
Our hope for years to come,
Our shelter from the stormy blast,
And our eternal home!

2 Before the hills in order stood,
Or earth received her frame,
From everlasting thou art God,
To endless years the same.

3 Time, like an ever-rolling stream,
Bears all its sons away;
They fly, forgotten, as a dream
Dies at the opening day.

4 Our God, our help in ages past,
Our hope for years to come!
Be thou our guard while troubles last,
And our eternal home.

757. L. M.

1 Swift years, but teach me how to bear,
To feel, and act, with strength and skill,
To reason wisely, nobly dare,
And speed your courses as ye will.

2 When life's meridian toils are done,
How calm, how rich, the twilight glow!
The morning twilight of a sun,
That shines not here, on things below.

3 Press onward through each varying hour;
Let no weak fears thy course delay;
Immortal being, feel thy power;
Pursue thy bright and endless way.

758. 8, 8, & 4s. M.

1 Alas! how poor and little worth
Are all those glittering toys of earth
That lure us here!—
Dreams of a sleep that death must break:
Alas! before it bids us wake,
They disappear.

2 Our birth is but a starting-place;
Life is the running of the race,
And death the goal:
There all those glittering toys are brought;
That path alone, of all unsought,
Is found of all.

3 O, let the soul its slumbers break,
Arouse its senses, and awake
To see how soon
Life, like its glories, glides away,
And the stern footsteps of decay
Come stealing on.

759. S. M.

1 The swift-declining day,
How fast its moments fly!
While evening's broad and gloomy shade
Gains on the western sky.

2 Ye mortals, mark its pace;
Improve the hours of light;
And know, your Maker can command
An instantaneous night.

3 On the dark mountain's brow
Your feet shall quickly slide,
And from its airy summit dash
Your momentary pride.

4 What most demands your care,
O, be it still pursued!
Lest, slighted once, the season fair
Should never be renewed.

760. C. M.

1 How swift, alas! the moments fly!
How rush the years along!

Scarce here, yet gone already by, —
The burden of a song.

2 See childhood, youth, and manhood pass,
And age, with furrowed brow;
Time was, — time shall be, — but, alas!
Where, where, in time, is now?

3 Time is the measure but of change;
No present hour is found;
The past, the future, fill the range
Of time's unceasing round.

4 Then, pilgrim, let thy joys and fears
On time no longer lean;
But henceforth all thy hopes and fears
From earth's affections wean.

5 To God let grateful accents rise:
With truth, with virtue, live;
So all the bliss that time denies,
Eternity shall give.

761. C. M.

1 Forth to the land of promise bound,
Our desert path we tread;
God's fiery pillar for our guide,
His Captain at our head.

2 E'en now we faintly glimpse the hills,
And catch their distant blue;
And the bright city's gleaming spires
Rise dimly on our view.

3 There love shall have its perfect work,
And prayer be lost in praise,
And all the servants of our God
Their endless anthem raise.

IX.

DEATH.

I.

DYING OF CHILDREN.

(p. 537.)

II.

DYING OF THE BELIEVER.

(p. 542.)

III.

FUNEREAL.

(p. 546.)

DYING OF CHILDREN.

---

762. L. M.

1 As the sweet flower that scents the morn,
But withers in the rising day,
Thus lovely was this infant's dawn,
Thus swiftly fled its life away.

2 It died ere its expanding soul
Had ever burnt with wrong desires,
Had ever spurned at Heaven's control,
Or ever quenched its sacred fires.

3 Yet the sad hour that took the boy
Perhaps has spared a heavier doom,—
Snatched him from scenes of guilty joy,
Or from the pangs of ills to come.

4 He died to sin; he died to care;
But for a moment felt the rod;
Then, rising on the viewless air,
Spread his light wings and soared to God.

763. 7 & 6s. M.

1 In the broad fields of heaven,—
In the immortal bowers
By life's clear river dwelling,
Amid undying flowers,—
There hosts of beauteous spirits,
Fair children of the earth,
Linked in bright bands celestial,
Sing of their human birth.

2 They sing of earth and heaven;
Divinest voices rise
To God, their gracious Father,
Who called them to the skies:
They all are there,—in heaven,—
Safe, safe, and sweetly blest;
No cloud of sin can shadow
Their bright and holy rest.

764. S. M.

1 Go to thy rest, fair child!
Go to thy dreamless bed,
While yet so gentle, undefiled,
With blessings on thy head.

2 Ere sin has seared the breast,
Or sorrow woke the tear,
Rise to thy throne of changeless rest,
In yon celestial sphere.

3 Because thy smile was fair,
Thy lip and eye so bright,
Because thy loving cradle-care
Was such a fond delight,—

4 Shall love, with weak embrace,
Thy upward wing detain?
No! gentle angel, seek thy place
Amid the cherub train.

765. C. M.

1 Calm on the bosom of thy God,
Young spirit, rest thee now!
E'en while with us thy footsteps trod,
His seal was on thy brow.

2 Dust, to its narrow house beneath!
Soul, to its place on high!
They that have seen thy look in death
No more may fear to die.

3 Lone are the paths, and sad the bowers,
Whence thy meek smile is gone;
But, oh! a brighter home than ours,
In heaven, is now thine own.

766. 8 & 7s. M.

1 Fare thee well, thou fondly cherished,
Dear, dear spirit, fare thee well;
He who lent thee hath recalled thee,
Back with him and his to dwell.

2 Like a sunbeam, through our dwelling
Shone thy presence, bright and calm;
Thou didst add a zest to pleasure;
To our sorrows thou wert balm.

3 Yet while mourning, O our lost one!
Come no visions of despair!
Seated on thy tomb, Faith's angel
Saith thou art not, art not, there.

4 Where, then, art thou? with the Saviour,
Blest, for ever blest to be;
'Mid the sinless little children,
Who have heard his "Come to me."

5 Passed the shades of Death's dark valley,
Thou art leaning on his breast,
Where the wicked may not enter,
And the weary are at rest.

6 Plead that, in a Father's mercy,
All our sins may be forgiven;
Angel! plead, that thou mayst greet us,
Ransomed, at the gates of heaven.

767. 6 & 5s. M.

1 Saviour, now receive him
To thy bosom mild;
For with thee we leave him,
Blessed, blessed child!

2 Though his eye hath brightened
Oft our weary way,

And his clear laugh lightened
 Half our hearts' dismay.

3 Now let thought behold him
 In his angel rest,
Where those arms enfold him
 To a Saviour's breast.

4 We yield but what was given
 At thy holy call;
The beautiful to heaven,
 Thou who givest all!

5 Still 'mid heavy mourning,
 Look thee now to God!
There, thy spirit turning,
 Kneel beside the sod.

DYING OF THE BELIEVER.

---

768. C. M.

1 Thou must go forth alone, my soul!
Thou must go forth alone,
To other scenes, to other worlds,
That mortal hath not known.
Thou must go forth alone, my soul,
To tread the narrow vale;
But He whose word is sure hath said
His comforts shall not fail.

2 Thou must go forth alone, my soul!
To meet thy God above:
But shrink not, — He hath said, my soul,
He is a God of love.
His rod and staff shall comfort thee
Across the dreary road,
Till thou shalt join the blessed ones
In heaven's serene abode.

769. C. M.

1 Behold the western evening light!
It melts in deeper gloom;
So calm the righteous sink away,
Descending to the tomb.
The winds breathe low, — the yellow leaf
Scarce whispers from the tree!
So gently flows the parting breath,
When good men cease to be.

2 How beautiful, on all the hills,
The crimson light is shed!
'T is like the peace the dying gives
To mourners round his bed.
How mildly on the wandering cloud
The sunset beam is cast!
So sweet the memory left behind,
When loved ones breathe their last.

3 And lo! above the dews of night
The vesper star appears!
So faith lights up the mourner's heart,
Whose eyes are dim with tears.
Night falls, but soon the morning light
Its glories shall restore;
And thus the eyes that sleep in death
Shall wake to close no more.

770. L. M.

1 How blest the righteous when he dies!
When sinks a trusting soul to rest,

How mildly beam the closing eyes,
How gently heaves the expiring breast!

2 So fades a summer cloud away,
So sinks the gale when storms are o'er;
So gently shuts the eye of day,
So dies a wave along the shore.

3 Farewell, conflicting hopes and fears,
Where lights and shades alternate dwell;
How bright the unchanging morn appears!
Farewell, inconstant world, farewell!

4 Life's duty done, as sinks the day,
Light from its load the spirit flies;
While heaven and earth combine to say,
"How blest the righteous when he dies!"

771. 8 & 7s. M.

1 Sister, thou wast mild and lovely,
Gentle as the summer breeze;
Pleasant as the air of evening,
When it floats among the trees.

2 Peaceful be thy silent slumber,
Peaceful in the grave so low;
Thou no more wilt join our number;
Here, no more our songs shalt know.

3 Dearest sister, thou hast left us;
Here thy loss we deeply feel;
But 't is God that hath bereft us:
He can all our sorrows heal.

4 Yet again we hope to meet thee,
When the day of life has fled,
Then in heaven with joy to greet thee,
Where no farewell tear is shed.

772. 7s. M.

1 VITAL spark of heavenly flame,
Quit, O, quit this mortal frame!
Trembling, hoping, lingering, flying,
O the pain, the bliss of dying!
Cease, fond nature, cease thy strife,
And let me languish into life.

2 Hark! they whisper! angels say,
"Sister spirit, come away!"
What is this absorbs me quite,
Steals my senses, shuts my sight,
Drowns my spirit, draws my breath?
Tell me, my soul, can this be death?

3 The world recedes; it disappears;
Heaven opens on my eyes; my ears
With sounds seraphic ring.
Lend, lend your wings! I mount, I fly!
O grave, where is thy victory?
O death, where is thy sting?

FUNEREAL.

773. L. M.

1 Unveil thy bosom, faithful tomb!
   Take this new treasure to thy trust,
And give these sacred relics room
   To slumber in the silent dust.

2 Nor pain, nor grief, nor anxious fear,
   Invade thy bounds; no mortal woes
Can reach the peaceful sleeper here,
   While angels watch the soft repose.

3 So Jesus slept; God's dying Son
   Passed through the grave, and blest the bed.
Then rest, dear saint, till from his throne
   The morning break and pierce the shade.

4 Break from his throne, illustrious morn!
   Attend, O earth, his sovereign word!
Restore thy trust! the glorious form
   Shall then arise to meet the Lord.

774. L. M.

1 Asleep in Jesus! blessed sleep!
From which none ever wakes to weep;
A calm and undisturbed repose,
Unbroken by the dread of foes.

2 Asleep in Jesus! peaceful rest!
Whose waking is supremely blest;
No fear, no woes, shall dim that hour,
Which manifests the Saviour's power!

3 Asleep in Jesus! time nor space
Debars this precious hiding-place;
On India's plains or Lapland's snows
Believers find the same repose.

4 Asleep in Jesus! far from thee
Thy kindred and their graves may be;
But thine is still a blessed sleep,
From which none ever wakes to weep.

775. 12 & 11s. M.

Thou art gone to the grave; but we will not deplore thee;
Though sorrows and darkness encompass the tomb;
The Saviour has passed through its portals before thee;
And the lamp of his love is thy guide through gloom.

2 Thou art gone to the grave; we no longer behold thee,
Nor tread the rough paths of the world by thy side:
But the wide arms of mercy are spread to enfold thee,
And sinners may hope, since the Saviour hath died.

3 Thou art gone to the grave; and, its mansion forsaking,
Perchance thy weak spirit in doubt lingered long;
But the sunshine of heaven beamed bright on thy waking,
And the sound thou didst hear was the seraphim's song.

4 Thou art gone to the grave; but we will not deplore thee;
Since God was thy Refuge, thy Guardian, thy Guide;
He gave thee, he took thee, and he will restore thee;
And death has no sting, since the Saviour hath died.

776. 10s. M.

1 Go to the grave in all thy glorious prime,
In full activity of zeal and power;
A Christian cannot die before his time,
The Lord's appointment is the servant's hour.

2 Go to the grave; at noon from labor cease;
  Rest on thy sheaves, thy harvest-work is done;
Come from the heat of battle, and in peace,
  Soldier, go home; with thee the field is won.

3 Go to the grave, for there thy Saviour lay,
  In Death's embraces, ere he rose on high;
And all the ransomed, by that narrow way,
  Pass to eternal life beyond the sky.

4 Go to the grave; — no, take thy seat above;
  Be thy pure spirit present with the Lord,
Where thou for faith and hope hast perfect love,
  And open vision for the written word.

777. C. M.

1 O, NOT when the death-prayer is said,
  The life of life departs;
The body in the grave is laid,
  Its beauty in our hearts.

2 This frame, O God, this feeble breath,
  Thy hand may soon destroy;
We think of thee, and feel in death
  A deep and holy joy.

3 Dim is the light of vanished years
  In glory yet to come;
O idle grief, O foolish tears,
  When Jesus calls us home!

778. C. M.

1 Dear as thou wast, and justly dear,
We would not weep for thee;
One thought shall check the starting tear, —
It is — that thou art free.

2 And thus shall faith's consoling power
The tears of love restrain;
O, who that saw thy parting hour
Could wish thee here again?

3 Gently the passing spirit fled,
Sustained by grace divine;
O, may such grace on us be shed,
And make our end like thine!

779. 8 & 7s. M.

1 Brother, rest from sin and sorrow!
Death is o'er, and life is won;
On thy slumber dawns no morrow:
Rest! thine earthly race is run.

2 Brother, wake! the night is waning;
Endless day is round thee poured;
Enter thou the rest remaining
For the people of the Lord.

3 Brother, wake! for He who loved thee,
He who died that thou might'st live,
He who graciously approved thee,
Waits thy crown of joy to give.

4 Fare thee well! though woe is blending
With the tones of early love,
Triumph high and joy unending
Wait thee in the realms above!

780. 6 & 4s. M.

1 LOWLY and solemn be
Thy children's cry to thee,
Father divine!
A hymn of suppliant breath,
Owning that life and death
Alike are thine.

2 O Father, in that hour
When earth all succoring power
Shall disavow,
When spear and shield and crown
In faintness are cast down,
Sustain us thou!

3 By him who bowed to take
The death-cup for our sake,
The thorn, the rod,
From whom the last dismay
Was not to pass away,
Aid us, O God!

4 Tremblers beside the grave,
We call on thee to save,
Father divine!
Hear, hear our suppliant breath;
Keep us in life and death,
Thine, only thine.

781. S. M.

1 SERVANT of God, well done!
Rest from thy loved employ;
The battle fought, the victory won,
Enter thy Master's joy.

2 Tranquil amidst alarms,
Death found him on the field,
A veteran slumbering on his arms,
Beneath his red-cross shield.

3 The pains of death are past;
Labor and sorrow cease;
And, life's long service closed at last,
His soul is found in peace.

4 Soldier of Christ, well done!
Praise be thy blest employ;
And while eternal ages run,
Rest in thy Saviour's joy.

782. P. M.

1 BROTHER, thou art gone before us,
And thy saintly soul is flown,
Where tears are wiped from every eye,
And sorrow is unknown:
From the burden of the flesh,
And from care and fear released,
Where the wicked cease from troubling
And the weary are at rest.

2 Sin no more can taint thy spirit,
Nor can doubt thy faith assail;
Thy soul its welcome has received,
Thy strength shall never fail:
And thou 'rt sure to meet the good,
Whom on earth thou lovedst best,
Where the wicked cease from troubling
And the weary are at rest.

3 To thy grave we sadly bear thee,
There in dust we place thy head;
We lay the turf above thee now,
And seal thy narrow bed:
But thy spirit soars away,
Free, among the faithful blest,
Where the wicked cease from troubling
And the weary are at rest.

783. C. M.

1 Why do we mourn departing friends,
Or shake at death's alarms?
'T is but the voice that Jesus sends,
To call them to his arms.

2 Why should we tremble to convey
Their bodies to the tomb?
'T is but the consecrated way
To their eternal home.

784. L. M.

1 Farewell! what power of words can tell
The sorrows of a last farewell,
When, standing by the mournful bier,
We mingle with our prayers a tear!

2 O God, extend thy arms of love!
A spirit seeketh thee above:
Ye heavenly palaces, unclose,
Receive the weary to repose!

3 Redeemer! thou didst mourn the dead;
Be with us in the time of need,
And grant us all, from sin set free,
At length to rest in heaven with thee!

785. L. M.

1 O God! whose thunder shakes the sky,
Whose eye this atom-globe surveys;
To thee, my only rock, I fly,
Thy mercy in thy justice praise.

2 The mystic mazes of thy will,
The shadows of celestial night,
Are past the power of human skill;
But what the Eternal does is right.

3 O, teach me, in this trying hour,
When anguish swells the rising tear,
To still my sorrows, own thy power,
Thy goodness love, thy justice fear.

4 The gloomy mantle of the night,
Which on my sinking spirit steals,
Will vanish at the morning light,
Which God, my hope and trust, reveals.

786. 7 & 8s. M

1 Lift not thou the wailing voice;
Weep not when a Christian dieth:
Up, where blessed saints rejoice,
Ransomed now, the spirit flieth:
High in heaven's own light it dwelleth;
Full the song of triumph swelleth:
Freed from earth and earthly failing,
Lift for them no voice of wailing.

2 They who die in Christ are blest;
Ours be, then, no thought of grieving;
Sweetly with their God they rest,
All their toils and troubles leaving:
So be ours the faith that saveth,
Hope that every trial braveth,
Love that to the end endureth,
And, through Christ, the crown secureth.

X.

IMMORTALITY.

I.

JUDGMENT.

(p. 559.)

II.

THE DEAD.

(p. 562.)

III.

HEAVEN.

(p. 575.)

JUDGMENT.

---

787. L. M.

1 That day of wrath, that dreadful day,
When heaven and earth shall pass away, —
What power shall be the sinner's stay?
How shall he meet that dreadful day?

2 When, shrivelling like a parchèd scroll,
The flaming heavens together roll,
When louder yet, and yet more dread,
Swells the high trump that wakes the dead, —

3 O, on that day, that wrathful day,
When man to judgment wakes from clay,
Be thou the trembling sinner's stay,
Though heaven and earth shall pass away!

788. L. M.

1 The Lord will come; the earth shall quake,
The hills their fixèd seat forsake;

And, withering, from the vault of night
The stars withdraw their feeble light.

2 The Lord will come, but not the same
As once in lowly form he came,
A silent Lamb to slaughter led,
The bruised, the suffering, and the dead.

3 Can this be he who wont to stray
A pilgrim on the world's highway,
By power oppressed, and mocked by pride?
O God, is this the Crucified?

4 Go, tyrants, to the rocks complain;
Go, seek the mountain's cleft in vain;
But faith, victorious o'er the tomb,
Shall sing for joy, "The Lord is come!"

789. L. M.

1 ETERNITY! Eternity!
How long art thou, Eternity!
Yet onward still to thee we speed,
As to the fight th' impatient steed,
As ship to port, or shaft from bow,
Or swift as couriers homeward go.
Mark well, O man, Eternity!

2 Eternity! Eternity!
How long art thou, Eternity!
As in a ball's concentric round
Nor starting-point nor end is found;
So thou, Eternity, so vast,
No entrance and no exit hast.
Mark well, O man, Eternity!

3 Eternity! Eternity!
How long art thou, Eternity!
Came there a bird, each thousandth year,
One sand-grain from the hills to bear,
When all had vanished, grain by grain,
Eternity would still remain.
Mark well, O man, Eternity!

THE DEAD.

---

790. S. M.

1 Our fathers, where are they,
With all they called their own?
Their joys and griefs, and hopes and cares,
And wealth and honor gone.

2 God of our fathers, hear,
Thou everlasting Friend!
While we, as on life's utmost verge,
Our souls to thee commend.

3 Of all the pious dead
May we the footsteps trace,
Till with them, in the land of light,
We dwell before thy face.

791. C. M.

1 Give me the wings of faith to rise
Within the veil, and see

The saints above,—how great their joy
And bright their glories be!

2 I ask them whence their victory came;
They, with united breath,
Ascribe their conquest to the Lamb,
Their triumph to his death.

792. S. H. M.

1 Friend after friend departs;
Who hath not lost a friend?
There is no union here of hearts,
That finds not here an end.
Were this frail world our only rest,
Living or dying, none were blest.

2 There is a world above,
Where parting is unknown,—
A whole eternity of love
And blessedness alone;
And faith beholds the dying here
Translated to that happier sphere.

3 Thus, star by star declines,
Till all are passed away,
As morning high and higher shines
To pure and perfect day.
Nor sink those stars in empty night,—
They hide themselves in heaven's own light.

793. C. M.

1 The great Apostle, called by grace,
Weaned from all works beside,
Preached the same faith he once abhorred,
And Christ, whom he denied.

2 In perils and in troubles oft,
His toilsome life he past;
But he who turned his heart at first
Upheld him to the last.

3 A chosen vessel of his will,
He fought the fight of faith;
And gained the crown of righteousness,
Obedient unto death.

4 Thus, Lord of grace, to all thy will
Obedient may we be;
And follow meekly in his steps,
E'en as he followed thee.

794. 11s. M.

1 How cheering the thought, that the spirits in bliss
Will bow their bright wings to a world such as this;
Will leave the sweet joys of the mansions above,
To breathe o'er our bosoms some message of love.

2 They come, — on the wings of the morning they come, —
Impatient to lead some poor wanderer home,

Some pilgrim to snatch from this stormy abode,
And lay him to rest in the arms of his God.

3 They come when we wander, they come when we pray,
In mercy to guard us wherever we stray;
A glorious cloud, their bright witness is given;
Encircling us here, are these angels of heaven.

795. P. M.

1 Jews were wrought to cruel madness,
Christians fled in fear and sadness,
Mary stood the cross beside.

2 At its foot her foot she planted,
By the dreadful scene undaunted,
Till the gentle sufferer died.

3 Poets oft have sung her story,
Painters decked her brow with glory,
Priests her name have deified;

4 But no worship, song, or glory
Touches like that simple story, —
" Mary stood the cross beside."

5 And when under fierce oppression
Goodness suffers like transgression,
Christ again is crucified.

6 But if love be there, true-hearted,
By no grief or terror parted,
Mary stands the cross beside.

796. C. M.

1 THE dead are like the stars by day,
Withdrawn from mortal eye,
Yet holding unperceived their way
Through the unclouded sky.

2 By them, through holy hope and love,
We feel, in hours serene,
Connected with a world above,
Immortal and unseen.

3 For death his sacred seal hath set
On bright and bygone hours;
And they we mourn are with us yet,
Are more than ever ours;—

4 Ours, by the pledge of love and faith,
By hopes of heaven on high;
By trust, triumphant over death,
In immortality.

797. P. M.

1 CALL them from the dead
For our eyes to see;
Prophet-bards, whose awful word
Shook the earth, " Thus saith the Lord,"
And made the idols flee,—
A glorious company!

2 Call them from the dead
For our eyes to see;

Sons of wisdom, song, and power,
Giving earth her richest dower,
And making nations free, —
A glorious company!

3 Call them from the dead
For our eyes to see;
Forms of beauty, love, and grace,
"Sunshine in the shady place,"
That made it life to be, —
A blessed company!

4 Call them from the dead, —
Vain the call would be;
But the hand of death shall lay,
Like that of Christ, its healing clay
On eyes which then shall see
That glorious company!

798. 6 & 4s. M.

1 Mortal, the angels say,
Peace to thy heart!
We, too, O mortal, have
Been as thou art, —
Hope-lifted, doubt-depressed,
Seeing in part,
Tried, troubled, tempted,
Sustained, as thou art.

2 Ye, too, they gently say,
Angels shall be;
Ye, too, O mortals,
From earth shall be free:

Yet in earth's loved ones
  Still shall have part,
Bearing God's strength and love
  To the torn heart.

3 Mortal, they sweetly say,
  Be our thoughts one;
Bend thou with us and pray,
  "Thy will be done!"
Our God is thy God;
  Willeth the best;
Trust him as we trusted,—
  Rest as we rest!

799. L. M.

1 The kings of old have shrine and tomb
In many a minster's haughty gloom;
And green, along the ocean's side,
The mounds arise where heroes died;
But show me on thy flowery breast,
Earth! where thy nameless martyrs rest;—

2 The thousands that, uncheered by praise,
Have made one offering of their days;
For truth, for heaven, for freedom's sake,
Resigned the bitter cup to take;
And silently, in fearless faith,
Have bowed their noble souls to death.

3 What though no stone the record bears
Of their deep thoughts and lonely prayers,

May not our inmost hearts be stilled,
With knowledge of their presence filled,
And by their lives be taught to prize
The meekness of self-sacrifice?

800. C. M.

1 Glory to God! whose witness-train,
Those heroes bold in faith,
Could smile on poverty and pain,
And triumph even in death.

2 O, may that faith our hearts sustain,
Wherein they fearless stood,
When, in the power of cruel men,
They poured their willing blood.

3 God, whom we serve, our God, can save;
Can damp the scorching flame,
Can build an ark, can smooth the wave,
For such as love his name.

4 Lord! if thine arm support us still
With its eternal strength,
We shall o'ercome the mightiest ill,
And conquerors prove, at length.

801. C. M.

1 Another hand is beckoning us,
Another call is given;
And glows once more with angel steps
The path that leads to heaven.

2 O, half we deemed she needed not
The changing of her sphere,
To give to heaven a shining one,
Who walked an angel here.

3 Unto our Father's will alone
One thought hath reconciled;
That he whose love exceedeth ours
Hath taken home his child.

4 Fold her, O Father, in thine arms,
And let her henceforth be
A messenger of love between
Our human hearts and thee.

5 Still let her mild rebukings stand
Between us and the wrong,
And her dear memory serve to make
Our faith in goodness strong.

802. L. M.

1 Why weep for those, frail child of woe,
Who fled and left thee mourning here?
Triumphant o'er their latest foe,
They glory in a brighter sphere.

2 Space cannot check, thought cannot bound,
The high-exulting souls whom he,
Who formed these million worlds around,
Takes to his own eternity.

3 Weep, weep no more; their voices raise
The song of triumph high to God,
And wouldst thou join their song of praise,
Walk humbly in the path they trod.

803. L. M.

1 O, why should friendship grieve for those
Who safe have reached the heavenly shore,
Released from all their fears and woes?
They are not lost, — but gone before.

2 Dear is the spot where Christians sleep,
And sweet the strain which angels pour;
O, why should we in anguish weep?
They are not lost, — but gone before.

804. 6s. M.

1 Flung to the heedless winds,
Or on the waters cast,
Their ashes shall be watched,
And gathered at the last:
And from that scattered dust,
Around us and abroad
Shall spring a plenteous seed
Of witnesses for God.

2 The Father hath received
Their latest living breath;
Yet vain is Satan's boast
Of victory in their death:
Still, still, though dead, they speak,
And trumpet-tongued proclaim
To many a wakening land
The one availing name.

805. C. M.

1 Answer me, burning stars of night!
Where is the spirit gone,
That past the reach of human sight,
E'en as a breeze, hath flown?

2 O many-toned and chainless wind!
Thou art a wanderer free;
Tell me if thou its place canst find,
Far over mount or sea?

3 Ye clouds, that gorgeously repose
Around the setting sun,
Answer! have ye a home for those
Whose earthly race is run?

4 O, speak, thou voice of God within!
Thou of the deep low tone!
Answer me through life's restless din,
Where is the spirit flown?

5 And the voice answers, "Be thou still;
Enough to know is given:
Clouds, winds, and stars their part fulfil;
Thine is to trust in Heaven!"

806. C. M.

1 The triumphs of the martyred saints
The joyous lay demand;
The heart delights in song to dwell
On that victorious band,—

Those whom the senseless world abhorred,
Who cast the world aside,
Deeming it worthless, for the sake
Of Christ, their Lord and Guide.

2 For him they braved the tyrant's rage,
The scourge's cruel smart;
The wild beast's fang their bodies tore,
But vanquished not the heart;
Like lambs before the sword they fell,
Nor cry nor plaint expressed;
For patience kept the conscious mind,
And armed the fearless breast.

3 What tongue can tell the crown prepared
The martyr's brow to grace?
His shining robe, his joys unknown,
Before thy glorious face?
Vouchsafe us, Lord, if such thy will,
Clear skies and seasons calm;
If not, the martyr's cross to bear,
And win the martyr's palm.

807. C. M.

1 THERE is a state unknown, unseen,
Where parted souls must be;
And but a step doth lie between
That world of souls and me.

2 I see no light, I hear no sound,
When midnight shades are spread;
Yet angels pitch their tents around
And guard my quiet bed.

3 The things unseen, O God, reveal;
My spirit's vision clear,
Till I shall feel, and see, and know,
That those I love are near.

4 Impart the faith that soars on high,
Beyond this earthly strife;
That holds sweet converse with the sky,
And lives eternal life.

HEAVEN.

---

808. C. M.

1 Ye golden lamps of heaven! farewell,
With all your feeble light:
Farewell, thou ever-changing moon,
Pale empress of the night!

2 And thou, refulgent orb of day!
In brighter flames arrayed,
My soul, which springs beyond thy sphere,
No more demands thine aid.

3 Ye stars are but the shining dust
Of my divine abode,
The pavement of those heavenly courts,
Where I shall reign with God.

4 No more the drops of piercing grief
Shall swell into mine eyes,
Nor the meridian sun decline,
Amid those brighter skies.

5 There all the millions of his saints
Shall in one song unite;
And each the bliss of all shall view
With infinite delight.

809. C. M.

1 BLEST be the everlasting God,
The Father of our Lord;
Be his abounding mercy praised,
His majesty adored.

2 When from the dead he raised his Son,
And called him to the sky,
He gave our souls a lively hope
That they should never die.

3 There 's an inheritance divine
Reserved against that day;
'T is uncorrupted, undefiled,
And cannot waste away.

4 Saints by the power of God are kept
Till the salvation come;
We walk by faith, as strangers here,
Till Christ shall call us home.

810. C. P. M.

1 ALL earthly charms, however dear,
Howe'er they please the eye or ear,
Will quickly fade and fly;

Of earthly glory faint the blaze,
And soon the transitory rays
In endless darkness die.

2 The nobler beauties of the just
Shall never moulder in the dust,
Or know a sad decay;
Their honors time and death defy,
And round the throne of heaven on high
Beam everlasting day.

811. C. M.

1 Nor eye hath seen, nor ear hath heard,
Nor sense nor reason known,
What joys the Father has prepared
For those that love his Son.

2 Pure are the joys above the sky,
And all the region peace;
No wanton lips nor envious eye
Can see or taste the bliss.

3 Those holy gates for ever bar
Pollution, sin, and shame;
None shall obtain admittance there,
But followers of the Lamb.

812. C. M.

1 There is a land of pure delight,
Where saints immortal reign,
Infinite day excludes the night,
And pleasures banish pain.

2 There everlasting spring abides,
And never-withering flowers;
Death, like a narrow sea, divides
This heavenly land from ours.

3 Sweet fields, beyond the swelling flood,
Stand dressed in living green:
So to the Jews old Canaan stood,
While Jordan rolled between.

4 But timorous mortals start and shrink,
To cross this narrow sea,
And linger shivering on the brink,
And fear to launch away.

5 O, could we make our doubts remove,
Those gloomy doubts that rise,
And see the Canaan that we love,
With unbeclouded eyes, —

6 Could we but climb where Moses stood,
And view the landscape o'er, —
Not Jordan's stream, nor death's cold flood,
Should fright us from the shore.

813. S. M.

1 O, WHERE shall rest be found,
Rest for the weary soul?
'T were vain the ocean depths to sound,
Or pierce to either pole:

2 The world can never give
The bliss for which we sigh;
'T is not the whole of life to live,
Nor all of death to die.

3 Beyond this vale of tears,
There is a life above,
Unmeasured by the flight of years,
And all that life is love.

814. L. M.

1 O, WHEN the hours of life are past,
And death's dark shade arrives at last,
It is not sleep, it is not rest,—
'T is glory opening to the blest.

2 There parted hearts again shall meet,
In union holy, calm, and sweet;
There, grief find rest; and never more
Shall sorrow call them to deplore.

3 No storms shall ride the troubled air;
No voice of passion enter there;
But all be peaceful as the sigh
Of evening gales, that breathe and die.

815. L. M.

1 THERE is a glorious world on high,
Resplendent with eternal day;
Faith views the blissful prospect nigh,
While God's own word reveals the way.

2 There shall the servants of the Lord
With never-fading lustre shine;
Surprising honor, vast reward,
Conferred on man by love divine!

3 The shining firmament shall fade,
And sparkling stars resign their light;
But these shall know nor change nor shade,
For ever fair, for ever bright.

4 On wings of faith and strong desire,
O, may our spirits daily rise,
And reach at last the shining choir
In the bright mansions of the skies!

816. S. M.

1 "For ever with the Lord,"
Amen. So let it be;
Life from the dead is in that word;
'T' is immortality.
Here in the body pent,
Absent from him I roam;
Yet nightly pitch my moving tent
A day's march nearer home.

2 My Father's house on high,
Home of my soul, how near,
At times, to faith's aspiring eye,
Thy golden gates appear!
Yet doubts still intervene,
And all my comfort flies;
Like Noah's dove, I flit between
Rough seas and stormy skies.

3 "For ever with the Lord!"
Father, if 't is thy will,
The promise of thy gracious word,
E'en here, to me fulfil.
Be thou at my right hand,
So shall I never fail:
Uphold me, and I needs must stand;
Fight, and I shall prevail.

4 So, when my latest breath
Shall rend the veil in twain,
By death I shall escape from death,
And life eternal gain.
Knowing "as I am known,"
How shall I love that word,
And oft repeat before the throne,
"For ever with the Lord!"

817. 8 & 7s. M.

1 O THE hour when this material
Shall have vanished like a cloud!
And amid the wide ethereal
All the invisible shall crowd!
And the naked soul, surrounded
By realities unknown,
Triumphs in the view unbounded,
Feels herself with God alone!

2 Angels! let the anxious stranger
In your tender care be blest;
Hoping, waiting, free from danger,
Till the trumpet end her rest;

Till the trump which shakes creation
  Through the circling heavens shall roll,
Till the day of consummation,
  Till the bridal of the soul!

3 Can I trust a fellow-being?
  Can I trust an angel's care?
O thou merciful All-seeing,
  Guide me by thy presence there!
Jesus! blessed Mediator!
  Thou the airy path hast trod,
Thou, the Judge, the Consummator,
  Shepherd of the fold of God!

4 Blessed fold! no foe can enter,
  And no friend departeth thence;
Jesus is their Sun, their Centre,
  And their shield Omnipotence!
Blessed, for the Lamb shall feed them,
  And their tears shall wipe away,
To the living Fountain lead them,
  Till fruition's perfect day!

5 Lo, it comes,—that day of wonder!
  Louder thunders shake the skies!
Hades' gates are burst asunder!
  See the new-clothed myriads rise!
Thought, repress thy weak endeavor,
  Here must reason prostrate fall;
O the ineffable Forever!
  And the eternal All in All!

818. C. M.

1 When I can read my title clear
To mansions in the skies,
I bid farewell to every fear,
And wipe my weeping eyes.

2 Let cares like a wild deluge come,
And storms of sorrow fall,
May I but safely reach my home,
My God, my heaven, my all!

3 There shall I bathe my weary soul
In seas of heavenly rest,
And not a wave of trouble roll
Across my peaceful breast.

819. 8 & 6s. M.

1 There is an hour of peaceful rest
To mourning wanderers given;
There is a joy for souls distressed,
A balm for every wounded breast;
'T is found alone in heaven.

2 There is a home for weary souls
By sins and sorrows driven,
When tossed on life's tempestuous shoals,
Where storms arise, and ocean rolls,
And all is drear but heaven.

3 There faith lifts up the tearless eye,
The heart no longer riven,

And views the tempest passing by,
Sees evening shadows quickly fly,
And all serene in heaven.

820. 8, 8, & 7s. M.

1 Lo! the seal of death is breaking;
Those who slept its sleep are waking;
Heaven opes its portals fair!
There the harps of God are ringing,
There the seraphs' hymn is flinging
Music on immortal air.

2 There, no more at eve declining,
Suns without a cloud are shining
O'er the land of life and love;
There the founts of life are flowing,
Flowers unknown to time are blowing,
In that radiant scene above.

3 There no sigh of memory swelleth;
There no tear of misery welleth;
Hearts will bleed or break no more;
Past is all the cold world's scorning,
Gone the night, and broke the morning,
Over all the golden shore.

821. L. M.

1 This life 's a dream, an empty show;
But the bright world to which I go
Hath joys substantial and sincere:
When shall I wake and find me there?

2 O glorious hour! O blest abode!
I shall be near and like my God!
And flesh and sin no more control
The sacred pleasures of my soul.

3 My flesh shall slumber in the ground
Till the last trumpet's joyful sound;
Then burst the chains with sweet surprise,
And in my Saviour's image rise.

822. L. M.

1 HEAVEN is a place of rest from sin;
But all who hope to enter there
Must here that holy course begin,
Which shall their souls for rest prepare.

2 Clean hearts, O God, in us create,
Right spirits, Lord, in us renew;
Commence we now that higher state,
Now do thy will as angels do.

3 In Jesus' footsteps may we tread,
Learn every lesson of his love;
And be from grace to glory led,
From heaven below to heaven above.

823. L. M.

1 WHAT must it be to dwell above,
At God's right hand, where Jesus reigns,
Since the sweet earnest of his love
O'erwhelms us on these earthly plains!

No heart can think, no tongue explain,
What joy it is with Christ to reign.

2 When sin no more obstructs our sight,
When sorrow pains our hearts no more,
How shall we view the Prince of Light,
And all his works of grace explore!
What heights and depths of love divine
Will there through endless ages shine!

3 This is the heaven I long to know;
For this, with patience, I would wait,
Till, raised from heaven here below,
I mount to my celestial seat,
And wave my palm, and wear my crown,
And, with the elders, cast them down.

824. S. M.

1 Far from these scenes of night
Unbounded glories rise,
And realms of infinite delight,
Unknown to mortal eyes.

2 There sickness never comes;
There grief no more complains;
Health triumphs in immortal bloom,
And purest pleasure reigns.

3 No strife nor envy there
The sons of peace molest;
But harmony, and love sincere,
Fill every happy breast.

4 No cloud those regions know,
For ever bright and fair;
For sin, the source of mortal woe,
Can never enter there.

5 There night is never known,
Nor sun's faint, sickly ray;
But glory from the eternal throne
Spreads everlasting day.

825. C. M.

1 Jerusalem! my happy home!
Name ever dear to me!
When shall my labors have an end
In joy, and peace, and thee?

2 There happier bowers than Eden's bloom,
Nor sin nor sorrow know:
Blest seats! through bright or stormy scenes
I onward press to you.

3 Apostles, martyrs, prophets, there
Around my Saviour stand;
And soon my friends in Christ below
Will join the glorious band.

4 Jerusalem! my happy home!
My soul still pants for thee;
Then shall my labors have an end,
When I thy peace shall see.

826. C. M.

1 Blest hour, when virtuous friends shall meet,
Shall meet to part no more,
And with celestial welcome greet,
On an immortal shore.

2 The parent finds the long-lost child;
Brothers on brothers gaze;
The tear of resignation mild
Is changed to joy and praise.

3 Each tender tie, dissolved with pain,
With endless bliss is crowned;
All that was dead revives again,
All that was lost is found.

4 Congenial minds, arrayed in light,
High thoughts shall interchange;
Nor cease, with ever-new delight,
On wings of love to range.

5 Their Father marks their generous flame,
And looks complacent down;
The smile that owns their filial claim
Is their immortal crown.

827. P. M.

1 When shall we meet again?
Meet ne'er to sever?
When will peace wreathe her chain
Round us for ever?

Our hearts will ne'er repose
Safe from each blast that blows
In this dark vale of woes, —
  Never, — no, never!

2 Up to that world of light
  Take us, dear Saviour;
May we all there unite,
  Happy for ever:
Where kindred spirits dwell,
There may our music swell,
And time our joys dispel
  Never, — no, never!

3 Soon shall we meet again,
  Meet ne'er to sever;
Soon shall peace wreathe her chain
  Round us for ever:
Our hearts will then repose
Secure from fears or woes;
Our songs of praise shall close
  Never, — no, never!

828. 11s. M.

1 I WOULD not live alway; I ask not to stay,
Where storm after storm rises dark o'er the way;
I would not live alway, thus fettered by sin,
Temptation without, and corruption within.

2 I would not live alway; no, welcome the tomb,
Since Jesus has lain there, I dread not its gloom;
There sweet be my rest, till he bid me arise,
To hail him in triumph descending the skies.

3 Who, who would live alway, away from his God,
Away from yon heaven, that blissful abode?
Where the rivers of pleasure flow o'er the bright plains,
And the noontide of glory eternally reigns;—

4 Where the saints of all ages in harmony meet,
Their Saviour and brethren transported to greet;
While the anthems of rapture unceasingly roll,
And the smile of the Lord is the feast of the soul.

829. C. M.

1 O HALLOWED memories of the past,
Ye legends old and fair,
Still be your light upon us cast,
Your music on the air.

2 For hearts the beautiful that feel,
Whose pulse of love beats strong
The opening heavens new light reveal,
Glory to God! their song.

3 And while from out our dying dust
Light more than life doth stream,
We bless the faith that bids us trust
The heaven that we dream.

830. L. M.

1 THINE earthly Sabbaths, Lord, we love;
But there 's a nobler rest above;
To that our longing souls aspire,
With earnest hope and strong desire.

2 No more fatigue, no more distress,
Nor sin nor death shall reach the place;
No groans to mingle with the songs
Which warble from immortal tongues.

3 No rude alarms of raging foes;
No cares to break the long repose;
No midnight shade, no clouded sun,
But sacred, high, eternal noon.

4 O long-expected day, begin!
Dawn on these realms of woe and sin;
Fain would we leave this weary road,
And sleep in death, to rest with God.

831. 8s. M.

1 Let me not, thou King eternal,
Enter hell's domains infernal!
Where is sorrow, where is sadness,
Where is horror, where is madness,
Where the shameless are astounded,
Where the guilty are confounded,
Where the rack is ever slaying,
Where the worm is ever preying;

2 Me may Zion welcome, savèd,
Tranquil city, seat of David;
God its builder, light immortal,
Wood of holy cross its portal,
Peter's tongue its key, the nation
Of the blest its population,
Living rock the walls that bound it,
Christ the guard that dwells around it.

3 O, with what congratulations
Throng thy gates the festive nations!
What the warmth of their embracing,
What the gem thy walls enchasing!
Through that city's streets are wending
Holy throngs their anthems blending;
There may I, among the pious,
Sing with Moses and Elias!

XI.

THE YEAR.

THE YEAR.

---

832. 7s. M.

1 While, with ceaseless course, the sun
Hasted through the former year,
Many souls their race have run,
Never more to meet us here:
Fixed in an eternal state,
They have done with all below;
We a little longer wait,
But how little none can know.

2 As the wingèd arrow flies,
Speedily the mark to find;
As the lightning from the skies
Darts and leaves no trace behind;—
Swiftly thus our fleeting days
Bear us down life's rapid stream:
Upward, Lord, our spirits raise;
All below is but a dream.

3 Thanks for mercies past receive;
Pardon of our sins renew;
Teach us henceforth how to live,
With eternity in view;
Bless thy word to old and young;
Fill us with a Saviour's love;
When our life's short race is run,
May we dwell with thee above.

833. 7s. M.

1 Bless, O Lord, each opening year
To the souls assembling here:
Clothe thy word with power divine,
Make us willing to be thine.

2 Where thou hast thy work begun,
Give new strength the race to run;
Scatter darkness, doubts, and fears,
Wipe away the mourner's tears.

3 Bless us all, both old and young;
Call forth praise from every tongue:
Let our whole assembly prove
All thy power and all thy love!

834. 10, 4, & 6s. M.

1 Another year is swallowed by the sea
Of sumless waves!
Another year, thou past Eternity!
Hath rolled o'er new-made graves.

2 They open yet, — to bid the living weep,
Where tears are vain ;
While they, unswept into the ruthless deep,
Storm-tried and sad, remain.

3 But there are things which time devoureth not:
Thoughts whose green youth
Flowers o'er the ashes of the unforgot;
And words, whose fruit is truth.

4 Are ye not imaged in the eternal sea,
Things of to-day?
Deeds which are harvest for eternity
Ye cannot pass away.

XII.

SUPPLEMENT.

SUPPLEMENT.

---

835. 8 & 4s. M.

New and Old.

1 O BACKWARD-LOOKING son of time! —
The new is old, the old is new,
The cycle of a change sublime
Still sweeping through.

2 So wisely taught the Indian seer;
Destroying Seva, forming Brahm,
Who wake, by turns, earth's love and fear,
Are one, — the same.

3 As idly as in that old day
Thou mournest, did thy sires repine;
So, in his time, thy child grown gray,
Shall sigh for thine.

4 Yet not the less for them art thou:
The eternal step of Progress beats
To that great anthem, calm and slow,
Which God repeats!

5 Take heart! — the waster builds again, —
A charmèd life old goodness hath:
The tares may perish, — but the grain
Is not for death.

6 God works in all things: all obey
His first propulsion from the night:
Ho, wake and watch! — the world is gray
With morning light!

836. P. M.

Easter Hymn.

ANGELS.

Christ hath arisen!
Joy to our buried Head!
Whom the unmerited,
Trailing inherited
Woes, did imprison!

WOMEN.

Costly devices
We had prepared,
Shrouds and sweet spices
Linen and nard.
Woe the disaster!
Whom we here laid,
Gone is the Master,
Empty his bed.

ANGELS.

Christ hath arisen
Loving and glorious,

Out of laborious
Conflict victorious,
Christ hath arisen.

DISCIPLES.

Hath the inhumated
Upward aspiring,
Hath he consummated
All his desiring?
Is he in being's bliss
Near to creative joy?
Wearily we in this
Earthly house sigh:
Empty and hollow, us
Left he unblest.
Master! thy followers
Envy thy rest.

ANGELS.

Christ hath arisen
Out of corruption's womb.
Burst every prison!
Vanish death's gloom!
Active in charity,
Praise him in verity!
His feast prepare it ye!
His message bear it ye!
His joy declare it ye!
Then is the Master near,
Then is he here.

837. 8, 7, & 4s. M.

Progress.

1 Everlasting! changing never!
Of one strength, no more, no less:
Thine almightiness for ever,—
All the same thy holiness:
Thee eternal,
Thee all-glorious we possess!

2 But we weak ones, but we sinners,
Would not in our poorness stay;
We, the low ones, would be winners
Of what holy height we may,
Ever nearer
To thy pure and perfect day.

3 Shall things withered, fashions olden,
Keep us from life's flowing spring?
Waits for us the promise golden,—
Waits each new diviner thing?
Onward! onward!
Why this faithless tarrying?

4 By the old aspirants glorious,
By the hearts that hopèd all,
By the strivers, half victorious,
By each soul heroical,
By thy dearest,
By thy Milton and thy Paul,—

5 By their holy, high achieving,
By their visions more divine,
By each gift of our receiving

From these mighty ones of thine,
By the radiance
That on us from them doth shine, —

6 By each saving word unspoken,
By thy truth, as yet half-won,
By each idol still unbroken,
By thy will, yet poorly done, —
Hear us! hear us!
Our Almighty, help us on!

7 Nearer to thee would we venture,
Of thy truth more largely take,
Upon life diviner enter,
Into day more glorious break;
To the ages
Fair bequests and costly make.

8 Ours must be a nobler story
Than was ever writ before:
After-comers! dim our glory;
Be your smiles and winnings more
Everlasting!
Fuller grace incessant pour!

838. P. M.

The Silent Land.

1 Into the Silent Land!
Ah! who shall lead us thither?
Clouds in the evening sky more darkly gather,
And shattered wrecks lie thicker on the strand!
Who leads us with a gentle hand,
Whither, O, thither,
Into the Silent Land?

2 Into the Silent Land!
To you, ye boundless regions
Of all perfection! tender morning visions
Of beauteous souls! eternity's own band!
Who in life's battle firm doth stand
Shall bear hope's tender blossoms
Into the Silent Land!

3 O Land! O Land!
For all the broken-hearted
The mildest herald by our fate allotted,
Beckons, and with inverted torch doth stand,
To lead us with a gentle hand
Into the land of the great departed,
Into the Silent Land!

839. 6 & 5s. M.

Onward.

1 Life is onward,—use it
With a forward aim;
Toil is heavenly, choose it
And its welfare claim.
Look not to another
To perform your will,
Let not your own brother
Keep your warm hand still.

2 Life is onward,—try it,
Ere the day is lost;
It hath virtue,—buy it
At whatever cost.
If the world should offer
Every precious gem,
Look not at the scoffer,
Change it not for them.

3 Life is onward, — heed it
In each varied dress,
Your own act can speed it
On to happiness.
His bright pinion o'er you
Time waves not in vain,
If Hope chants before you
Her prophetic strain.

4 Life is onward, — prize it
In sunshine and in storm;
O, do not despise it
In its humblest form.
Hope and Joy together,
Standing at the goal,
Through life's darkest weather,
Beckon on the soul.

840. 11 & 10s. M.

"Still with Thee."

1 Still, still with Thee, when purple morning breaketh,
When the bird waketh, and the shadows flee;
Fairer than morning, lovelier than the daylight,
Dawns the sweet consciousness, I am with Thee!

2 Alone with Thee, amid the mystic shadows,
The solemn hush of nature newly born;
Alone with Thee in breathless adoration,
In the calm dew and freshness of the morn.

3 As in the dawning, o'er the waveless ocean,
The image of the morning star doth rest,

So in this stillness Thou beholdest only
Thine image in the waters of my breast.

4 When sinks the soul, subdued by toil, to slumber,
Its closing eye looks up to Thee in prayer,
Sweet the repose beneath thy wings o'ershading,
But sweeter still, to wake and find Thee there.

5 So shall it be at last, in that bright morning
When the soul waketh, and life's shadows flee;
O, in that hour, fairer than daylight dawning,
Shall rise the glorious thought, I am with thee!

841. 7s. M.

At Sea.

1 Lord! whom winds and seas obey,
Guide us through the watery way;
In the hollow of thy hand
Hide and bring us safe to land.

2 Father, let our faithful mind
Rest, on thee alone reclined:
Every anxious thought repress,
Keep our souls in perfect peace.

3 Keep the friends whom now we leave;
Bid them to each other cleave;
Bid them walk on life's rough sea,
Bid them come by faith to thee.

4 Save, till all these tempests end,
All who on thy love depend;
Waft our happy spirits o'er,
Land us on the heavenly shore.

842. 11 & 10s. M.

The Calm of the Soul.

1 WHEN winds are raging o'er the upper ocean,
And billows wild contend with angry roar,
'T is said, far down beneath the wild commotion,
That peaceful stillness reigneth, evermore.

2 Far, far beneath, the noise of tempests dieth,
And silver waves chime ever peacefully,
And no rude storm, how fierce so e'er it flieth,
Disturbs the Sabbath of that deeper sea.

3 So to the heart that knows thy love, O Purest!
There is a temple, sacred evermore,
And all the babble of life's angry voices
Dies in hushed stillness, at its peaceful door.

4 Far, far away, the roar of passion dieth,
And loving thoughts rise calm and peacefully,
And no rude storm, how fierce so e'er it flieth,
Disturbs the soul that dwells, O Lord, in thee.

5 O rest of rests! O peace, serene, eternal!
Thou ever livest, and thou changest never;
And in the secret of thy presence dwelleth
Fulness of joy, for ever and for ever.

843. 10 & 9s. M.

"Domine ne in Furore."

1 FROM profoundest depths of tribulation,
Lord! I lift my earnest cry to thee!
O, rebuke me not in indignation,
Nor in thy displeasure chasten me.

2 With my groaning I am very weary;
All the night I wet my couch with tears;
All the day my plaintive *miserere*
Bears to thee the burden of my fears.

3 O'er my soul have rolled the floods of anguish:
Every light has faded from my sky;
And in darkness I am left to languish,
Till thou send me succor from on high.

4 From my weary foot hath passed the lightness
Of the bounding step of earlier years,
And mine eye hath lost its youthful brightness,
Dimmed by sorrow and continual tears.

5 Sick and helpless, and of hope divested,
In my weakness and my sore distress
Be thy healing mercy manifested,
And with peace my troubled spirit bless.

6 Wherefore should I die? since with the living
Only dwell remembrances of thee;
From the grave ascendeth no thanksgiving,
Psalm, or laud, or *benedicite!*

844. 10 & 9s. M.

"*In Te, Domine, confido.*"

1 Not in vain I poured my supplication,
Voiced in anguish that was nigh despair;
God — henceforth the Rock of my salvation —
Hears in pity and receives my prayer.

2 On his name from midst the darkness calling,
He my soul hath ransomed from its fears;

By his strength my feet are saved from falling,
And his love hath dried my flowing tears.

3 Therefore come I to his altars, bringing
Hymns and vows my gratitude would pay;
Hallelujahs and the voice of singing
Best interpret all this heart would say.

4 Henceforth, with a spirit meek and lowly,
With a faith that nothing can appall,
Hopes serene and purpose high and holy,
I will meet whatever may befall.

5 If around me clouds and darkness gather,
Lo the brighter day that dawns beyond!
Through the gloom the Everlasting Father
Sends a voice that bids me not despond.

6 By his mercy, which hath never failed me,
Over hate and falsehood's brood abhorred,
Over all the foes that have assailed me,
I shall triumph greatly through the Lord!

845. 8 & 7s. M.

Liberty of Prophesying.

1 All conviction should be valiant, —
Tell thy truth, if truth it be;
Never seek to stem its current, —
Thoughts, like rivers, find the sea;
It will fit the widening circle
Of eternal verity.

2 Where would be all great inventions,
Each from by-gone fancies born,

Issued first in doubt and darkness,
Launched 'mid apathy or scorn?
How could noontide ever light us,
But for dawning of the morn?

3 Where would be our free opinion,
Where the right to speak at all,
If our sires, like thee, mistrustful,
Had been deaf to duty's call,
And concealed the thoughts within them,
Lying down for fear to fall?

4 Should an honest thought, outspoken,
Lead thee into chains or death, —
What is life, compared with virtue?
Shalt thou not survive thy breath?
Hark! the future age invites thee!
Listen, trembler! what it saith!

5 It demands thy thought in justice,
Debt, not tribute, of the free;
Have not ages long departed
Groaned and toiled and bled for thee?
If the Past have lent thee wisdom,
Pay it to Futurity.

846. 11 & 10s. M.

Ministering Spirits.

1 WHY come not spirits from the realms of glory,
To visit earth as in the days of old,
The times of sacred writ and ancient story?
Is heaven more distant? or has earth grown cold?

2 To Bethlehem's air was their last anthem given,
When other stars before The One grew dim?
Was their last presence known in Peter's prison,
Or where exulting martyrs raised their hymn?

3 And are they all within the veil departed?
There gleams no wing along the empyrean now;
And many a tear from human eyes has started,
Since angel touch has calmed a mortal brow.

4 No: earth has angels, though their forms are moulded
But of such clay as fashions all below;
Though harps are wanting and bright pinions folded,
We know them by the love-light on their brow.

5 I have seen angels by the sick one's pillow;
Theirs was the soft tone and the soundless tread;
Where smitten hearts were drooping like the willow,
They stood "between the weeping and the dead."

6 And if my sight, by earthly dimness hindered,
Beheld no hovering cherubim in air,
I doubted not, for spirits know their kindred,
They smiled upon the wingless watchers there.

7 There have been angels in the gloomy prison,
In crowded halls, by the lone widow's hearth:
And where they passed, the fallen have uprisen,
The giddy paused, the mourner's hope had birth.

8 O, many a spirit walks the world unheeded,
That, when its veil of sadness is laid down,
Shall soar aloft with pinions unimpeded,
And wear its glory like a starry crown.

847. 10 & 9s. M.

"Why thus longing?"

1 Why thus longing, thus for ever sighing,
For the far-off, the unattained and dim;
While the beautiful, all round thee lying,
Offers up its low, perpetual hymn?

2 Wouldst thou listen to its gentle teaching,
All thy restless yearnings it would still;
Leaf and flower and laden bee are preaching,
Thine own sphere, though humble, first to fill.

3 Poor indeed thou must be, if around thee
Thou no ray of light and joy canst throw;
If no silken cord of love hath bound thee
To some little world through weal and woe;—

4 If no dear eyes thy fond love can brighten,
No fond voices answer to thine own;
If no brother's sorrow thou canst lighten,
By daily sympathy and gentle tone.

5 Not by deeds that win the crowd's applauses,
Not by works that give thee world-renown,
Not by martyrdom, or vaunted crosses,
Canst thou win and wear the immortal crown.

6 Daily struggling, though unloved and lonely,
Every day a rich reward will give;

Thou wilt find, by hearty striving only,
And truly loving, thou canst truly live.

7 Dost thou revel in the rosy morning,
When all nature hails the lord of light,
And his smile, the mountain-tops adorning,
Robes yon fragrant fields in radiance bright?

8 Other hands may grasp the field and forest,
Proud proprietors in pomp may shine;
But with fervent love if thou adorest,
Thou art wealthier, — all the world is thine!

9 Yet if through earth's wide domains thou rovest,
Sighing that they are not thine alone,
Not those fair fields, but thyself, thou lovest,
And their beauty and thy worth are gone.

10 Nature wears the colors of the spirit;
Sweetly to her worshipper she sings;
All the glow, the grace she doth inherit,
Round her trusting child she fondly flings.

848. L. M.

Voyage of Life.

1 How often, as we beat along,
With wind ahead and blowing strong,
We hear our watchful captain cry,
"Near! nothing off! and full and by!"

2 So when in life our steps begin
To tread the devious paths of sin,
May conscience wake our timely fear,
Uttering her warning cry of "Near!"

3 And when from truth's unerring line
Our coward lips would dare decline,
Then may we heed, though fools should scoff,
Her stern injunction, "Nothing off!"

4 Virtue and vice to win us try;
Be then our watchword, "Full and by!"
Safe course through this world to another,
Is "full" of one and "by" the other.

849. P. M.

"Miserere, Domine!"

1 DARK the faith of days of yore,
And at evening evermore
Did the chanters, sad and saintly,
Yellow tapers burning faintly,
Doleful masses chant to thee,
"Miserere, Domine!"

2 Bright the faith of coming days,
And when dawn the kindling rays
Of heaven's golden lamp ascending,
Happy hearts and voices blending
Joyful anthems chant to thee,
"Te laudamus, Domine!"

3 Night's sad cadence dies away
On the yellow moonlit sea;
The boatmen rest their oars, and say,
"Miserere, Domine!"

4 Morn's glad chorus swells alway
On the azure, sunlit sea;
The boatmen ply their oars, and say,
"Te laudamus, Domine!"

850. P. M.

Action for the Future.

1 Men of thought! be up, and stirring
Night and day:
Sow the seed, withdraw the curtain,
Clear the way!
Men of action, aid and cheer them,
As ye may!
There 's a fount about to stream,
There 's a light about to beam,
There 's a warmth about to glow,
There 's a flower about to blow;
There 's a midnight blackness changing
Into gray.
Men of thought and men of action,
Clear the way!

2 Once the welcome light has broken,
Who shall say
What the unimagined glories
Of the day?
What the evil that shall perish
In its ray?
Aid the dawning, tongue and pen;
Aid it, hopes of honest men;
Aid it, paper, — aid it, type, —
Aid it, for the hour is ripe,
And our earnest must not slacken
Into play.
Men of thought and men of action,
Clear the way!

3 Lo! a cloud 's about to vanish
From the day;

And a brazen wrong to crumble
    Into clay;
Lo! the right 's about to conquer:
    Clear the way!
With the right shall many more
Enter smiling at the door;
With the giant wrong shall fall
Many others, great and small,
That for ages long have held us
    For their prey.
Men of thought and men of action,
    Clear the way!

851. L. M.

The Alpine Shepherd.

1 When on my ear your loss was knelled,
    And tender sympathy upburst,
A little spring from memory welled,
    Which once had quenched my bitter thirst;

2 And I was fain to bear to you
    A portion of its mild relief,
That it might be as cooling dew
    To steal some fever from your grief.

3 After our child's untroubled breath
    Up to the Father took its way,
And on our home the shade of death
    Like a long twilight haunting lay,

4 And friends came round with us to weep
    The little spirit's swift remove,
This story of the Alpine sheep
    Was told to us by one we love.

5 They, in the valley's sheltering care,
Soon crop the meadow's tender prime,
And when the sod grows brown and bare,
The shepherd strives to make them climb

6 To any shelves of pasture green
That hang along the mountain-side,
Where grass and flowers together lean,
And down through mists the sunbeams glide

7 But naught can lure the timid thing
The steep and rugged path to try,—
Though sweet the shepherd call and sing,
And seared below the pastures lie,—

8 Till in his arms their lambs he takes,
Along the dizzy verge to go,
When, heedless of the rifts and breaks,
They follow on o'er rock and snow.

9 And in those pastures lifted fair,
More dewy soft than lowland mead,
The shepherd drops his tender care,
And sheep and lambs together feed.

10 This parable, by nature breathed,
Blew on me as the south wind free
O'er frozen brooks that float unsheathed
From icy thraldom to the sea.

11 A blissful vision through the night
Would all my happy senses sway,
Of the good shepherd on the height,
Or climbing up the starry way,

12 Holding our little lamb asleep;—
  And like the burden of the sea
Sounded that voice along the deep,
  Saying, "Arise, and follow me!"

852. P. M.

Luther's Psalm.

1 A MIGHTY fortress is our God,
  A bulwark never failing;
Our helper he amid the flood
  Of mortal ills prevailing.
For still our ancient foe
Doth seek to work us woe,
His craft and power are great,
And, armed with cruel hate,
  On earth is not his equal.

2 Did we in our own strength confide,
  Our striving would be losing,—
Were not the right man on our side,
  The man of God's own choosing.
Dost ask who that may be?
Christ Jesus, it is he,
Lord Sabaoth his name,
From age to age the same,
  And he must win the battle.

3 And though this world, with devils filled,
  Should threaten to undo us,
We will not fear, for God hath willed
  His truth to triumph through us.
The Prince of Darkness grim,—
We tremble not for him,

His rage we can endure,
For lo! his doom is sure,
One little word shall fell him.

4 That word above all earthly powers—
No thanks to them—abideth,
The spirit and the gifts are ours
Through Him who with us sideth.
Let goods and kindred go,
This mortal life also;
The body they may kill,
God's truth abideth still,
His kingdom is for ever.

853. 5 & 4s. M.

True Rest.

1 SWEET is the pleasure
Itself cannot spoil!
Is not true leisure
One with true toil?

2 Thou that wouldst taste it,
Still do thy best;
Use it, not waste it,
Else 't is no rest.

3 Wouldst behold beauty
Near thee? all round?
Only hath duty
Such a sight found.

4 Rest is not quitting
The busy career;

Rest is the fitting
Of self to its sphere.

5 'T is the brook's motion,
Clear without strife,
Fleeing to ocean
After its life.

6 Deeper devotion
Nowhere hath knelt;
Fuller emotion
Heart never felt.

7 'T is loving and serving
The Highest and Best!
'T is onwards! unswerving,
And that is true rest.

854. 6 & 5s. M.

The Choice.

1 The future hides in it
Good hap and sorrow;
We press still thorow,
Naught that abides in it
Daunting us, — onward.

2 And solemn before us
Veiled, the dark portal,
Goal of all mortal;
Stars silent rest o'er us,
Graves under us silent.

3 But heard are the voices,
Voices of sages,
The worlds and the ages;
Choose well, your choice is
Brief and yet endless.

855. 6 & 4s. M.

Pilgrim Ode.

1 Sons of renownèd sires,
Join in harmonious choirs,
Swell your loud songs;
Daughters of peerless dames,
Come with your mild acclaims,
Let their reverèd names
Dwell on your tongues.

2 From frowning Albion's seat,
See the famed band retreat,
On ocean tost;
Blue tumbling billows roar,
By keel scarce ploughed before,
And bear them to this shore,
Fettered with frost.

3 Not winter's sullen face,
Not the fierce tawny race
In arms arrayed;
Not hunger shook their faith,
Not sickness' baleful breath,
Nor Carver's early death
Their souls dismayed.

4 Watered by heavenly dew,
The germ of empire grew,
Freedom its root;

From the cold northern pine,
Far toward the burning line,
Spreads the luxuriant vine,
  Bending with fruit.

5 Columbia, child of heaven,
The best of blessings given
  Rest on thy head;
Beneath thy peaceful skies,
While prosperous tides arise,
Here turn thy grateful eyes, —
  Revere the dead.

6 Here trace the moss-grown stones,
Where rest their mouldering bones,
  Again to rise;
And let thy sons be led
To emulate the dead,
While o'er their tombs they tread
  With moistened eyes.

7 Sons of renownèd sires,
Join in harmonious choirs,
  Swell your loud songs;
Daughters of peerless dames,
Come with your mild acclaims,
Let their reverèd names
  Dwell on your tongues.

856. 10s. M.

City of God.

1 My feet are worn and weary with the march
  Over the rough road and up the steep hill-side;

O city of our God! I fain would see
  Thy pastures green, where peaceful waters glide.

2 My hands are weary, toiling on,
  Day after day, for perishable meat;
O city of our God! I fain would rest,—
  I sigh to gain thy glorious mercy-seat.

3 My garments, travel-worn and stained with dust,
  Oft rent by briers and thorns that crowd my way,
Would fain be made, O Lord, my righteousness!
  Spotless and white in heaven's unclouded ray.

4 My eyes are weary looking at the sin,
  Impiety, and scorn upon the earth;
O city of our God! within thy walls
  All—all are clothed again with thy new birth.

5 My heart is weary of its own deep sin,—
  Sinning, repenting, sinning still again;
When shall my soul thy glorious presence feel,
  And find, dear Saviour, it is free from stain?

6 Patience, poor soul! the Saviour's feet were worn;
  The Saviour's heart and hands were weary too;
His garments stained, and travel-worn, and old;
  His vision blinded with a pitying dew.

7 Love thou the path of sorrow that he trod;
  Toil on, and wait in patience for thy rest;
O city of our God! we soon shall see
  Thy glorious walls,—Home of the loved and blest.

857. 8 & 7s. M.

The Father's Hand.

1 When my life-bark, richly freighted,
In the light of morning lay,
Came my Father's hand so gently,
And its treasures bore away.

2 Beggared by the sore affliction,
Eagerly my heart pursued,
As, 'mid clouds his face concealing,
The receding hand I viewed.

3 Wings of faith its flight supporting,
Lo! it cleaves the upper sky;
There my heart its treasure greeting,
Both within his hand shall lie.

858. 10s. M.

The Future Life.

1 How shall I know thee in the sphere which keeps
The disembodied spirits of the dead,
When all of thee that time could wither sleeps,
And perishes among the dust we tread?

2 For I shall feel the sting of ceaseless pain,
If there I meet thy gentle presence not;
Nor hear the voice I love, nor read again
In thy serenest eyes the tender thought.

3 Will not thy own meek heart demand me there,—
That heart whose fondest throbs to me were given?

My name on earth was ever in thy prayer,
  Shall it be banished from thy tongue in heaven?

4 In meadows fanned by heaven's life-breathing wind,
  In the resplendence of that glorious sphere,
And larger movements of the unfettered mind,
  Wilt thou forget the love that joined us here?

5 The love that lived through all the stormy past,
  And meekly with my harsher nature bore,
And deeper grew, and tenderer, to the last,
  Shall it expire with life, and be no more?

6 A happier lot than mine, and larger light,
  Awaits thee there; for thou hast bowed thy will
In cheerful homage to the rule of right,
  And lovest all, and renderest good for ill.

7 For me, the sordid cares in which I dwell
  Shrink and consume the heart, as heat the scroll;
And wrath hath left its scar — that fire of hell
  Has left its frightful scar upon my soul.

8 Yet though thou wear'st the glory of the sky,
  Wilt thou not keep the same belovèd name, —
The same fair, thoughtful brow, and gentle eye,
  Lovelier in heaven's sweet climate, yet the same?

9 Shalt thou not teach me, in that calmer home,
  The wisdom that I learned so ill in this, —
The wisdom which is love, — till I become
  Thy fit companion in that land of bliss?

859. L. M.

Creation.

1 The Spirit moved upon the waves
That darkly rolled, a shoreless sea;
He spake the word, and light broke forth,
A glorious, bright immensity.

2 At his command, the mountains heaved
Their rocky pinnacles on high,
Island and continent displayed
Their desert grandeur to the sky.

3 The voice of God was heard again,
And lovely flowers and graceful trees
Appeared on every vale and plain,
And perfumes floated on the breeze.

4 The word went forth, and vast and high
The heavenly orbs gave out their light,
O'er all the earth and sea and sky,
The rulers of the day and night.

5 Glory to God! the angels sang,
With harps of gold, and tongues of flame:
And all the heavenly arches rang
Reëchoing with the awful theme.

860. P. M.

Hear our Prayer.

1 Hear! Father, hear our prayer!
Thou who art Pity where sorrow prevaileth,
Thou who art Safety when mortal help faileth,
Strength to the feeble, and Hope to despair,
Hear! Father, hear our prayer!

2 Hear! Father, hear our prayer!
Wandering unknown in the land of the stranger,
Be with all travellers in sickness or danger,
Guard thou their path, guide their feet from the snare:
Hear! Father, hear our prayer!

3 Hear! Father, hear our prayer!
Still thou the tempest, night's terrors revealing,
In lightning flashing, in thy thunder pealing;
Save thou the shipwrecked, the voyager spare:
Hear! Father, hear our prayer!

4 Hear thou the poor that cry!
Feed thou the hungry, and lighten their sorrow,
Grant them the sunshine of hope for the morrow;
They are thy children, their trust is on high:
Hear thou the poor that cry!

5 Dry thou the mourner's tear!
Heal thou the wounds of time-hallowed affection,
Grant to the widow and orphan protection,
Be in their trouble a friend ever near:
Dry thou the mourner's tear!

6 Hear! Father, hear our prayer!
Long hath thy goodness our footsteps attended;
Be with the pilgrim whose journey is ended;
When, at thy summons, for death we prepare,
Hear! Father, hear our prayer!

861. 8 & 7s. M.

Charity.

1 Meek and lowly, pure and holy,
Chief among the blessed three,

Turning sadness into gladness,
  Heaven-born art thou, Charity!
Pity dwelleth in thy bosom,
  Kindness reigneth o'er thy heart,
Gentle thoughts alone can sway thee,
  Judgment hath in thee no part.
Meek and lowly, &c.

2 Hoping ever, failing never,
  Though deceived, believing still;
Long abiding, all confiding
  To thy Heavenly Father's will;
Never weary of well-doing,
  Never fearful of the end;
Claiming all mankind as brothers,
  Thou dost all alike befriend.
Meek and lowly, &c.

862. C. M.

Call to Action.

1 Away, ye ceaseless doubts and fears,
  That weaken and enthrall;
Wipe off, my soul, thy faithless tears,
  And rise at wisdom's call.

2 Awake, my soul, to duty wake;
  Go pay the debt thou ow'st;
Go forward,—and the night shall break
  Around thee as thou go'st.

3 Swift fly the hours, and brief the time
  For action or repose;
Fast flits this scene of woe and crime,
  And soon the whole shall close.

4 The evening shadows deeper fall,
The daylight dies away;
Wake, slumberer, at the Master's call,
And work while it is day!

863. 8 & 7s. M.

Be thou ready.

1 Be thou ready, fellow-mortal,
In thy pilgrimage of life,
Ever ready to uphold thee
In the toil and in the strife.
Let no hope, however pleasant,
Lure thy footsteps from the right;
Nor the sunshine leave thee straying
In the sudden gloom of night.

2 Be thou ready when thy brother
Bows in dark affliction's shade;
Be thou ready when thy sister
Needs thy kindness and thy aid;
Let thine arm sustain and cheer them,—
They have claims upon us all,—
And thy deeds like morning sunlight
On their weary hearts shall fall.

3 Be thou ready when the erring
List to sin's enchanting strain,
Ready with kind words to woo them
Back to virtue's path again.
Be thou ready, in thy meekness,
To do good to friend and foe,
As thy Father sheddeth freely
Light on all that dwell below.

4 Be thou ready for the morrow,
When delight shall please no more;
When the rose and lily fadeth,
And the charm of song is o'er.
When the voices of thy kindred
Faintly move thy dying ear,
Be thou ready for thy journey
To some higher, brighter sphere.

864. C. M.

Death and Judgment.

1 The day approacheth, O my soul,
The great, decisive day,
Which from the verge of mortal life
Shall bear thee far away.

2 Another day, more awful, dawns;
And, lo! the Judge appears;
Ye heavens, retire before his face,
And sink, ye darkened stars.

3 Yet does one short, preparing hour,
One precious hour, remain;
Rouse thee, my soul, with all thy power,
Nor let it pass in vain.

4 For this, thy temple, Lord, we throng;
For this, thy board surround;
Here may our service be approved,
And in thy presence crowned.

865. P. M.

"The Lord gave the Word."

1 "The Lord gave the word," 't was the word of his truth,
And the word of salvation for all men to be:
Then forth went its preachers, the aged, the youth,
And "great was the company."

2 "The Lord gave the word," — it was not as of old,
When the ark of his strength to the temple was brought,
With the clanging of steel, and the gleaming of gold,
And spoils of a battle fought.

3 But the Gospel of faith in the spirit of love
Is the true "King of Glory" the Church has enshrined;
And "the chariots of God" are the "thousands" that move
As "angels" to bless mankind.

4 O Lord! give this word its triumphant success;
Be its mercy and peace on thy worshippers here;
And clothe all thy saints with its righteousness,
With its earnest joy and fear.

866. 7s. M.

The Last Judgment.

1 In the sun, and moon, and stars,
Signs and wonders there shall be;
Earth shall quake with inward wars,
Nations witn perplexity.

2 Soon shall ocean's hoary deep,
Tost with stronger tempests, rise;
Darker storms the mountain sweep,
Redder lightning rend the skies.

3 Evil thoughts shall shake the proud,
Racking doubt, and restless fear;
And amid the thunder-cloud
Shall the Judge of men appear.

4 But though from that awful face
Heaven shall fade, and earth shall fly,
Fear not ye, his chosen race,—
Your redemption draweth nigh.

867. C. M.

The Judge of Nations.

1 God, to correct a guilty world,
In wrath is slow to rise,
But comes at length in thunder clothed,
And darkness veils the skies.

2 Dark and mysterious is the course
Of his tremendous way;
His path is in the trackless winds,
And in the foaming sea.

3 Yet, though enveloped in the cloud,
And from our view concealed,
The righteous Judge will soon appear,
In majesty revealed.

4 Then will he curb the lawless power,
The deadly wrath, of man,
And all the windings will unfold
Of his own gracious plan.

868. P. M.

Prayer for all Men.

1 God of the mountain, God of the storm,
God of the flowers, God of the worm!
Hear us, and bless us,
Forgive us, redress us;
Breathe on our spirits thy love and thy healing;
Teach us content with thy fatherly dealing;
Teach us to love thee,
To love one another, brother his brother,
And make us all free,—
Free from the shackles of ancient tradition;
And show us 't is manly, 't is God-like, to labor!

2 God of the darkness, God of the sun,
God of the beautiful, God of each one,—
Clothe us and feed us,
Illume us and lead us;
Show us that avarice holds us in thrall,—
That the land is all thine, and thou givest to all.
Scatter our blindness,
Help us do right all the day and the night.—
To love mercy and kindness;
Aid us to conquer mistakes of the past;
Show us our future to cheer us and arm us,
The upper, the better, the mansions thou hast;
And, God of the grave, that the grave cannot harm us.

869. C. M.

Christmas.

1 Jesus has lived! and we would bring
The world's glad thanks to-day;

And at his feet, while anthems ring,
The grateful offering lay.

2 Jesus has lived! and his pure life,
So perfect and sublime,
Shall conquer man's dark sin and strife
Through every rank and clime.

3 Jesus has died! and o'er the stars
Gone home to God on high:
He burst the grave's cold prison-bars,
And said, "Man cannot die."

4 Jesus yet lives! and from the sky
Where victory he wrote,
Before the good man's closing eye,
Visions of glory float.

5 Jesus yet lives! and oh! may we,
While in this valley dim,
So feel our immortality,
That we may be like him.

870. 12s. M.

A Supplication.

1 O Love Divine! lay on me burdens, if thou wilt;
Burdens to break, in mercy, my fond, feverish sleep;
Turn comforts into awful prophets to my guilt,
Let me but at thy wondrous footstool fall and weep!

2 Visit and change, uplift, ennoble, recreate me!
Ordain whatever masters in thy saving school;
Let the whole eager host of Fashion's flatterers hate me,
So thou wilt henceforth guide me by thy loving rule.

3 I pray not, Lord, to be redeemed from mortal sorrow;
Redeem me only from my vain and mean self-love;
Then let each night of grief lead in a mourning
morrow,
Fear shall not shake my trust in Thee,—my Peace
above.

4 Yet while the Resurrection waves its signs august,
Like morning's dewy banners on a cloudless sky,
My weak feet cling enamored to the parching dust,
And, on the sand, poor pebbles lure my roving eye.

5 Ye witnessings of silent, sad Gethsemane,—
That shaded garden whence light breaks for all our
earth,—
Around my anguish let your faithful influence be!
Ye prayers and sighs divine, be my immortal birth!

6 Vales of Repentance mount to hills of high desire;
Seven times seven suffering years earn the Sab-
batic Rest;
Earth's fickle, cruel lap—alternate frost and fire—
Tempers beloved disciples for the Master's breast.

7 O Way for all that live! heal us by pain and loss;
Fill all our years with toil, and bless us with thy rod.
Thy bonds bring wider freedom; climbing, by the
cross,
Wins that brave height where looms the city of our
God!

8 O Sunshine, rising ever on our nights of sadness!
O Best of all our good, and Pardoner of our sin!
Look down with pity on our unbelieving madness!
To Heaven's great welcome take us, homesick pil-
grims, in!

9 Spirit that overcame the world's long tribulation
Try faltering faith, and make it firm through much enduring;
Feed weary hearts with patient hopes of thy salvation;
Make strait submission, more than luxury's ease, alluring.

10 Hallow our wit with prayer; our mastery steep in meekness;
Pour on our study inspiration's holy light;
Hew out, for Christ's dear Church, a Future without weakness,
Quarried from thine Eternal Beauty, Order, Might!

11 Met, there, mankind's great Brotherhood of souls and Powers,
Raise thou full praises from its farthest corners dim;
Pour down, O steadfast Sun, thy beams on all its towers;
Roll through its world-wide spaces Faith's majestic hymn.

12 Come, age of God's own Truth, after man's age of fables!
Seed sown in Eden, yield the nations' healing tree!
Ebal and Sinai, Mamre's tents, the Hebrew tables,
All look towards Olivet, and bend to Calvary.

13 Fold of the tender Shepherd! rise, and spread!
Arch o'er our frailty roofs of everlasting strength!
Be all the Body gathered to its living Head!
Wanderers we faint: O, let us find our Lord at length!

871. 8 & 4s. M.

" God speed the Right!"

1 Now to Heaven our prayers ascending,
God speed the right!
In a noble cause contending,
God speed the right!
Be their zeal in heaven recorded,
In the better land rewarded,
Who serve the right.

2 Be that prayer again repeated,
God speed the right!
Ne'er despairing, though defeated,
God speed the right!
Like the good and great in story,
If they fail, they fail with glory:
God speed the right!

3 Still their onward course pursuing,
God speed the right!
Every foe at length subduing,
God speed the right!
Truth thy cause, whate'er delay it,
There 's no power on earth can stay it:
God speed the right!

872. L. M.

Noonday Hymn.

1 Up to the throne of God is borne
The voice of praise at early morn,

And he accepts the punctual hymn
Sung as the light of day grows dim.

2 Nor will he turn his ear aside
From holy offerings at noontide;
Then, here assembling, let us raise
Our song of gratitude and praise.

3 In heaven, behold, the industrious sun
Already half his race hath run!
He cannot halt or go astray,
But our immortal spirits may.

4 Lord, since his rising in the east,
If we have faltered or transgressed,
Guide from thy love's abundant source
What yet remains of this day's course:

5 Help with thy grace, through life's short day,
Our upward and our downward way;
And glorify for us the west,
When we shall sink into our rest.

www.ingramcontent.com/pod-product-compliance
Lightning Source LLC
LaVergne TN
LVHW021050110826
845150LV00001B/37

9781425567729